Elise Boulding

Elise Boulding

A Life in the Cause of Peace

by MARY LEE MORRISON

Foreword by Mary Catherine Bateson

McFarland & Company, Inc., Publishers
Jefferson, North Carolina, and London

LIBRARY OF CONGRESS CATALOGUING-IN-PUBLICATION DATA

Morrison, Mary Lee.
Elise Boulding : a life in the cause of peace / by Mary Lee Morrison ; foreword by Mary Catherine Bateson.
p. cm.
Includes bibliographical references and index.

ISBN 0-7864-2055-3 (softcover : 50# alkaline paper) 

1. Boulding, Elise. 2. Quakers—United States—Biography.
3. Sociologists—United States—Biography. I. Title.
BX7795.B56M67 2005
289.6'092—dc22

2005009056

British Library cataloguing data are available

Cover photograph: Elise at Dartmouth College in the early 1980s.

Manufactured in the United States of America

McFarland & Company, Inc., Publishers
Box 611, Jefferson, North Carolina 28640
www.mcfarlandpub.com

To the millions of people around the globe
who work every day to build
a more hopeful and peaceful world

Acknowledgments

I am deeply grateful for the loving support I have received throughout the process of completing this book. I am particularly grateful to the following people:

To Elise Boulding, who has opened her heart and home to me over the course of the last eight years and who has taught me so much,

To my husband, Bill Upholt, who has been a constant source of love and companionship for the last 25 years,

To my children, Gretchen and Boyce Upholt, who have taught me that at times there are things more important than the completion of this book and who have provided laughs at just the right moment,

To Mary Catherine Bateson, for writing the foreword and for her consultation on issues related to her mother, Margaret Mead,

To the faculty of the University of Connecticut Neag School of Education, who were so supportive and allowed me very early on in my graduate work to study the life and work of Elise Boulding.

I thank also the members of the Boulding family who allowed me to interview them: Christine Boulding Graham, Philip Boulding and Russell Boulding.

Thanks also go to the colleagues, former students and friends of Elise who shared their stories with me: Linda Reney Forcey, Michael Greenstein, Robert Irwin, Ann and George Levinger, Marty Gonzales, LeRoy Moore, Ruth Correll, Guy Burgess, Holly Giffin, Vivian Wilson, Laurel Schneider, Gilbert White, Clinton Fink, Kevin Clements, Dortha Meredith, Mary Garman and Judith Harvey.

Gratitude is due to Robin and Jack Powelson, who opened their home to me in Boulder, Colorado, while I was doing archival work and who have since become friends,

and to the members of Boulder Friends Meeting, who shared anecdotes with me about Elise.

To the staff of Woolman Hill Conference Center in Deerfield, Massachusetts, where I spent many hours by the woodstove in a one-room cabin, writing.

And to Donn and Diane Weinholtz, who gave me the use of their cabin in New Hampshire one cold January, I owe thanks.

I must thank David Hayes and the staff at the University of Colorado Library Archives, who so patiently answered my questions and helped with the voluminous amount of Boulding material.

I send heartfelt thanks to the archivists at the Bentley Historical Library at the University of Michigan for their help while I was there for such a brief time.

Margaret Hope Bacon, Quaker biographer, who shared with me stories of her craft, has my sincere gratitude.

I thank also Melinda (Armstrong) Salazar and Anna Spradlin, whose earlier biographical works on Elise Boulding helped me with key ideas. I am grateful for Melinda's help in brainstorming concepts with me.

I thank the members of Hartford Friends Meeting for deep and ongoing spiritual support.

Finally, my thanks go to the many friends and colleagues, too numerous to mention, who have offered their love and suggestions at just the right time.

Contents

PART III. TEACHER, PREACHER AND HEAVENBOUND REACHER: THE LATER YEARS

Foreword

One of the by-products of the new wave of feminism in the second half of the twentieth century was a flood of biographies, autobiographies, and memoirs by and about women, followed by new thinking about the nature of these genres and their relevance to the search for equality. One rationale was to make examples of successful and creative women available as role models and as arguments for female potential, but this goal has given way to a new understanding of the relationship between personal life and public achievement. Elise Boulding is an important subject for biographical study for, in a very real sense, she is a model of the process of the personal becoming political.

Of course it has been important that society become aware of the achievements of particular women, which are so often glossed over. Of course it has been important for female readers, from early childhood to old age, to have their imaginations stretched by new models for courage and creativity. But in the process of generating this wealth of books and studies it has become clear that there is an especially close relationship between these genres and the way women learn and live their lives, and gradually that insight has been applied to the lives and achievements of men, where it is often more deeply camouflaged.

The old division between public and private, on which so many masculine careers are built, has not been workable for women. The female experience has historically been one of multitasking, of divided attention and multiple commitments, of seeing events and decisions in context rather than in isolation, of composing lives from many diverse elements. Similarly, the distinction between objectivity and subjectivity has felt uncomfortable to women, who have repeatedly challenged objectivity as an illusion or a pretended blindness and who have insisted that there is wisdom to be found in reflection on feeling and response. This reflexive turn is now being played out in works by and about men as well.

Elise (I believe I may call her that, although I have known her only slightly) had a dislike of dichotomies, like the dichotomy between public and private life or between research and activism. She enlarged upon that dislike with an insistence that spirituality is not an occasional or marginal aspect of human life but central to the process of becoming fully human. In the areas of research, education, and action that are so often kept separate, we see a crosscutting pattern of ongoing learning and listening, a spiritually grounded willingness to learn that is often formalized as research, a movement toward relationship that includes both teaching and learning, and a commitment to change—individual, social, and global. Elise's spirituality stretches from an emphasis on listening—both to the inner voice and to others—to a spiritual imagination with the capacity to envision and pursue the possibility of genuine globalization, which would lead to mutually respectful interdependence and, above all, to peace.

Elise put great emphasis on the developmental character of pacifism. She saw that peace is not a state but a process, a fabric woven in the daily activities of families and communities and reinforced by congruent educational programs intimately tied to ongoing research. Just as the institution of warfare is humanly created, the human potential for violence is shaped by experiences in and out of school, so the challenge is not only to end particular wars but to create cultures of peace in which institutional commitments support peaceful potentials in individuals and vice versa.

Inevitably, Elise's work has had multiple separate constituencies. Some see her as a pioneer in understanding the role of NGOs or as a futurist. Some read her books on women. Some read her work out of an interest in education. And some, no doubt, read only her Quaker writings in publications of the Society of Friends. But what this biography makes clear is that all of these areas of interest are interconnected and grounded in the developmental character of pacifism. They are part of the same epistemology. Understanding this epistemology requires us to understand its author as daughter and wife, immigrant and teacher, mother of five and now grandmother of sixteen with several great-grandchildren, someone inevitably and deeply committed to a future of peace.

Mary Catherine Bateson
Cambridge, Massachusetts

Frequently Used Acronyms

AAAS	American Association for the Advancement of Science
ACUNS	Academic Council for the United Nations System
AFSC	American Friends Service Committee
ASA	American Sociological Association
CASBS	Center for the Advanced Study of the Behavioral Sciences
COPRED	Consortium on Peace Research, Education and Development
CRCR	Center for Research on Conflict Resolution
EXPRO	Exploratory Project on the Conditions of Peace
FAHE	Friends Association for Higher Education
FRIHER	Friends Responsibility in Higher Education and Research
FPT	Friends Peace Teams
INGOs	International nongovernmental organizations
IPRA	International Peace Research Association
ISA	International Sociological Association
NGOs	Nongovernmental organizations
PEC	Peace Education Commission (of IPRA)
WILPF	Women's International League for Peace and Freedom
UN	United Nations
UNESCO	United Nations Educational, Scientific and Cultural Organization
UNU	United Nations University
WOMP	World Order Models Project
WSP	Women's Strike for Peace

Preface

It was a beautiful New England September day in 1998, with the leaves beginning to turn their golden and red hues. The Office of Religious Life at Wellesley College outside of Boston had inaugurated a program on the role of spirituality in higher education with a conference at the college. Eight hundred participants gathered to hear a variety of speakers address the main theme, "Education as Transformation." One of those participating was a tall, stately octogenarian, recognizable by her statuesque walk and her traditional white, braided hair, reminders that her roots lay in Scandinavia. Elise Boulding had been invited as one of the speakers at the conference. Her workshop was entitled "Communities of Learning as Cultures of Peace."

As Elise's workshop began in one of the campus classroom buildings, participants gathered in what would soon become much too small a conference room for the more than forty participants. As more and more people entered the room, some arriving after the starting time, Elise greeted each one and invited them to find a place, often apologizing for not having adequate space for them to sit. Numerous Wellesley students, all women, mostly in their teens and twenties, came in, drawn to hear Elise, and many stayed afterward to talk and share with her.

I had been trailing Elise Boulding for several years, seeking to learn more about her life and work for the story of her life. As she had often done in our travels together, she asked me to help her out this day, to provide her with a typed transcript of the workshop, as she had realized that I was taping the proceedings. Later she and I were grateful for this, as her talk represented a wonderful encapsulation of her philosophy of educating toward a culture of peace.

Her book *Cultures of Peace: The Hidden Side of History* (Syracuse, 2000) was almost complete at the time of the Wellesley conference. The book represented the culmination of her life's work researching, writing, networking and organizing in three key areas: peace, women's studies and futures. As was usual for her, the Wellesley talk was largely autobiographical, as she shared the importance of her own experiences in shaping her life views, particularly as they related to educating toward a culture of peace. She told of how she came to see a peace culture as a "listening, learning, mutually nurturant culture that deals creatively with conflict and difference and freely shares its resources without the aid of structured power difference." Elise spoke of her own spiritual journey as it had related to all of her other endeavors.

The importance of community and acting within communities is central to Elise's concept of educating for peace. Speaking at the workshop, Elise said, "In developing peace studies programs, the first step is to legitimate academically the linking of the mind and the heart and then to translate the learning and the search process into the community itself."

Elise Boulding has been called the matriarch of the twentieth century peace research movement. Sociologist emeritus from Dartmouth College and the University of Colorado, she has been in on the ground floor in the movements of peace, women's studies and futures and has played pivotal roles in each. Prior to her scholarly career, formally beginning at age fifty, however, she was making major contributions in other areas, most notably as a peace educator and an activist, a leader in the Women's International League for Peace and Freedom (WILPF) and a member of the Religious Society of Friends (Quakers). Boulding has been the recipient of over nineteen awards for her work in peace and was a 1990 nominee for the Nobel Peace Prize.

This book weaves together Elise Boulding's life and work, using peace education and its historical and conceptual dimensions as a unifying theme. Boulding's theoretical work on the role of the family in educating toward social change and the roles women have played in peacemaking predates much of the work discussing women's unique capacities for connections, networking and peace (Gilligan, Ruddick, Belenky et al.). The various stages of her life—child, student, young wife, Quaker, activist, sociologist and scholar, retiree and elder—are bound together metaphorically as a hologram. Always eschewing dichotomy, her life has been a constant attempt to integrate, both privately and publicly, the human need for both autonomy and connectedness. Elise Boulding's ideas on transnational networks and their relationship to global understanding are considered seminal contributions to twentieth-century peace education thought.

The book has three parts. The first and the third deal chronologically with the life of Elise Boulding, including her prolific peace, Quaker, educational and activist work. Part II departs from a strictly chronological format to include elements of Elise's philosophy of education, the influence of Quakerism on her educational endeavors, the conceptual evolution of a culture of peace and Elise's theoretical work in women's and futures studies. Because I wished for readers to understand some of the idioms used by Elise in our interviews, and to take a rather "organic" approach in order that the flow reflect what she really said, any irregularities of syntax have remained in quoted conversations.

Two trips to the Boulding archives in Boulder, Colorado, were made, four years apart, to complete the research. The first trip was in 1999 and resulted in the completion of my doctoral dissertation, the revision of which is this book. The second trip occurred in 2003. During the interval, extensive reorganizing and cataloguing of the Boulding archival material was accomplished, resulting in a different form of cataloguing for some of the material. Therefore, the reader may note that there are some inconsistencies in notations.

Introduction

Elise Boulding was a key player in the beginning of academic peace studies in the 1950s and early 1960s, and she continued this work through the 1970s when peace studies established itself as a legitimate academic discipline. She has long advocated, often at her own professional peril, for an integration of peace education, research and activism. Early perceptions of peace education were that it was education toward the abolition of war and that it was an "arm" of the peace research movement. In the years following the Second World War, and particularly in the last thirty years, new ideas have expanded the concept of peace education. Elise's writings and those of other feminists in the 1970s laid the groundwork for the work of later educators who embraced ideas of connectedness, caring and imaging and the importance of thinking globally and acting locally. Many of Boulding's ideas predated contemporary thinking on the importance of ecological sustainability and the dangers inherent in "cultures of war."

Elise Boulding's contributions to peace and the grounding she received for her subsequent theoretical work began in her early life, as an immigrant child born to parents with high expectations, and in her marriage to internationally known Quaker economist and poet Kenneth Boulding. Throughout her life, Elise always used her immediate experiences to add meaning to her existence. She has always grounded whatever she has done in the basic human experience that begins with the child and involves the family. To paraphrase a family friend, she "is a person who has been able to stretch so far the limits of human experience that she could address the United Nations with no problem and then, in the next second, stoop to tie a child's shoe and be aware of the needs of both at the same time."[1]

Elise's dynamic partnership with Kenneth Boulding, together with some of their conflicts, is explored in the book, as their relationship helped to contribute to her theoretical ideas on cultures of peace. The grounding she received from her Quaker spirituality, also explored in the book, has played an important role in influencing the focus and content of her work in many areas.

In a field long dominated by men, Elise Boulding has left an indelible mark and has made major contributions to the ongoing theoretical work on peace and social change, including the importance of linking individuals to their communities and to the global world. Her life and work speak to the significant presence of cultures and societies of peace, while most media attention and scholarly publications focus on the extreme violence in today's society. *Cultures of Peace* was written as a recognition of her long-time associations with UNESCO and the United Nations, the UN having designated the current decade (2000–2010) as the Decade for a Culture of Peace and Nonviolence for the Children of the World.

Elise Boulding's Contributions to Peace Education: Some Historical and Conceptual Dimensions

Peace education is currently considered to be both a philosophy and a process involving skills that include listening, reflection, problem-solving, cooperation and conflict resolution.[2] The process involves empowering people with the skills, attitudes and knowledge to create a safe world and to build a sustainable environment. The philosophy teaches nonviolence, love, compassion and reverence for all life. The Peace Education Commission of the International Peace Research Association further clarifies the definition to take into account both *explicit* and *implicit* peace education.[3] Explicit education, also sometimes traditionally associated with *peace studies*, involves the processing of facts elicited from peace research.[4] Implicit peace education is the attempted means of approaching a peace culture and the process of educating students toward this. Betty Reardon of Columbia University offers what is probably the most comprehensive definition of peace education. She argues that the purpose of peace education is the promotion of the "development of an authentic planetary consciousness that will enable us to function as global citizens and to transform the present human conditions by changing social structures and patterns of thought that have created it."[5] Reardon believes that at the center of peace education must be the potential for transformation, both inward and outward.

UNESCO has defined peace education as "international by nature, global in perspective and action-oriented in its aspirations."[6]

These contemporary views on peace education reflect the evolution of the concept from its beginnings in the 1940s and 1950s to what we now know as the current peace movement. In the early years, peace education was seen as the process of propagating the findings of peace research. Peace research, in the modern sense, began in the decades following World War II with the establishment of various research institutes for the study of peace.[7] One of the first was that established by Johan Galtung in Oslo, Norway, in the late 1950s. These institutes were founded as independent entities because finding universities that would support such projects was nearly impossible.[8] The International Peace Research Association, founded in part by Elise and Kenneth Boulding and funded by UNESCO, began in 1965 as an outgrowth of work done by the Quakers and the Women's International League for Peace and Freedom. Peace research institutes were founded in order to study war, its causes and cures. The key players in these institutes were, for the most part, male.

Early scholars of the peace movement recognized the inherent relationship linking peace research, education and activism. Elise Boulding has used metaphor to relate her conception of this relationship. She believes that peace research and action can be related metaphorically to medical education and practice. Whereas doctors train to heal patients, peace people train to heal the world. Elise sees peace research, education and action as essentially equal in importance. Quoted in an interview in the 1990s with Judith Porter Adams, Elise stated, "My goal has been to initiate a dialogue between the action and the research perspectives.... [M]y mediation role has been between peace researchers and peace activists, each of whom thinks the other is failing to address the real needs of our time."[9] The founding of COPRED (the Consortium on Peace, Research, Education and Development) in 1970 by the Bouldings was a conscious effort to unite these three disparate elements.

Peace education in the late nineteenth century was begun in earnest in the U.S. by social reformers such as Jane Addams and Fanny Fern Andrews. Addams, as a founder of WILPF, was one of the first to connect the social conditions underlying the oppression of women and families to the violence propagated in communities and in the world. Elise's early ideas on educating for peace were inspired and grounded in the work of these women reformers.

Later-evolving ideas of peace education, including its relational and transformative potential, arose partly as a result of the women's movement and its influence on the field of peace studies.[10] Feminists such as Elise

Boulding, who taught women's studies at the University of Colorado, were concerned about the emphasis within the peace movement, largely dominated by males, on the technical aspects of the arms race and the resulting neglect of the more human and personal consequences of violence. Elise's research project on the women who participated in the Women's Strike for Peace in the early 1960s showed that women were overwhelmingly concerned about these social issues. Elise discussed this research in a report to UNESCO in the early 1980s.[11]

In the 1960s there was intense discussion among academics of the relationship between peace and feminist issues, largely missing from the earlier nineteenth-century work of reformers such as Addams and Andrews. The Women's International League for Peace and Freedom, of which Elise was international chair in the late 1960s, again took up the banner of pacifism in relation to women's issues.[12] Connections were seen between poverty, racism and ecological danger, and physical, structural and psychological violence. Peace began to be seen as a state of harmonious relationships, intra-personal, interpersonal and intra-global.

At that time, some "second-wave" feminists felt that peace studies were a diversion from the struggle for liberation from oppressive structures. However, in the early '70s, a generation of feminists came into "new ways of knowing." [13] Different ways of looking at connectedness and its relation to nurturance and how women learn and process moral thinking provided the grounding for the work of such thinkers as Elise Boulding, Betty Reardon, Birgit Brock-Utne, Nell Noddings and Sara Ruddick.[14] Elise, at this time, was teaching and writing about women. Her work celebrated women's capacities as peacemakers, mediators and nurturers and discussed the fact that the peace work of women goes largely unnoticed, particularly in the developing world. She has called this part of the globe the "two-thirds" or the "five-sixths" world, thus placing "development" in its proper perspective. Elise was also struggling, as were many feminists such as Jean Baker-Miller and Carol Gilligan, not to exclude men in her thinking.

These views of women as nurturers, caretakers and carriers of the values of their cultures came to be seen by some, with the rise of feminism's third wave (postmodernism), as "essentialist." The essentialist position is that women are inherently different from men in a *relational* sense and that they possess characteristics such as the capacity to nurture, to care and to connect in ways that men do not. Because of this, women are expected to be kinder and gentler than are men. A few of her associates felt that some of Elise's ideas were out of touch with part of the current feminist thinking. Interestingly, when I raised these issues in the course of our work together, Elise vehemently denied that her ideas could be considered "essentialist."[15]

In fact, the criticism of some of her views did not alter her belief that men have much to learn from women about partnering, nurturing, sharing, and connecting.

During the mid–1970s, when she was doing much of her work in women's studies and in particular with the American and International Sociological Associations, Elise became aware that the U.S. State Department had major concerns about her "leftist views." Her journal entry of January of 1976 reveals the following:

> I was very troubled yesterday with a letter from a colleague who described a visit to the woman officer in the State Department in charge of IWY [the International Women's Year, 1975]. The colleague mentioned my work on women and the officer said they could have nothing to do with my work because I am too "leftist." This was the second such message. The first was during an IWY panel at the UN when Jessie Bernard [prominent sociologist] told me she had not been allowed by the State Department to quote me in a speech.

Conclusion

In 1996 Elise received the first Peacemaker of the Year award, given by the Rocky Mountain Peace and Justice Center in Boulder, Colorado. The following poem was written and read for the occasion by the center's longtime founder and director, LeRoy Moore, and, in some sense, may be considered a summation of much in the life of Elise Boulding.

Elise, how do I prize you?
Is it for the breadth and depth of your knowledge?
    for your wonderful curiosity?
    for your love of children?
    or for your great rolling laugh?
    or is it that you speak for women?
    or that you champion those who are despised
        and misunderstood?
    and what about your insistence that action
        without reflection is empty
        but that nothing changes without action?
When I hear your name
    so many words, thoughts, images come to mind—
"the 200 year present" you say we carry with us,
development, whether of the child, the global civic culture,
    the economy—none really separate from the others

simplicity
sustainability
"the family in the world and the world in the family"
play: as essential for adults as for children
    —is it true that the revolution you seek
    is one where you'll be absent if you can't play?
the trinity of thinking, feeling, acting
your challenge that we explore cracks in the technological shield
    that separates us from the essential reality
    of our own bodies, our own souls, our earth house
INGO, no not Bingo, but INGO:
    international non-governmental organizations,
    the abundance of which you have charted,
    some of which you have chartered, many charged.
You remind us, Elise, in this age
    when the nation-state is simultaneously
    so destructive and so outmoded,
    so predictable, yet so predatory—
    you remind us that we already are creating

Receiving recognition for the peacework she has done has always meant a great deal to Elise, although her pleasure is largely a private matter. The Boston Research Center for the 21st Century honored her in 1995 with their first Global Citizen Award. The mission of the BRC is "to bring together scholars and activists in dialogue on common values across cultures and religions, seeking in this way to support an evolving global ethic for a peaceful twenty-first century." The BRC motto reads, to "[B]e the heart of a network of global citizens. Be a bridge for dialogue between civilizations. Be a beacon lighting the way to a century of life." More apt words to describe the life of Elise Boulding would be difficult to find.

Chronology

1920 born in Oslo, Norway to Birgit Marianne and Josef Biörn-Hansen

1923 family immmigrates to the U.S., joining an active Scandanavian community in New Jersey

1940 Norway invaded by the Nazis—time of personal crisis and turning to pacifism and the Society of Friends (Quakers)

1941 marries Kenneth Boulding, move to Princeton, New Jersey

1942 move to Nashville so that Kenneth can teach at Fisk University

1944 move to Ames, Iowa, where Kenneth teaches economics establishes with Kenneth the Friends Student Colony

1947 Russell, first child, born

1949 receives a Master's in sociology from Iowa State

1949 second child, Mark, born

1949 family relocates to Ann Arbor, Michigan

1951 Christine Boulding born

1953 Philip Boulding born

1953 family sabbatical in Jamaica, Kenneth teaching at the University of the West Indies

1954–55 family sabbatical at Stanford University, meets Fred Polak and translates his book *The Future* into English

1955 William Boulding born

1963 first research project on the Women's Strike for Peace

1963 continues her research during a family sabbatical in Japan

1963 begins IPRA newsletter

1965 return to graduate school on a Danforth fellowship at the University of Michigan

1965 founding of IPRA in Clarens, Switzerland

1966 runs for Congress on a write-in Peace Party platform

1967 family relocates to Boulder, CO, begins teaching sociology at the University of CO

1967 appointed International Chair of WILPF

1969 receives a doctorate in sociology from the University of Michigan, dissertation is on the effects of global industrialization on women

1970 founding of COPRED in Boulder

1970 begins work on climate, population, the environment and arms control with the American Association for the Advancement of Science

1970 begins editing the *The American Sociologist*

1970 founding work with the International Sociological Association on sex roles and society

1972 begins key leadership positions on several committees of the American Sociological Association on women and world conflict

1973 joins the board of directors of the Institute for World Order (later to become the World Policy Institue)

1974 "burn-out"—retreats to a newly built "hermitage" for year of solitude, begins to write *The Underside of History*

1976 *The Underside of History: A View of Women Through Time* is published

1977 begins consultative work with the United Nations University

1978 move to Dartmouth and 8 year "commuter marriage"

1978 begins consultative work with UNESCO

1979 appointed by Jimmy Carter to the Congressional Commission on Proposals for the National Academy of Peace and Conflict Resolution (later to become the U.S. Institute for Peace)

1984 appointed to the board of the National Peace Institute Foundation

1985 retires and returns to Boulder

1987 appointed to the American Friends Service Committee Corporation

1988 appointed Secretary-General of IPRA

1988 begins to chair the board of the Boulder Parenting Center

1988 board co-chair, Exploratory Project on Conditions for a Just World Peace

1989 accepts for IPRA UNESCO's annual peace prize

1989 Visiting Professor, Center for Conflict Analysis and Resolution, George Mason University

1989 helps to found and becomes president of the IPRA Foundation

1991 Project Director, IPRA's Commission on Peacebuilding in the Middle East

1992 becomes Senior Fellow of the Dickey Center for International Understanding at Dartmouth

1993 Kenneth Boulding dies

1993 begins to edit *the International Nonviolent Peace Teams Services*

1993 invited to the inaugural world gathering of the Interfaith Peace Council in England

1995 appointed to the Committee for the Quaker UN Office (QUNO)

1996 moves to Wayland, MA

1996 receives the Global Citizens's Award from the Boston Research Center for the 21st Century

1997 receives the World Futures Studies Federation Award

2000 moves into North Hill retirement community in Needham, MA

I

From Norway to the Halls of Academia: The Early and Middle Years

Chapter 1

Seeds and Soil: Forebears and Early Life

Ancestors

Elise Boulding was born in 1920 in Oslo, Norway, the eldest child of Birgit Marianne Johnsen and Josef Biörn-Hansen. Her forebears were seafarers on both sides of her family: sea captains, shipbuilders and international traders who sailed the oceans and brought goods from around the world to their homes on the islands off the southern coast of Norway. Her parents were second cousins, having known each other since childhood on these islands. Her maternal grandfather was the captain of a clipper ship. Her maternal grandmother, for whom Elise was named, often sailed with him, until she lost a baby while at sea. Afterwards she stayed home, and, when her husband died at the same time clipper ships were being replaced by steam powered boats, her grandmother sold the ship and then bought and managed a farm.

Elise's mother's family moved to Oslo from the islands, but many descendants have remained there, and Elise considers the islands her ancestral home. When she was ten, Elise and her parents returned there (the only time the family did so), and Elise felt strongly that she was part of a very tightly-knit, warm and loving clan.

One of Elise's earliest memories is of her mother standing at the window in their new home in New Jersey, crying. Birgit had not wanted to move to the United States, believing that Americans were terribly crass and materialistic. Soon after arriving, Birgit's younger sister Tulla, who had

Elise as a baby with her mother.

come shortly after Elise and her family arrived, died of cancer, leaving Birgit bereft. Elise's mother always dreamed of returning to Norway, though the family had only the one trip back during Elise's growing years.

Her mother profoundly influenced Elise, who said, "I grew up seeing the world through my mother's eyes." As part of the last wave of Norwegian immigration to America, the family emigrated when Elise was three. There was an economic depression at that time, 1923, in Norway, and Elise's father feared for his job as an engineer. They relocated to the Newark, New Jersey, area, where Joseph worked for Carrier, helping to design the air conditioners. Partly due to her mother's influence, Elise retained the idea that Norway was a "safe place" until the Nazis invaded in the early 1940s during her last year in college. This was a time of profound personal crisis for her and an epiphany that was to determine the course of the rest of her life.

Elise Boulding's immigrant status profoundly affected her life views. Her sense of being both a part of a culture and standing away from it developed as a result of living equally in both the Norwegian and American worlds. Elise's family spoke only Norwegian in the home until her younger sisters arrived, one when Elise was nine, the other when she was eleven. Elise's sisters, in her view, were much more American than she. Elise took a large role in caring for her two younger sisters, especially once her mother had returned to work as a therapeutic masseuse in order to bring in money during the economic depression of the 1930s. Her father lost his engineering job briefly during that time, a cause of worry to young Elise.

The family's recreational activities were mainly with a group of Scandinavians, all of whom had emigrated about the same time. Summers were spent either at the home of two elderly American women clients of her mother's who owned a home in New Brunswick, Canada, or at a lake in Pennsylvania, where swimming continued to be the favorite family activity. Though Elise's status as an immigrant played a central role in shaping her life views, just as influential was the role of her parents and *their* status as immigrants, in addition to their expectations for her as a first-generation American child.

Birgit Marianne Johnsen, Elise's mother, as a young woman.

The Biörn-Hansens' move to America was part of the last wave of Norwegian immigration to the U.S. The first documented journey of this so called "modern" wave was in 1825, when the ship *Restoration* departed from Stavanger, Norway. The *Restoration* is known as the "Norwegian *Mayflower*" and holds a significant place in Scandinavian-American history, though the boat itself was only one fourth the size of the original *Mayflower*.

There is a paucity of material about the early immigrants, many of whom eventually settled in the northern and midwestern areas of the United States. It is believed, however, that among the early arrivals were many Quakers, hoping to find freedom of religion from the state-imposed Evangelical Lutheran faith, established when Norway gained its independence from Denmark. The Constitution of 1814 mandated that the king profess Lutheranism, thus imposing a state religion. Elise connected with the descendents of some of these Quakers while living in Iowa during the 1940s as a young wife and mother.

Though most of the Norwegian immigrants who arrived on American shores were nominally Lutheran, only about half formally joined any congregation, partly because fierce individualism was an inherent part of their

Elise with her parents, Josef and Birgit, probably around 1927.

character. The existing Lutheran churches in America could not accommodate the thousands of recent arrivals. The official State Church of Norway had done little in the way of support and preparation for those who emigrated.[1]

The large migrations from Norway ended in the mid–1920s. Between 1825 and 1930, more than 800,000 people left to settle in the United States and Canada, with most arriving between 1865 and 1915.[2] Emigration from Scandinavia reached its peak in 1882. In the 1920s, there was a deep economic depression in Europe. Josef, Elise's father, had worked briefly in the United States during the first World War. He was employed by two different American corporations, General Electric and Goodrich, after completing his degree at Edinburgh University. Being familiar with the American culture, he was much more ready to emigrate than Birgit.

Most of the Scandinavian immigrants to the United States settled near others who had come before them. This was also true of Elise's parents, who first settled in East Orange, New Jersey, shortly thereafter relocating to more rural Livingston, and then to Hillside, where Elise's memories of her childhood began. Most of the Scandinavian engineers of this last wave of migration, such as Josef, and their families settled either in the Schenectady or the Newark area, near the industrial hubs where they could find work. Though many immigrants stayed together in tightly knit communities, Norwegians generally disdained formal organizations related to their immigrant status. They did not readily form clubs, as did other groups such as the Italian-Americans. There are very few Scandinavian-American associations on record, due in part to a deep love of freedom and a commitment to individuality, characteristics found in the "Norwegian personality."[3] One exception to this trend is that many did join the Sons of Norway, founded in the late 1890s as an organization devoted to aiding fellow Norwegians when the U.S. was enduring a deep economic recession. Subsequently, the organization evolved into an association that has helped to keep alive the history and culture of Norway and that of Norwegian-Americans.[4]

Elise's parents never joined any formal immigrant associations. Elise herself had some contact with the Sons of Norway during her adult life while she was living in Colorado. She was invited to one of their meetings to talk about peace. The group was amazed to learn of the birth of peace research in Norway, "that part of Norway they didn't know anything about." In Elise's view, the organization was "culturally oriented—conservative, but not right-wing, just conservative." And so was her extended family in Norway. She explained,

> If I go to Norway now I am talking with people who live in a totally different world politically than I do ... but ... and I am very conscious of that because I spend part of my time at the Peace Research Institute in Oslo with my peace research colleagues and then I go over to my family and they are just two different worlds, but you have the same in this country.... It would be as if they were conservative Republicans.[5]

Elise was named after her paternal grandmother, Elise Marie, as well as her mother's mother. There were several ancestral Elises, including, in addition to her maternal grandmother, her great-great-grandmother on her mother's side.

Elise's father was the youngest of five siblings. His mother, to whom he was deeply attached, died when he was seventeen, and he did not get along well with his father. Josef did not have a happy childhood. He rarely spoke of his family in Norway, in contrast to Birgit who retained such utopian memories. Josef's family moved to Edinburgh, Scotland, when he was a child. Subsequently, he taught briefly at Edinburgh College before coming to America the first time. Josef had kept in touch with his young cousin, Birgit Johnsen, and eventually he persuaded her to marry him, after which the couple settled in Oslo, where he found work.

Though a quiet man, her father was the more affectionate of her parents. In a poignant letter to her younger sister Vera in 1990, after Vera's inquiry about Josef, Elise wrote:

> The people who spoke about father in his youth all remarked on the great change that came over him when he married mother at age 27 (I was probably conceived a month before their marriage). He became outgoing and cheerful. Everyone said mother "brought him out," "rescued him." People had feared he might be suicidal, so pronounced was his melancholy at times.... He loved being a father, we all had wonderful fathering. He loved public speaking and he loved singing, these were all things mother helped him discover in himself and develop as talents. He was much more demonstrative and affectionate than mother. His own mother must have been an affectionate person.

Though Elise carried fond memories of her father, it was her mother who had a much greater influence on her throughout her childhood. In 1935, when Elise was fifteen, she dedicated her journal, which she had begun keeping, to both her mother and humanity, "my two beloveds."[6] It was her mother who insisted Elise carry on with her Norwegian heritage. On coming home from school as a girl, her mother helped her with her lessons, always insistent that she repeat them in Norwegian in order for her to keep the culture alive. She explained,

> I don't remember disliking it, but I remember being impatient, because I wanted to go out and play. But I did it, and I am *very, very* glad that I did it. Because I think growing up bilingual is *so* much better than growing up monolingual. I wouldn't be able to read and write Norwegian now if she hadn't done that when I was a child. The fact that I grew up seeing the world through my mother's eyes, and it was primarily my mother, you know, she was always telling me how good everything was in Norway. The medicine was better, education was better, the care of the environment was better, people were healthier, they were more moral, you know ... and that America was a materialistic country where people were, she never used words like degenerate, but you know now that I think of it, there was sort of the flavor of that. Well-meaning but not up to snuff, really by her standards [*she laughs*]. And the fact that I had that view and then got the view in school of America, the land of opportunity and the great democracy and the country that had really pioneered the good life and civic virtue and inventiveness and creativity and that it was the land of opportunity where everybody could make a wonderful life and I remember reading ... all the biographies of people who came from, you know, immigrants who wrote the story of how they had come ... and made it ... and always in the vein that this was the land of opportunity. So the fact that I could look at this country I was growing up in and see it in two totally different ways I think was very, very important in my own development because in a sense ... I knew both were true.... So I could set myself up in a Norwegian context and view things, or I could set myself up in an American context and view things, and I could give a coherent account of what was happening from two perspectives, and the fact that I could do that was a very special part of my intellectual and social maturation, I think.[7]

Birgit's move to Oslo from the islands when she was a young girl was hard on her after the freedom and closeness to nature she had experienced on the islands. The extended family homestead remained on the island of Askerøen. Elise and her mother and younger sister returned there when Elise was ten, but her father did not go back to Norway until after Birgit died (when Elise was a young adult), and he did so only at the insistence of his second wife. The memory of the islands, through the eyes of her mother, and her visit there as a child inspired Elise to write *Mor*, her memoir of her mother, in 1981, written for Elise's grandchildren.

Birgit was an accomplished pianist, and as a young adult she had hopes of studying at the Oslo Conservatory. But financial setbacks when she was a young girl in Norway precluded this, and she trained as a nurse and masseuse.

Elise's maternal grandmother was a strong, domineering woman who was stern with her children and later equally so with their spouses. Birgit found her joy in nature and coped with her mother as best she could. Birgit grieved deeply over the loss of her younger sister, Tulla, when the family arrived in America. Issues of loss and depression in the extended family are significant and have been carried down through several generations. At that time, Elise, as a small child of three or four, became for her mother a comforter. She wrote in *Mor*, "I did everything a little girl could to let her know that I was happy.... [C]hildren are often more adaptable than their parents think." Shortly after this, Elise came down with diphtheria, and her mother nursed her back to health. Elise heard her mother laughing again for the first time since Tulla's death several years earlier as she helped Elise learn to walk again.

Birgit's family considered her a bit of a radical as a young adult in Norway, as she helped to organize clubs and activities for women factory workers and worked as a social worker. She marched in peace parades and was part of the annual May 17 celebrations, when Norwegians and Norwegian-Americans traditionally celebrate on the anniversary of the founding of the Constitution of 1814. Birgit's friends and her family did not approve of some of these activities, particularly her views on class distinctions in Norway. While the country traditionally has had few income differentials, there have historically been strong distinctions between the working and middle classes. Birgit refused to use servants and insisted on doing her own housework. This was true also in America until she became too busy with her professional work. Then the family hired outside help, releasing Elise—by that time a young adolescent—from housework. However, whatever political activism her mother may have engaged in in Norway was left behind as the family made their way to America, where they were fearful of reprisals if they were openly political or critical of the government. One incident stands out:

> I remember the summer after I graduated from college I worked in New York for awhile and then decided that wasn't for me and moved up to Syracuse (her parents had relocated there) and entered graduate school, and of course I was politically very active through Norman Thomas and all that, and once I wrote a letter, I was living at home and eating with the family, and once I told them at the supper table that I had just sent a letter to our Congressman.... I don't remember what the issue was now ... it had something to do

> ... it was about 1940 it certainly had something to do with war, we shouldn't go to war or whatever ... and Father and Mother were both very upset.... Mother said, "you go right down to that mailbox and stand there until the mailman comes to pick up the mail and get that letter back," and I did. They were terrified of ... that his job would be in jeopardy if any member of the family criticized the government.... Isn't that interesting? I still puzzle over that.... I can still remember standing there.... I was so embarrassed.... Fortunately for their peace of mind the evening mail was picked up ... at a time when I was able to go to retrieve it.... The mailman just grinned.... They are not supposed to do that, but of course he knew who I was.[8]

Birgit had come to America as a young woman and had worked as a nurse at a sanitarium in New Jersey for two years. This time in America was a happy time for her. She made many friends, among them two sisters, whom Elise later would call her aunts, who lived across the street from the inn where Birgit worked. The family, after their move to Hillside and on through Elise's childhood, would summer with these two women at their country home in New Brunswick, Canada, along with their myriad servants, including nurses, maids, chauffeurs and cooks. Despite her earlier pleasant experiences, Birgit was unhappy about the move to the U.S. However, Josef did not harbor the same ill will toward Americans and did not have the same attachment to Norway as did Elise's mother.

Family Values

It was not until the family's move to Maplewood, when Elise was in high school, that they finally found compatibility with others who held similar socio-economic and educational values. Birgit was tremendously popular with her clients, often being invited to their homes with Elise sometimes accompanying her. Elise's two younger sisters, Sylvia having been born when Elise was nine and Vera when she was eleven, spoke English at home among themselves and considered themselves Americans. This relocation meant for the family a move toward fuller integration into mainstream middle-class American culture. Yet for Elise, it was never a full integration.

Elise's mother had worried earlier about the social contacts Elise was developing in the blue collar city of Hillside, a factory town. In *Mor*, Elise wrote, "All of my mother's middle-class Norwegianness, which she rebelled against in Norway, came out as her own in America." Elise struggled with trying to please her parents, at the same time she was loving the "gang of children always ready to play ... the cinder street with its oddly assorted houses.... I was always accepted in their games."[9] At one point, Elise knew she had displeased her mother with a friend she brought home from school:

> I remember having long conversations with her after my friend left, explaining to her that I should be friends with everybody. It was to be the first of many such conversations. The wonderful thing about mother was that she did converse with me in that way. She took my opinions seriously—sometimes.[10]

Elise's mother compartmentalized in her mind her concern for working-class children and her concern for Elise:

> I must have the best, the most constructive and culturally developed environment and contacts at all times, because I was going to grow up and to achieve great things in America. We belonged to the last great wave of immigrants, but we were not just any old immigrants, we were *Norwegians*. The Biörn-Hansens and the Johnsens had been somebody in Norway. We owned and sailed fleets of clipper ships. We were descended from barons. And anyway, we were the ones who had discovered this country a few centuries ago.... [M]y training emphasized that I must always carry myself like a Norseman, walk erect, and look people in the eye. I was also trained to great politeness. I had to curtsey to adults in a country where no one curtsied any more. Mother had a program of toughening me up which involved sloshing ice water over me each morning before I got out of bed.[11]

Her mother refused to allow Elise to use the telephone to call her friends because, in Elise's words, "I would become like Americans and lose the use of my legs." Birgit insisted she walk to meet her friends, face to face.

Her mother insisted that Elise learn to play the piano and cello. She continued with the cello but fought with her mother over playing the piano. Her parents monitored her school work closely and her mother often invited her elementary school teachers home for coffee. Birgit organized mother-daughter clubs, which was the way her mother channeled her activist energies once the family settled in the United States.

Elise's mother was stubborn, having a "very unyielding Nordic strain," as described by Elise. She tearfully remembered a childhood incident after having won a scholarship to scout camp as one of the group of daughters in the mother-daughter club which Birgit started:

> We were all sitting together, the mothers and daughters.... It was announced that I was going to be awarded the two week scholarship ... and I was very happy, and then mother heard that one of the other mothers said, "oh well, that's because she is Birgit's daughter that she got it." And mother had given some leadership to the group, so mother said, "Elise, you can't have it." And that was hard enough but then in the group of mothers ... the mother who had said this got on her knees in front of mother ... it is terrible even now to remember it ... and *begged* her to let me have the scholarship and she said "no." The principle of "no special privilege" was a very important one, and it was always drilled into me never, never special privileges ... wrong for anybody ever anywhere unless there was a handicap, and I realize that that meant for me that when my own children were in school that other mothers would dash down to the school and fight for their kid's rights about this or that, and it was very hard for me to do that ... and I think it goes back to my own mother ... and special privileges.[12]

Her mother often splashed cold water on Elise in the morning, a Norwegian practice considered to strengthen body and character. Elise's daughter Christine, amazed at what her mother has had to overcome, spoke of her thus: It was a "Norwegian household where we would consider the behavior abusive. Her mother was very driven for her, and you add that to a person who was very driven for themself.... She and Dad bent over backwards not to do that to their children."[13]

Birgit died at age 52, when Elise was 25, after a two year struggle with Amyotrophic Lateral Sclerosis, a debilitating and degenerative neurological disease which, in its course, often strikes adults during their middle years. Her mother had severely overworked herself during the years in New Jersey and when Elise was in college. While she did not actively work as a masseuse after the move to Syracuse, by then the damage had been done.

With Kenneth's blessing, Elise, who had been married to him only a short time, came home during her mother's last days to be with her and care for her, reading the Bible to her as she slipped away. Her mother had burned all her papers, "her own Viking funeral pyre," as Elise describes it, leaving only her "legacy of love" to Elise, the 13th chapter of Paul's Epistle to the Corinthians.[14] During Elise's year away, in her own mid-life at the Hermitage, these memories would return with the realization that she had unfinished business with her mother, that "it is never too late to bring love into any relationship."[15]

In her own words, Elise's thoughts about her mother and their relationship were summed up:

> She wasn't charismatic, but she had a wonderful outgoing personality and people always responded very positively to her ... so I think probably in some ways I am like her, in SOME ways.... So she would ... whenever we went anywhere she always talked to the bus driver, getting in or off the bus, you know, talk to the person she was sitting next to ... embarrass the tears out of me, but I do the same thing [she laughs].[16]

And in 1981 in *Mor* Elise wrote:

> Perhaps none of us realized how deeply mother loved her family, because she was not as physically demonstrative as father. She was a person of very deep feelings, but she needed to keep space between her own feelings and other people, even her own family. For mother all beauty and truth came through art and she could not imagine that the pursuit of art could do other than ennoble and enrich any person. She nourished all of us on music because she thought that was the best she could possible do for us. At bottom, I think she was right. She provided the nourishment, and it was up to us to determine how to use that nourishment. I was always eager to talk with her about the new ideas that came to me through my studies, and we often reached a sense of real sisterhood in those discussions. We loved to be asked if we were sisters when we were out walking. When I compared our family with the family of my friends, I knew that we had more *family being* than any of my friends. Mother communicated the centrality of family to the whole of one's life in many ways, both through her working and her home-centered years, and we three girls have all been blessed by that. It has helped each of us to strive for, and to a significant extent achieve, a sense of wholeness in the family life we have fostered in our own households. That same wholeness will, I trust and pray, be passed on to the fourth generation.

Later that same year, 1981, Elise's younger sister Sylvia committed suicide in her early fifties, a victim, Elise believes, of her mother's relentless pursuit of Sylvia's musical prodigy as a child and of her attempts at living out her frustrated career as a concert musician through her daughter. Elise wrote a journal entry during January 1974 describing Sylvia as:

> a genius unfulfilled which is the tragic legacy of mother's misguided aspirations for her.... [I]n a strange way, we both share that sense of being blocked and limited.... [O]ddly I feel it both in my intellectual work and in my imaginative capacities.

Childhood

Elise as a young child often played alone and found herself a special playhouse in the family's back yard where she sat for long periods of time, cutting out paper dolls and making up stories and plays. She loved school all through her growing years, and her parents took great pride in her accomplishments. Her parents bought a set of *Encyclopedia Britannica*, even though at the time they could not afford it. In *Mor*, Elise recalled the excitement of her first research using the encyclopedia, a report on the attar of roses production in Bulgaria in fourth grade. She was an excellent student, perpetually stood out in her class and was, at times, verbally cited in class by teachers as a model student whom others should emulate. To Elise, this was quite embarrassing.

Elise particularly enjoyed writing stories and researching for projects, and she greatly enjoyed studying ancient Greece and Rome.[17] She disdained any sort of arts and crafts and remembers penmanship as a dismal experience, citing hers as awful. When the family moved to Maplewood during her second year of high school, this was quite a change for her, as she no longer was the brightest student in the class. But she relished in the opportunities for practicing her musicianship, as by then she was an accomplished cellist and began performing with a group of young people who became her friends, though none of the relationships became particularly close. She excelled in social studies and English, but enjoyed less her mathematics courses. One of her favorite classes was a "Problems in Democracy" class, an honors course for which only a few students were selected. It was an interdisciplinary class taught by an English and a social studies teacher. She recalled, "We felt really grown up.... It was a special privilege."[18]

Yet for all her accomplishments, at times Elise felt that she was not doing enough. As a fifteen year old, she wrote in her journal of July 7, 1935:

> [Y]esterday ... I became fifteen years old ... and strange as it may seem I am sorry. I have lived for fifteen long years and have accomplished almost nothing. I am so ignorant, know so little, and have done so little that I am ashamed of myself.... I have read almost nothing of the classics and worthwhile literature. I know the lives of so few great people, I know no philosophy, or anything about politics, our government and world history, I know practically nothing about music.

Beginning as a child, Elise felt the presence of God, and this sense of listening for the Spirit has remained with her ever since. She was led in her elementary school years to a Protestant church near Hillside. She began

Elise was a serious cello player in college and as a young adult. Here she is pictured (with cello) with Frankin (far left) and Libuse Miller (center back), and an unidentified fourth. It was partly through her music that she found the Quakers.

attending this church regularly by herself, and eventually the minister's wife, Mrs. Northwood, befriended her and invited her to tea, to read and to talk. She was to remain, in Elise's eyes, one of several women she considers mentors and role models.

It was a happy day for the family when Elise won a scholarship to what was then called the New Jersey College for Women, now Douglas College and part of Rutgers University. Elise was preparing to work her way through college as a waitress until she realized her parents would not allow her to do this, as "no daughter of theirs would wait on other people." Fortunately, her father had put a little money aside during the Depression for her spending money.[19]

Finishing college in three years, music continued to be central in her life. Elise continued to play, sometimes earning money as a cellist while participating in trios and quartets. She spent time at "musical evenings," playing at the homes of certain faculty. These relationships were very

Elise, as a college student at Douglas College, continued her love of the outdoors.

important parts of her college experience, often extending into conversations and shared meals. During college Elise wrote musical reviews for the school newspaper. In 1939, when she was nineteen, she reviewed a concert given by the New York Philharmonic Orchestra.[20]

It was in college, partly through spending time at the Rutgers research library, that Elise began to realize the possibility of becoming a more serious scholar. She majored in English and minored in French and German. One of her plans early on was to study the influence of the Viking invasions on English literature. At that time, she became intensely interested in the nature and structure of language. Elise had no other scholarly ambitions, however, than to teach English at a local high school when she finished college. Soon, however, her move to New York City would lead her toward new paths and into new associations.

Chapter 2

Young Adult and Wife

After graduating from Douglas College, Elise moved to New York City and stayed there for a brief but influential five months, working at two consecutive jobs which entailed, in her words, "first running a billing machine in one publishing house and then rewriting impossible high school texts in another."[1] This period in her life was a time of "reckoning," of coming to terms with the values with which she had been raised, and it marked the beginning of the integration of her inner commitment to social justice and her developing sense of spirituality. She literally fled New York to return home to Syracuse, where her parents had relocated, at the end of that time.

Elise had had no previous experience with the kind of social life with which she was confronted in the city, including frequent office parties involving what she considered highly superficial conversations and associations. It was a jarring experience for her. She befriended a co-worker who was Catholic and who volunteered his time at a local Catholic Worker hospitality house. The Catholic Worker Movement, a loose association of radical anarchists who lived with and worked among the poor and disenfranchised, had been started earlier in the century in New York City by Dorothy Day, who was the editor of a newspaper by the same name. Elise found Day's writings during that time and also came under the influence of Catherine de Hueck, a woman whom she called "the Baroness," a Russian émigré who directed one of the houses in Harlem where her friend worked. This woman who had forsaken her wealthy and upper class roots to live among the poor, made a tremendous impression upon Elise, and, as she recalled, she does not believe Catherine de Hueck even realized this, so humble was she. Elise remembered, "She wore her poverty like court jewels," and to her, the Baroness "saw all social reality as at core spiritual reality."[2] It was through her that Elise discovered that people could love God unashamedly and profess this love through acts of charity in loving kindness.

It was in New York that Elise began to have first-hand experiences with those who were working to better the lot of African-Americans. Her parents at that time did not approve of her associations with blacks, with the reminder that "birds of a feather flock together." For Elise, the idea of living among blacks was foreign to her, having grown up in her insular Scandinavian-American community. Later, after she and Kenneth moved to Princeton, they incurred the disfavor of some members of the Princeton Quaker Meeting when they entertained blacks in their home during the years prior to the Civil Rights movement.

Elise could understand the pacifism of the radical Catholics, as she believed that, at heart, her mother was a pacifist. Though Birgit had become fearful of exhibiting this side of herself once the family emigrated, Elise remembers when she was in high school her mother writing plays, essays and poems about peace, particularly as the United States moved toward entering the Second World War. It was during this time in New York, 1939 to 1940, that Elise became involved in the socialist movement, joining the youth campaign for two candidates.

Finding Friends (The Quakers)

These experiences were Elise's first real forays into the peace movement. She also worshipped among pacifists and occasionally attended Quaker Meetings. Elise had discovered Quakerism while still a student at Douglas College in the late 1930s. Her high school and college years had been a time of spiritual questioning and, as she wrote in her autobiographical piece, "Born Remembering," a time of "torrential denial of religious belief" and of "stiff, intellectually impeccable deportment." She also recalls that "[in college] I saw my love of God as a weakness ... as a crutch.... I must learn to walk alone, to be strong."[3] Attending the Meeting for Worship sporadically during those years, she became acquainted with several Quaker musicians in New Brunswick. She was impressed with their deep sense of social activism and spiritual commitment, and, when she left New York City after five months, she began regularly attending the Syracuse Monthly Meeting. As she was to recall, "The silence of the meeting was a reminder of my own childhood listening space," where she felt at peace and at home.[4]

As a young girl growing up in her Scandinavian-American household, Elise had not been introduced to any formal church liturgy, though their family was, as were most of the other immigrants in their community, nominally Lutheran. Nor did the family regularly attend church. Nevertheless, as a young child, her mother and she nightly recited together the Lord's Prayer in Norwegian, which well into her seventies Elise still recalled verbatim. Christmases were happy occasions in their household, as they were celebrated in the traditional Scandinavian way, and Christmas Eve was a special time when her father would take out the old family bible and read joyously from the Gospel of Luke. To Elise, God was an unseen presence:

> [L]istening to God is one of my clearest childhood memories. There was always a quiet inner space I could go into, a listening place. I listened while I picked blueberries in a sweet-smelling meadow; while lying in the bottom of a rowboat rocking on the ripples of a small mountain lake; while curled up on the living room couch leafing through the reproductions of Norwegian paintings that were among the few treasures brought from our home in Norway.[5]

It seemed natural that Elise would find deep compatibility with the Quaker method of worship which is to sit in silence listening, "waiting on the Lord."[6] Founded in the mid–17th century, the Quaker movement represented a radical wing of that of the English Reformation. Early Quakers or Friends took to heart the message discovered and preached by the movement's founder, George Fox, "that Christ has come to teach his people himself," that no minister or priest need mediate between the experience of the individual and the divine. The concept of the "Inward Teacher" is central to Quakerism. "God as teacher" may be found within every living soul.[7]

The purpose of Quaker worship is to discover, through silent, expectant waiting, that truth which is universal and which can guide individuals into the right relationship both with God and with the world. As Paul Lacey, recently retired from teaching at Earlham, a Quaker college in Richmond, Indiana, notes, "The image of the Inward Teacher" stresses the primary saving work of the spirit as *pedagogical* rather than *priestly*. The priestly is subsumed under the pedagogical work. And the work of "answering that of God" in everyone invariably leads a seeker to "answer that of God in him or herself." This listening also leads to seeking an answer to the question of what God wishes the seeker to *do* in the world, or the pedagogical/spiritual call.[8]

Thus the basis of Friends' social testimonies is on answering the call of the Inward Light, the Inward Teacher, the Spirit of Christ, or God, seeking to discover "that of God" in individuals encountered in daily living and in the world at large. As Quaker scholar Howard Brinton points out, Quakers "cannot answer that of God in every one by any form of violence, physical or psychological, for violence moves only the external, not the internal spirit.[9] This is the basis for the historic Friends Peace Testimony, roots of which are found in the words that George Fox addressed to King Charles II in 1661:

> We utterly deny all outward wars and strife and fightings with outward weapons, for any end or under any pretense whatsoever. And this is our testimony to the whole world. The spirit of Christ, by which we are guided, is not changeable, so as once to command us from a thing as evil and again to move unto it; and we do certainly know, and so testify to the world, that the spirit of Christ, which leads us into all Truth, will never move us to fight any war against any man with outward weapons, neither for the kingdom of Christ, nor for the kingdoms of this world.[10]

Whirlwind Courtship

When she moved to Syracuse, Elise began attending Quaker Meeting more regularly, a meeting she has described as "famous for their activism." She also occasionally sought out a local Catholic Church. Soon thereafter, she met Kenneth Boulding, who was already well-known in Quaker circles as a gifted speaker and poet. Kenneth was visiting Syracuse for Quarterly Meeting. Quaker Quarters are monthly meetings gathered regionally that meet several times a year.

Three weeks after they met, Kenneth and Elise announced their engagement, and at the same time she applied for membership in the Syracuse Friends Meeting. She was 21 years old, Kenneth was ten years her senior. Though their courtship was brief, it was obvious to all of the Quakers in their respective meetings that they were meant for each other.[11]

As Elise wrote in "Born Remembering,"

> [W]hile in one way I had been preparing for the world [he] introduced me to all my life, in another way this was a new world to me.... Kenneth's own deep spirituality released the last of my own inhibitions about the religious dimension.... [W]hen he spoke in Meeting the tears often rolled down my cheeks in love and joy and compassion for this extraordinary man who was to be my husband.[12]

Courting Kenneth at Cooperstown, New York, spring of 1941.

For Elise, her marriage and her entrance into the Society of Friends, both occurring at the same time in 1941, were two experiences that were to transform her and ground all of her future work. Spiritual issues played pivotal roles both in bringing her deeply together with Kenneth and, later at times, driving them painfully apart.

Just before the Bouldings announced their engagement, Elise applied for and was accepted to civilian overseas service in a program run by the American Friends Service Committee, and she planned to begin training near Pendle Hill, the Quaker retreat center outside Philadelphia. She moved to Pennsylvania soon thereafter to begin the program.

Kenneth Boulding was an émigré from England, having already established himself as an academic economist, international peace researcher and Quaker poet. He had recently completed several years teaching at the University of Edinburgh. Kenneth came to the U.S. initially as a representative of Scottish Quakers to the 1937 World Gathering of Friends in Philadelphia. Offered a job at Colgate University in upstate New York, he decided to stay in America, and the next year he sent for his mother, a widow, who continued to live with him until his marriage.

Kenneth had discovered Quakers as a student at Oxford, having grown up in a fundamentalist Methodist church in lower-middle-class Liverpool, England. Always painfully aware of English class differences, this became more acute during his scholarship days in college. Throughout his life he continued to marvel at the relative lack of class differentials in the United States.[13] The eagerness with which he embraced the virtues of capitalism at times became a source of conflict and pain for Elise, whose ideas on the importance of frugality, simplicity of consumption and egalitarianism had been partly shaped by her Norwegian culture and further influenced by her study of those on the so-called "margins" of society, the poor and oppressed, women and children.

Those who describe Kenneth Boulding say he was an "iconoclast," a brilliant and a creative genius, defying categorization. A charismatic lecturer, large crowds would often gather around him after his talks. Later Elise began at times to feel "like a spectator" at some of these gatherings and realized over time that unless she were to find outlets for her own talents and creativity, she would forever be living in Kenneth's shadow at the expense of her own sense of self. While beginning his career as a rather conventional economist, by the time he retired, Kenneth was equally well known for his treatises and ideas on other things, most notably his work on social systems and peace research. Later at both the Universities of Michigan and Colorado, he was among the highest paid faculty. Colleagues describe his charisma and his ability to "spin off ideas" at fantastic rates.[14]

Yet from childhood he had a rather severe speech impediment that caused him to stutter. Some thought that this was an artifice that he used during his speeches, so artful was his speaking, but this was not the case.

After the couple had announced their engagement and Elise had left for her training outside Philadelphia, Kenneth made weekly visits to her, and they were married in late August of 1941, under the care of Syracuse Meeting. Thus began their long and fruitful relationship that lasted more than fifty years, until Kenneth's death in 1993. The summer of 1941, the beginning of their courtship and marriage, also marked the beginning of a long working relationship between the Bouldings and Pendle Hill that culminated in their both having several pamphlets published by the Pendle Hill Press.

Their marriage and the bombing of Pearl Harbor in December of that year put an end to Elise's plans for overseas work at that time. Elise had already, as she states, been "primed" to hear sociologists and political scientists talk about peace and war. When she met Kenneth, it was to begin a profound transformation for her in many ways. Elise often said that Kenneth was "the most important influence in my adult life ... a teacher about the world of social science and peace studies, lover, fellow Quaker activist, husband, father of our children and friend."

At that time, Elise had no further career ambitions than to be a homemaker, and, as she describes in *One Small Plot of Heaven*, her seminal work on families, she espoused, with Kenneth as her partner, to make their home a place of peace and love. Quakerism was the mold that drew the couple together and was to contain them in their long and eventful life together. Cynthia Kerman, in her intellectual biography of Kenneth Boulding, expressed this eloquently:

> Elise shared Kenneth's spiritual sensitivity, and together they centered their lives in Friends meetings wherever they were, holding meetings in their home when there was no meetinghouse, actively moving and shaping the lives of these small Friends gatherings, and finding, in their travels, a worldwide community of diverse but like-minded souls, both gaining and giving strength and joy and power.[15]

It was in their early life together that both of the Bouldings did their most prolific Quaker writing. Kenneth told Kerman as she interviewed him for her book that he did not think that he and Elise would have settled anywhere there was not a meeting and if there were not one there, they would have started one, so central in importance was their spiritual community. The Boulding children remember as they were growing up that both of their parents frequently spoke in Quaker Meeting.

For Elise when she met him, Kenneth's deep sense of the love of God was like a cool stream bathing her scarred and somewhat scared psyche. He was already well known, not just for his brilliance and his international reputation as a theoretical economist, but also as a deeply respected Quaker "elder." Kenneth's idea that their marriage was to be a "founding of a Colony of Heaven" was both exhilarating and a bit frightening to Elise.

Kenneth's first academic book, *Economic Analysis*, was published the same year they were married and went through many revisions as a popular college text. A few years later at Michigan he helped to pioneer the idea of interdisciplinary faculty seminars that were, "for adventurous minds to explore ideas together, from the points of view of many different specialties."[16] Later, this concept reached its fruition with the founding of the Center for Research on Conflict Resolution in 1959, an outgrowth of an earlier group, the Society for General Systems Research of which Kenneth was the first president.

In the only full-length biography written of Kenneth Boulding, Kerman, who had worked for him during his Michigan tenure, used a psychoanalytic framework to study his life and work. Using the Thematic Apperception Test as her basis, she discovered several conflicting themes running through his personality. She sensed his strong need for autonomy manifesting itself at times in his tendency to distance himself from the needs of others. Elise, Kerman believed, was everything Kenneth's mother was not: "beautiful rather than pretty, tall and statuesque rather than short and elfin, strong and assured rather than anxious, gently deflating rather than effusively praising."[17] Beginning with their courtship and continuing through the years of their marriage, Kenneth continued to write love sonnets to Elise. In 1957, many were published privately under the title *Sonnets for Elise*. Kerman described them as "full of tenderness and devotion, emphasizing the spiritual but not ignoring the comforts of love, and ... are a door opened up on the inner life of a richly imaginative and deeply feeling man."[18] Kerman noted the consistency through these poems of the figure of Elise as the strong, dominant and powerful partner, in contrast to Kenneth's weaker and submissive role.

XXXII

I thank God for thy body, and for mine,
That we are walled about with flesh and skin,
Lit with the life of coursing blood within,
The shining temple of our inner shrine.

***Opposite:* Elise at her wedding in the summer of 1941 with her two sisters, Sylvia *(right)* and Vera.**

I thank Him for the bones, the skull, the spine,
That gives us solid shape, and prove us kin
To brothers of the hoof and the wing and fin,
The heirs of earth's most noble, ancient line.
For were we spirits only, they would fly
Like two bright liquids shaken in a glass,
Into a dull and undistinguished mass
Of neutral Union, and love would die.
For love is not mere fusion, but a mesh
Uniting separateness: The Word Made Flesh!

XXXIII

Not if I sent thee sonnets every hour,
Nor every moment, at the speed of light,
With far more potent words than I can write,
Could I express my wonder at thy power:
For thou hast drawn my bud into a flower,
And glassed my gauzy vision into sight,
Lifted by groveling motion into flight
And built my ruins to a might tower.
I, who was poor, am rich, and will return
To thy domains the wealth that thou has made,
For only thus can love's unbalanced trade
Be made complete, its true result to earn.
And as between us both the current flow
Of sweet exchange, our mutual riches grow.[19]

Kerman noted that Kenneth wrote, after his marriage to her, that Elise "makes an excellent Elder and pulls my coat tails when I have said enough!"[20] Elise grounded Kenneth. "She was always the solid counterpart to Kenneth's flying all over the place and she was underground, you know...very solid, like Mother Earth.... [H]e was very fond of her, but he was also ... much more of a child," according to one longtime friend.[21] Elise at times greatly enjoyed Kenneth's exuberance and his sense of humor, and they could joke about her Nordic roots sometimes as preventing her from seeing life from the funny side. He called her "my gloomy Norwegian."[22] In a playful interview given for the Douglas College Alumni Bulletin in 1973, Elise recalled that "running our home was like running a combination hotel-theater."[23] As her daughter, Christine Boulding, noted:

> Dad loved to argue.... He would do it for the sake of arguing, he loved the process of thinking, creating an argument, and he could switch sides at the drop of a hat.... Mom argues from the heart, and it is because she *cares* so much, and it is very hard for those two

> kinds of people to argue because those of us who argue from the heart feel so angry.[24]

Everything Elise had been experiencing in her recent past, her experiences in New York City and contact with radical pacifists as well as the spiritual mentoring she received through her seeking, helped to "prime the pump" so to speak, for the extraordinary trajectory of her meeting and courtship with Kenneth Boulding. Though she often referred to her meeting him as an epiphany, and mentioned that in the beginning he was her primary teacher about social science and peace studies, her earlier solitary experiences as a child and her associations in college and in New York City had influenced her in ways perhaps less obvious, but real nevertheless.

One very vivid experience that profoundly affected her was the invasion of Norway by the Nazis in April of 1940. Prior to that time Elise had intended to apply for a scholarship to study Scandinavian literature in Oslo. When the invasion occurred, these hopes were dashed. Other more utopian dreams were also crushed, such as the idea that Norway was a safe haven to which to return should things in America become terribly bleak, the dream nurtured by Birgit through Elise's growing years.

Her last year of college had been one that involved giving up many of Elise's childhood fantasies and wishes. With characteristic determinism she had decided that if Norway was not safe, then perhaps there was nowhere safe, and that it was up to *her*, Elise, to work at making the world safe. Thus began, at least in her dim visioning, the course of her future life and work in peace. Meeting Kenneth at this time added to the inner transformations already under way.

In the beginning, Elise's and Kenneth's was a traditional marriage with gender-divided roles and responsibilities, one in which she fully expected to continue to be a housewife and mother for the foreseeable future. In a lecture she gave on the family during the early years of their marriage, these views of the differences between men's and women's roles were evident: "I don't mean to say that *all* women should stay in the kitchen but simply that ... men make better engineers [*author's italics*]." In another lecture given during that time she discussed the important role husbands might play in supporting their wives while the women cared for the children. Though relying on what at that time was a traditional separation of roles, evident also in these statements is the echo of the importance Elise placed on the work of women, traditional though it may sound. Though her ideas on feminism later greatly expanded to include partnering between women and men, through the years she continued to preach for the invaluable work of nurturance, the "breeder-feeder" roles that women have played throughout global history.

Elise's later writings and speeches on marriage and the family emphasized the importance of equality between partners in marriage, and her views evolved to include much role reciprocation between men and women, particularly as it related to child-rearing. A 1999 piece written for the *Historical Dictionary of Quakerism* for the section on marriage is the latest in what, for Elise, had been an evolving understanding of the institution of marriage. She wrote, "Quaker marriage is a commitment of two persons to live together in a partnership of equals, nurturing one another and dealing creatively with differences as they arise."[25] These are the very same words she used to describe a culture of peace. The above phrase aptly sums up the heart of the Boulding marriage of over fifty years. In the preface to the book she wrote with Kenneth, *The Future: Images and Processes*, published posthumously for him, Elise described their marriage.

> The different ways in which we experienced the world were the very spice of our life together. The differences came together in our love of creation, the Creator, and each other. They also came together in a passionate conviction that the world needs mending, and that what we do, whether in family, community, or the world itself, matters. I loved the way Kenneth's mind roamed the universe and created patterns in space and time—making unexpected connections that no one else would think of. Those patterns, no matter how vast, always included how humans *behave, learn*, and, at their best, *love*. My work was always to translate those patterns into the specifics of actual human behavior in everyday settings—first as a wife, mother, and community activist, then as a sociologist-peace researcher. The future—what lay before us as a human species—was never far from our thoughts.[26]

And in the forward to this volume, a colleague of Elise's at Dartmouth, the late Donella Meadows, wrote of Elise's and Kenneth's work:

> [T]ogether this couple makes one of the most powerful yin/yang combinations in intellectual history—Kenneth throwing out ideas like a pinwheel, letting them fall where they may; Elise picking up ideas from many peoples and cultures, especially ideas from the least-noticed and least-heard people ... and nurturing them into mature and useful combinations.... Kenneth thinks macro, Elise micro, but both are unusually aware of how the macro and the micro connect. Both are masters of the English language. Both have a sardonic sense of humor. Most important, both make a disciplined and wholehearted practice of centering everything they do, think and write in peace and love.[27]

Relocations

In 1941, shortly after the Bouldings were married, Elise and Kenneth moved to Princeton, New Jersey, where Kenneth took a job with the Economic Section of the League of Nations. Here, Elise first became interested in the concept of NGOs, or nongovernmental associations, as she began to learn about the workings of what would later become the United Nations system. It was here also that she first met and became friends with the Swedish sociologist, Alva Myrdal, wife of the economist, Gunnar Myrdal. Alva became at that time a strong role model for Elise, as she worked and advocated for peace and showed Elise the importance of integrating her life as a wife, mother, potential scholar and international traveler. Fifteen years her senior, Myrdal was to greatly influence Elise's thinking on the multiple roles of women. Elise learned from Alva to appreciate her immediate experiences and to use them as models for viewing the world. Elise began to see important connections between local grass-roots involvement and global civic culture. Alva Myrdal later became ambassador to the International Disarmament Commission.

The Bouldings joined the Princeton Quaker Meeting. It was shortly after the bombing of Pearl Harbor. Many members of their Meeting were uncomfortable with a statement that Kenneth wrote and that Elise endorsed, which they signed and passed out among their fellow Quakers. It called on Americans to resist taking up arms following the attack. The document was also publicly circulated. In a 1978 interview, Elise reported that

> technically it was a seditious document and there were a number of consequences. One was that Kenneth was asked by the League of Nations not to make statements on public issues. The upshot to that was that he left the League because he felt he had to be free to speak out.... [T]here was only a tiny community of support for speaking out about how things were and how they ought to be. Our own marriage was a continuing seminar on the state of the world. I had married a wonderful teacher![28]

The Bouldings then moved to Fisk University in Nashville for a year and became active members of the small Quaker Meeting there. Elise began a newsletter for the South Central Friends Yearly Meeting in the hope of uniting some of the smaller meetings scattered throughout the region.

At Fisk, Elise was exposed to eminent sociology faculty, including Robert Park. The interactions at Fisk and her relationship with Alva Myrdal had a marked influence on Elise's decision to study for her master's degree

Relaxing at George School in Pennsylvania, May 1942.

in sociology a few years later. The early years in Princeton and Nashville were years for her of establishing connections, beginning networking and expanding her horizons to include the teachings of social science. Many seeds were sown which would later bear fruit.

In the mid–1940s, the Boulding's moved to Ames, Iowa, where Kenneth took a teaching post at Iowa State University, then called Iowa State College. Elise decided to pursue her master's, beginning her studies in 1945 at age 25. She became a research assistant to Reuben Hill, her thesis advisor. Her work involved interviewing Iowa farm families about the effects of wartime separation. Later, in 1949, her master's thesis was incorporated into a book by Hill entitled *Families Under Stress*. It was also published in 1950 in the *Annals of the American Academy of Political and Social Science*, the outgrowth of a symposium on family stability. These were her early scholarly works in sociology.[29] She received her master's degree in 1949, having taken time off for the birth of Russell, the first born of the Boulding children.

Elise found collegiality among the faculty wives in Ames. The university community did not exclude spouses from the intellectual activity of the university, so common in other college settings. Elise felt very accepted.[30] She continued her involvement with music while in Ames, playing cello in the university orchestra. This would be her last extended experience of playing her instrument in community settings. In future years, Elise would confine the use of her cello to playing solos at home.

It was in Ames that the Bouldings founded their "Friends Student Colony," hosting many discussions in their home on the role of pacifism in public life. They invited a dozen or so students, including returning veterans and conscientious objectors, to live together in a big house near campus. They were hoping to bring a sense of integration of the concepts of peace, nonviolence and spirituality to students and to help them find their true calling in the world. This experience helped to provide the grounding for her later work introducing peace studies programs at both the University of Colorado and at Dartmouth.

Elise became active in the work of the American Friends Service Committee, volunteering out of the Des Moines office, traveling around the state on behalf of the mentally ill, and supporting conscientious objectors whose alternative service was working in the hospitals. Her involvement with AFSC would continue for years to come. Her first publication, "Where is our Sense of Sin?," was on the reciprocal roles between Quakers and AFSC and was published in 1947 in a Quaker weekly.[31] She fondly remembered traveling all over Iowa visiting many small Quaker Meetings representing the theological spectrum of Friends. Visiting meetings whenever they traveled and hosting many Quakers in their various homes continued through the years of their married life together.

Chapter 3

Foundations for Peacebuilding: The Boulding Family

Families as Co-Creators

Families are the "practice ground for making history." So Elise stated in her essay of the same name, reprinted in *One Small Plot of Heaven*, her seminal work on families published by Pendle Hill in 1989. As she became more involved in academia, Elise increasingly came to believe in the relevance of her own "apprenticeship" in the areas of homemaking, childrearing and community activism. She went on to explain,

> When we talk of "making history" we often think of dramatic public acts. Yet, history is really made by the painstaking accumulation of different kinds of experiences and skills in private and public settings. We can never really act "on the national scene" or "on the international scene." We can only act in specific geographical and social spaces which may serve as metaphors for larger scenes. It is our *intending the metaphor* that gives our actions significance. Work done on tax legislation in a local branch of the League of Women Voters is as much international as similar work done in the United Nations buildings in New York or Geneva, which are also only other localities. One of the frightening things abut professors, planners, policy makers, and politicians is that the metaphors often seem more real to them than the specific underlying human experience.[1]

The importance Elise placed on the family as the grounding of individuals for all their future endeavors cannot be underestimated. Herself rooted in her strong Norwegian family, Elise's ideas on how families are the link between individuals and the world took shape as her career as an academic family sociologist evolved. But always, as she often stated in interviews, "I learned much of what was needed to know about children and families through observing my children as they grew up." Her theoretical ideas on the links between the local and the global were partly rooted in her own attempts to make sense of each of the phases of her life. As Christine Boulding noted, "I learned from my mother that life can be lived in stages, that it isn't necessary to be doing everything at once."[2] Indeed, Elise often proudly stated publicly that for the first eighteen years of her married life she was a homemaker. Family laid the backdrop for Elise's subsequent theoretical work, and, as a long-time friend noted, after she was a more respected international sociologist, Elise "just dressed up her language in fancier terms but essentially she was talking about the same things," i.e., the role of the family in the grounding of all other peacemaking functions.[3]

Elise believed the family, as the foundation for the future of the child, offered the possibilities of "crafting individuals to become what they are."[4] This statement by her reflected her belief in the inherent worth of every child, based on her Quaker beliefs and also nurtured by her own experience with her parents. She remembered that she felt "listened to" in profound ways. While raising her own children, this quality of listening became the backdrop for the intentionality of her parenting. The Boulding children found this quality of "being taken seriously" to be of immense import in their growing years and that it separated them in some ways from most of their peers. As Elise's ideas on futurism evolved, she incorporated these ideas into her theoretical work on children as co-creators of visionary futures.

Writing that children allowed parents to further develop their own nurturing skills, Elise believed that in order for this to happen, adequate "listening and dialogue" must take place on the part of parents and that there must be an intentionality for the making of a partnering relationship. Ultimately this partnering can benefit both parents and children. Because children have not lost their imaging capacities as much as adults, Elise wrote that young people can "enliven our social imagination" and thus contribute new ways of looking at the world, including searching for ways to contribute toward building a more peaceful planet.[5] Parents must be open to the possibility of playing, of co-creating with their children. Children's greatest gift to parents is "the sensitivity to the needs of others and

In 1948, Kenneth Boulding became a U.S. citizen in Des Moines, Iowa, the first to be granted this status despite a refusal to take the oath to bear arms in wartime. Here he celebrates with Elise just after the ceremony. (Photograph courtesy of the Boulding family archives.)

the capacity to see the world anew."[6] Adults, recognizing the "personhood of children," could rediscover the child within themselves.[7]

Elise began her career as a family sociologist at the same time she and Kenneth began planning for a family. When Elise and Kenneth moved to Ames, Iowa, in the mid–1940s, at the time when she began work on her master's degree, she briefly considered a career as a marriage and family counselor. Her work on farm families had been grounded in her interest in parenting. The results of this work, published with Reuben Hill, found that fathers who had closer links prior to their going off to war had better success integrating back into family life. Elise's topic for her thesis was an interesting one, given that later the Bouldings lived apart during her years at Dartmouth in the early 1980s.

In 1949 the Bouldings moved to Ann Arbor, where Kenneth joined the economics faculty at the University of Michigan. Elise became a doctoral student for a year, taking baby Christine with her to classes until this became too much for her. Two years later, Elise had all but given up the idea of work on a Ph.D. and, instead, named their fourth child Philip Daniel, as her Ph.D.

Though Elise speaks of these years in Ann Arbor as "happy homemaker years," she was by no means confined to home and children. Elise began more actively speaking on family issues, especially for Quaker groups. This reflected her deep felt passion for the importance of parenting in intentional ways and of integrating this "intentionality" with spirituality. These experiences also helped her to find meaning in the day-to-day activities of running a very busy household. A fellow Quaker who knew her during that time related that when Elise spoke about parenting at Quaker gatherings, others felt the Boulding children were not as "disciplined" as they should be and that it was somewhat ironic that Elise should be speaking on how to parent when the perception was that her own children were somewhat out of control! Philosophically, Elise believed in giving her children a certain amount of freedom, and, with five young children, disciplining at times took a back seat to other activities.

There was a group of five families, all members of the Ann Arbor Meeting of Friends, who frequently acted as parental substitutes for one another. They were all activists, and this arrangement made it possible for all of the women in this group to keep up their participation in Quaker and other social concerns. The families have maintained close contact through the years. This arrangement was especially helpful for Elise, who was beginning her legendary travels on behalf of the Women's International League for Peace and Freedom and speaking at regional and national Quaker gatherings.

During Elise's early parenting days the question that was always in the back of her mind was, "Will this help the children to grow up to be peacemakers ... [will] our children choose the nonviolent path in their own lives?" Citing the importance of the small group of activist/Quaker mothers with whom she became involved in her community of Ann Arbor, Elise wrote in *One Small Plot of Heaven*, "[T]his [question] became the touchstone of how we judged all our actions, our lifestyle, everything. We were very conscientious (or thought we were) about leaving room for our children to choose their own way, but we wanted there to be good ways open to them."[8] Continuing on, she wrote of taking their children with them to most of the activist gatherings in which she was involved. "We women hardly ever did adults-only activities, except in the evening after the children had gone to bed."[9] Out of these experiences came the basis of many of her ideas which are written about in *Building a Global Civic Culture*, her most recognized treatise on education, and other writings connected with the rights of children.[10]

Elise and Kenneth had tried to conceive for several years. Considering adoption as an option, Elise finally became pregnant with their first child, Russell, shortly before they moved to Montreal for a year, in 1946, so that Kenneth could teach at McGill University. Elise did some additional graduate work there in sociology. She came back a bit early from their stay in Canada so that Russell could be born on U. S. soil in 1947.

Christine, the only Boulding girl, was born in 1949. Additional Boulding children came in two-year successions, Mark in 1951, Philip in 1953, and William in 1955 after the family had relocated to Ann Arbor. As her children grew, so did Elise's involvement in many of their activities, including helping to write a school peace curriculum for the Ann Arbor schools, involvement in the PTAs and leadership in the Scouts. Also, one or more of the Boulding children usually accompanied their parents to Quaker gatherings at which they were speaking. If not, some were left home with one or two of the students that lived with the Bouldings or one of the other Ann Arbor families. In exchange for some baby-sitting and household duties, the students received room and board. This arrangement allowed Elise a few hours each day for her own myriad activities, including work with the WILPF, the American Friends Service Committee and the Fellowship of Reconciliation, teaching Quaker Sunday School, and, prior to her returning to finish her Ph.D., her position as a research associate at the Center for Conflict Resolution at the University of Michigan. How did she do this all? A glimpse at her schedule shows her ability to organize her time:

6:30—heave out bed, run a hot bath and soak for 10 minutes, getting my soul back in my body
6:45—wake family
7:00—prepare breakfast, start laundry (Russell sets table)
7:15—everybody eat
7:30—clear breakfast, clean kitchen and dining room, get ready to leave house for day (Philip does breakfast dishes, bless him!)

7:55—leave house
8:00—Monday, Wednesday, Friday, class in Logic of Theory Construction (library work other days)
9:00—Wednesday, Friday, Advanced Theory Seminar (Sociological)
11:00—Class in National Integration and World Society, Monday, Wednesday, Friday.
12:00—lunch meeting to carry on a host of local responsibilities, or brown bag seminars (Mondays I conduct research development seminar for the Center for Conflict Resolution: Tuesdays there is a Social Organization lunch seminar; Wednesdays, religious advisors (I am one for the Friends Meeting) meets, once or twice a month, then our own religious advisory committee in Meeting meets once a month)
1–4:00—study in library, keep up with IPRA newsletter correspondence and business, keep up with secretarial correspondence for Friends Lake Community, Childhood Education Committee of WILPF, preparing Sunday School class, etc.
4–7:30—family time (cook, market, launder, clean, sew, mend, iron, talk to my family!)
7:30—study until midnight

Extra classes that meet only once a week but take lots of reading time:

5–7—Tuesdays, Sociological Method
1–3 Mondays—Theory of International Relations
Then Wednesday nights I meet with the student supper discussion group at Friends Center.[11]

This calendar was typical of the manner in which Elise organized her days, in order to devote time to the family needs and to her research and scholarly interests which had continued to evolve from the early days with Kenneth.

For the most part, the Boulding children seemed to have taken in stride their mother's very busy schedule during their growing years. Later, however, it became more apparent that at least one of them found it more difficult than was obvious at that time. Most now believe that, though their family was a bit unusual because of the high profile of both their parents, for the most part they felt the strong love and acceptance of their parents, particularly Elise, who was the primary parent during the children's growing years. They do believe, however, that there were unspoken expectations placed on them that they "make a contribution." As Philip Boulding said, "The most important element in this shaping was the freedom and encouragement given in subtle ways to think for ourselves."[12]

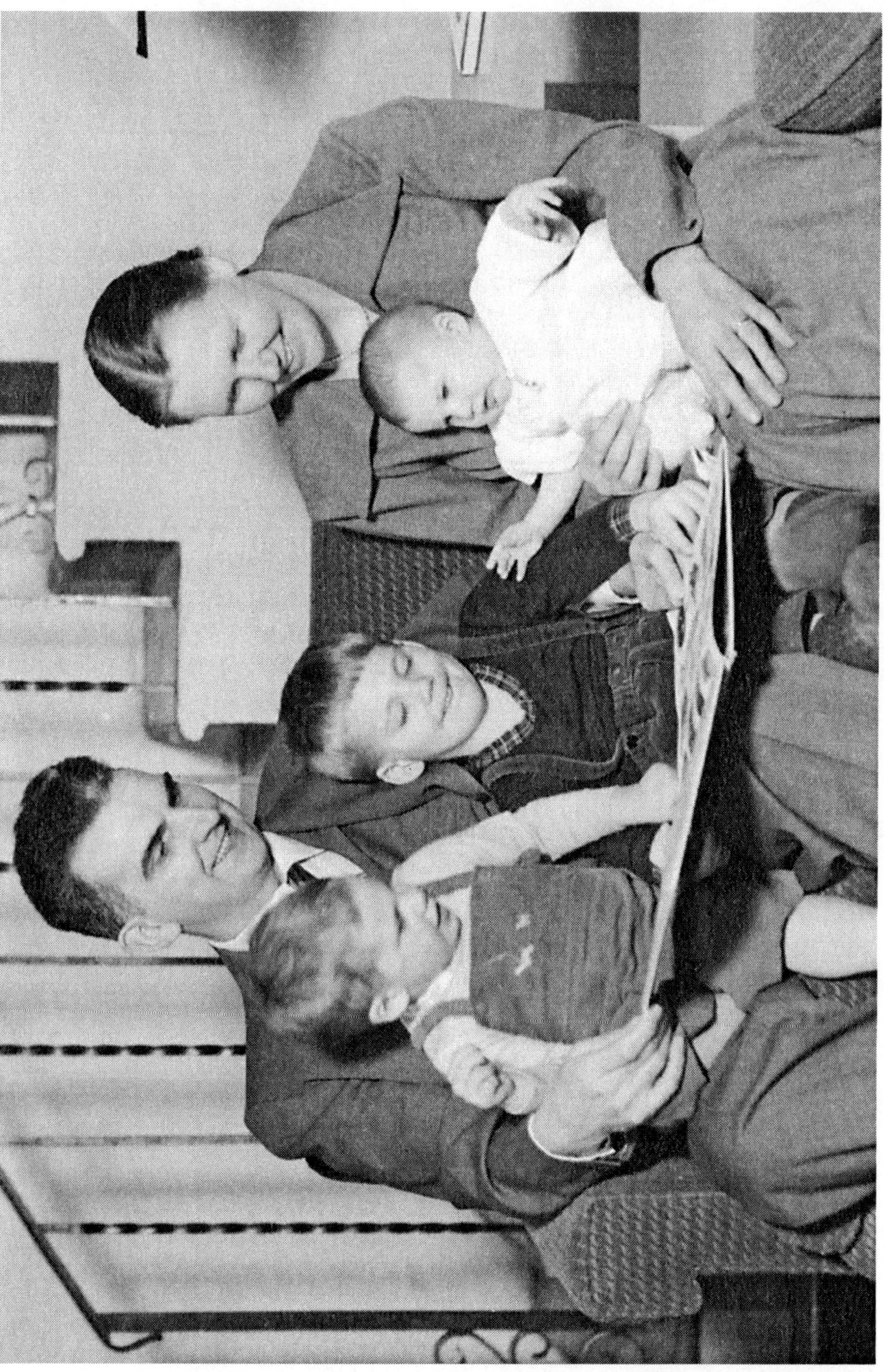

Christine admitted, however, that at times the freedom to find her own way was difficult for her, particularly during her late adolescence when she was choosing a college and career path. Neither parent ever gave much advice on various careers and none of the children was steered toward academia; nor were they apparently *not* steered that way. Only one child, William, the youngest, is in academia, teaching economics at Duke University. The others are all, as Russell put it "entrepreneurs," each in his own way. Russell is an environmental consultant and subsistence farmer in Indiana. Mark is the founder and owner of an artistic display company in Colorado. Philip, in an ironic twist to his naming, is the only Boulding child to not pursue higher education. With the blessing of Elise and Kenneth, he is a musician and instrument maker in the Seattle area. Christine is the vice-president and chief financial officer of a contracting company, which she co-owns with her husband in the Boston suburbs. None could be called activists in any of the same ways this could describe Elise and Kenneth. And yet, as Christine notes, she believes they are all living out the values given to them by their familial upbringing.

Understanding the grounding Elise received for her ideas on parenting and the important function families play in building peace helps to make clear the meaning of how these thoughts permeate most of her other theoretical work. Starting with her own family of origin, Elise felt somehow, as she described in *Mor* and noted earlier, that her family "had more family being" than those of any of her friends.[13] To Elise, this meant that the importance of family was somehow communicated, chiefly through her mother, who believed in "the centrality of family to the whole of one's life in many ways, both through her working and her home-centered years."[14] Elise and Kenneth attempted in the rearing of their own family, as they described in their 1945 annual letter to friends and family, to "create an island of healthy social tissue in the diseased body of the world." Here can be seen the idea of the family as a *utopia* and as a *culture of peace*.

One Small Plot of Heaven: Reflections on Family Life by a Quaker Sociologist is the book which represents, in their most complete form, Elise's thoughts on parenting and the important interplay between the family, God and Quaker worship. Published in 1989 by Pendle Hill press, the book is a series of essays that Elise had written over many years. She had originally been urged to consider submitting them for publication by her son Russell, who at that time owned a small press in Indiana. Some of the essays included are also printed as articles in other publications. *One Small*

Opposite: **The Boulding family at home in Ann Arbor in 1951—Kenneth, Mark, Russell, Elise and Christine (left to right).**

Plot of Heaven also includes much autobiographical reflection, most notably in "Born Remembering," her spiritual autobiography, originally published as a Pendle Hill pamphlet in 1975 shortly after Elise's year of solitude at her Hermitage in Colorado.

In *One Small Plot of Heaven* are many of Elise's ideas on "the personhood of children," the importance of times of solitude, creative play and interaction across age spans. In addition, one chapter is devoted more or less exclusively to a discussion of the Quaker testimonies as they relate to home and family. Though Quakers have traditionally eschewed creeds, believing them contrary to each individual's experience of God and to the continual individual and corporate search for Truth, what have evolved historically within the Society of Friends are a number of testimonies for "right living in relationship to God" coupled with queries which guide seekers to endeavor to do right by the Holy Spirit.

Probably the most well known testimony of Quakers is the historic peace testimony. A particular query which has evolved and is found in some form in several Quaker books of Faith and Practice is "Are you endeavoring to make your home a place of friendliness, refreshment, and peace, where God becomes more real to all who dwell there and to those who visit it?" This query reflects the deeply felt beliefs among Friends not only in the importance of nurturing the young, but also of treating with love all those who may cross the threshold of individual households. Elise directly addresses this query in her essay.

Elise, in the chapter entitled "Friends Testimonies in the Home," cited the importance of building a home which is a center of spiritual nurturance for families as well as for visitors. Also included were her ideas on the metaphoric role parenting plays in most of the world's religions, with God as Father, Mother, and/or Parent. In addition, she noted the application of four of the most famous Quaker testimonies to the family, citing the abundance of Quaker literature on this topic. These are community, harmony, equality and simplicity. She argued for the importance of family worship in the home, something the Boulding family practiced for years, often including one or more of the myriad guests or students in their home. In addition to citing what Quaker meetings can do to help families, she also wrote of the

> *developmental* character of pacifism, the fact that the peacemaker in us ripens slowly through a process of lifelong learning and discipline and prayer, that links the peace testimony so powerfully to the family.... [I]n the family we are willy-nilly whole.... [T]he family may help or hinder our growth, but it is definitely a part of the process.... [R]eceiving love and acceptance in early childhood,

> experiencing times of solitary reflection in puberty and adolescence, accepting early responsibility for self and others—this combination seems to produce peacemakers. Always we come back to what is happening is that most intimate setting of our lives, the household.[15]

Family as Metaphor

Though Elise in most of her writings argued passionately for partnering in parenting, through most of the parenting years she was the primary care giver. Kenneth, when home, was often to be found in his study with the door closed. While both she and Kenneth believed passionately in the idea that their family should be a heavenly colony, the nitty-gritty, day in and day out of raising children was left to Elise. Chuckling over the story, Russell told me:

> My father in many ways was not real present to us as children. I think he had a wonderful sense of playfulness, but I remember my mother once commenting to me that she used to get exasperated with my father when we were young and playing with blocks, essentially it would be like parallel play.... He would get so involved in building these wonderful towers out of blocks, they would go all the way to the ceiling, he wasn't really playing *with* us.[16]

Every Christmas, Kenneth would make a large gingerbread village. He enjoyed candlemaking and clay sculpturing as well. Toward the end of his life Kenneth regretted his lack of involvement with his offspring and to his children expressed sadness that he did not spend more time with them.

Though criticized by some feminists for not stressing enough the egregious effects of oppressive patriarchal structures, Elise nevertheless consistently argued against male dominated patriarchal parenting, particularly as it related to its effects on family functioning. Parenting as a positive social identifier is usually lacking in our modern western society, she argued that, as a result, mothers often minimize their subjective experiences and perceptions relating to their own peacebuilding capacities. Mothering is often associated with feelings of oppression and exclusion. Women's skills and perceptions must be affirmed and embraced because men have a more difficult time seeing local to global connections. For women it is easier to imagine peaceful change, though women often tend to deny the importance of this. Therefore, according to Elise, male dominance thwarts families' visioning capacities as well as the growth of parent-child partnerships. Communities must support these parent-child partnerships.[17]

Elise's use of metaphor is almost universal in her writings, and nowhere does it appear more often than in her writings on families. Families may be considered metaphors themselves for society as a whole. In her writings, she viewed the family as both the basic unit of society and society itself in microcosm. Again using metaphor, Elise, calling on her experiences of spending time in India, referred to a Hindu jeweled net to explain this phenomenon. Each family may be seen as an individual jewel within the net, the entire net being society. But each jewel (family) is reflected in the image of every other jewel, and all are necessary to make the entire net. Here is also seen the emphasis on the importance of families in relation to their communities, an interchange without which society cannot adequately function. One can see, using the jewel metaphor, that neither can any family sustain itself alone.

Each family is a culture itself, yet one in continual creation with other families around it. Frequently using analogy, Elise in *One Small Plot of Heaven*, wrote of the "analogy of back yard sand play and the disarmament campaign among the children of Bedford Road [their address in Ann Arbor] and the issues involved in international disarmament talks," thus forging a link between peacemaking functions involved in settling children's squabbles and conflict resolution among nation-states. Here are noted the similarities in the process of peacemaking on a very local (backyard) level and a global one, while at the same time lending credence to the important developmental work involved in social play.[18]

The use of analogy has allowed Elise to integrate issues related to locality with a view of the world, taking into account global issues and seeing the similarities between the two. This particular lens has not only allowed her to make sense of her experiences as she has lived them, but has grounded her in the importance of what she was doing at any particular time during her early years of raising five active children. It also helped her to realize the importance of reaching out to others in her community who were in similar situations.

Families are cultures where crucial peacemaking skills are learned and practiced, including negotiating, mediating, resolving conflicts and learning how to deal with differences in creative ways. Parenting itself offers practice in the crucial skills needed for peacebuilding, including listening, dialoguing and learning to reconcile. Women more often than men are exposed to these skills, but men need to learn them as well, and parenting can offer opportunities for men to learn.

Elise believed that this teaching and learning process worked both ways between parents and children. As a small child, Elise nurtured Birgit in the early years after their immigration, helping her mother through her difficulties accepting the move to America and then through her sister's death. Children have much to teach parents. In her sociology classes at the University of Colorado and at Dartmouth, Elise often asked her students to write about times they nurtured their parents through particular crises and events their parents might not have even recognized as such. The responses often surprised both Elise and her students, as they captured memories that might otherwise have gone unnoticed.

As units of social change, families are information processing entities, and in times of rapid social change, Elise found that they emerge as "units of activism."[19] Because various family members each go out into their individual "worlds" on a daily basis, coming back to the family unit allows an exchange of ideas which can be the basis for societal change. The various networks in which each family member participates are the basis of connections between the individual, the family, the community and the world. Nongovernmental organizations offer a more formal way to bridge these local to global connections. Grass roots groups, or GROs, are also a way for individuals to participate in social change. When leading her children's Scout troops, Elise would often point out to the group their connections to the world Scouts, thus offering a global view which might ordinarily have been lost. These connections, she believed, are the basis for a particular kind of "ministry" for social change, which links individuals to a world order and is based on citizen participation as an adjunct to and parallel to the international system of nation-states.[20] Elise argued, "If we are to have a more realistic and viable planning for world order, more people must see the connections between the family, the local habitat and the international sphere."[21] The key here is *participation*. Although Elise in her writings was not always specific about exactly how involvement might occur, her intent was clear: activism and involvement are necessary in order to affect change.

When teaching, Elise often gave her students an exercise asking them to list their own and their family's participation in transnational organizations such as the YWCA, the Rotary, the Scouts and so forth. As she states in *Building a Global Civic Culture*, "These transnational voluntary associations cover the whole range of human interests and ... [this] is based on the new-old perception that humankind has common interests."[22] At times Elise incorporated the idea of linkages and their unique form of world mapping into planning the workshops she subsequently conducted.

Through placing importance on the role of the family in creating a culture of peace, Elise's writings also reflected her belief that not all families are loving, nor are they all nurturing. The role of intentionality is important. By understanding that she herself wished to undo in her own child-rearing those things which she felt were egregious in her own childhood,

Elise placed importance on the possible roles families could play in visioning and building a more peaceful world. Families may not always be healthy, nor do they always offer continual love and support. Yet even the most dysfunctional families often provide some semblance of love and support. Elise, therefore, argued for the *fiction* of the family as a loving unit. As she mentioned in a 1982 lecture, later published as a pamphlet, a focus on families can overcome the despair about what to do about the world. This "fiction," imagining love as experienced in families, is needed because humans long to feel at home in a protected space.[23]

Of her two parents, Birgit was the stronger figure. A working mother being unusual in the 1930s of Maplewood, New Jersey, several of Birgit's Norwegian friends did not approve of her career. Yet for all of her attachment to her mother, Elise's ambivalence about her relationship with Birgit and her insecurities at times about her own parenting showed through in this 1959 entry from her journal:

> Last night after all the children were asleep I knelt for a long time by Christy's bed. What I make of my life will closely affect her life, more than it will affect the boys, because I am her pattern for a woman. I have felt so vividly just several days ago that my mother literally died of the despair of purposelessness and it is the fact of her defeat by life which shadows my own struggle. Will I shadow Christy's adult life in this way? Dear god, I know it need not be.

Even as an adult, Elise carried with her the legacies left by Birgit, which were to influence so much her subsequent theoretical work.

Chapter 4

Years as a "Happy Homemaker": The 1950s and Early 1960s

The 1950s marked for Elise the passage from a young wife married to an influential academic during a decade of heavy involvement writing and speaking for the Religious Society of Friends into a woman intensely involved with the Women's International League for Peace and Freedom (WILPF). Elise's activism reached its peak in the mid–1960s when she was led back to academia and to a life as a scholar, integrating activism while continuing her extensive networking.

The WILPF was to provide major grounding for much of Elise's future work in peace research and education, including her theories on women and peace and her evolving ideas on the role of nongovernmental associations in peacemaking.

It was in the closely-knit Ann Arbor Friends Meeting where Elise met many of the women who would remain her life-long friends and associates, many of whom would also help her develop her ideas on peace. It was with these women, along with other local activists in Ann Arbor, that Elise helped to start a small chapter, which was an off-shoot of the larger one in Detroit, of WILPF. Additionally, the chapter served as a local branch of the Fellowship of Reconciliation, the interfaith association founded in 1915, headquartered in Nyack, New York, and devoted to peace and justice. Elise at this time was also supporting the work of the local chapter of the American Friends Service Committee.

Elise's first work for WILPF was with the elementary school in Ann Arbor that her children attended. Elise became quite fond of the woman who was the principal of the school and who was very receptive to the ideas of Elise that involved developing programs and displays on peace for the library and other places in the school. Later these projects would evolve into national and international activities under the auspices of WILPF.

WILPF

Probably no other organization in which Elise Boulding has been involved has helped to define her subsequent life and work more than WILPF. From local work in the children's schools, Elise began chairing the national Childhood Education Committee, subsequently serving on the U.S. Section governing board. Moving into service on the international board, Elise was then elected International Chair of WILPF in 1967. This work took her all over the world and helped to solidify and ground her academic writing and speaking on women, including the writing of *The Underside of History.*[1] It also helped foster connections to many, if not most of the subsequent organizations in which she became involved during the decades of the '50s and '60s.

The Women's International League for Peace and Freedom evolved out of an International Congress of Women which convened at the Hague in 1915 with the aim of trying to end the slaughter of World War I. The congress had been organized by a group of European women and was attended by delegates from twelve countries. Jane Addams led the U.S. delegation. Out of this congress came a formulation for a just and lasting peace, which according to Frank Gordon, who wrote a brief history of WILPF, was said by President Woodrow Wilson to be "by far the best formulation which up to the moment has been put up by anybody."[2] Four years later the name of WILPF was adopted, and international committees were set up to work toward adoption of proposals for peace. Additional world members continued to join. Later, the headquarters moved to Geneva, Switzerland. The League continued its advocacy, organizing activist work right up until the Second World War. In 1931 Jane Addams received the Nobel Peace Prize.

During World War II, it became fairly clear that the League had never held a totally pacifist view, that is "peace at any price," as the leadership recognized that freedom held sway over the shadow of Nazi persecution in Germany and elsewhere. The League was active just prior to the war in aiding refugees. As an organization, the League survived the war, but, as

Gordon points out, "in truncated form."[3] In 1946 Emily Greene Balch, the recently elected international chair, was honored as a co-recipient of the Nobel Peace Prize under a newly renewed League. WILPF was granted NGO status with the United Nations at that time. During the 1950s, a big part of the League's agenda was in opposition to nuclear testing, followed by a call for universal disarmament in the 1960s. During the 1970s, League members were involved individually and corporately in protesting the war in Vietnam, the U.S. section in 1963 urging the government to end the war.

What Gordon fails to point out in his brief history of WILPF is the relationship between the organization and the women's suffrage movement. Catherine Foster, in her history, notes that it evolved out of the International Women's Suffrage Alliance in the early part of the 1900s.[4] These discrepancies in the focus of the early League activities point to tensions within the organization, which have maintained themselves through the years and reached their head in the second wave of feminism in the 1960s, during the time of Elise's active involvement. In the beginning both universal suffrage *and* peace were seen to be two sides of the same issue. Later it became clear that just getting the vote for women was not enough to insure not only that war would be abolished, but that full human rights for women would automatically evolve. This became particularly clear during the Vietnam War.

According to Foster, there have always been tensions in WILPF between the more radical pacifists and those who are willing to make accommodations for the use of violence in some situations.[5] During the 1960s it became clear to the WILPF leadership that there was an acute lack of "voice" from young people, particularly relating to the youth unrest on campuses. Kay Camp, the president of the U.S. Section, was concerned about the rising level of campus violence and the gaps in philosophy and representation between the young and old members of the League. As a result of some soul searching, some chapters of WILPF began more active tactics of civil disobedience, such as engaging in street theater in Washington, D.C. As part of its "Tuesdays in Washington Series," the D.C. chapter had a symbolic procession of coffins to protest the war.[6]

The 1960s were a time of introspection for the League in many ways. Elise headed a committee to discuss the future of the organization just prior to her tenure as international chair. The League began to question its role as an exclusively women's organization in the light of feminist assertions that real freedom meant moving away from what many saw as the founding values of the organization. These values were seen as too traditionally associated with women, "essentializing" them into the roles of nurturer and caretaker. The Danish chapter dropped "Women's" from its title in 1969, and Elise, as international chair, sent them a congratulatory note, saying, "perhaps our sisters are right and it is time for women to become people."[7] The philosophical gaps between the older women and the newer, younger members became more apparent, as each chapter was allowed to decide if they wanted to allow men to join. Foster quotes some members as saying, "[O]ur criticism is that some feminists equate equality and similarity—the idealization of masculine attributes."[8] During the 1980s a more conciliative stance was found, even as the organization continued to explore deeply its rationale as a women's organization and to seek to understand the unique contributions women make toward peacekeeping. As Foster notes, "While WILPF has not always embraced the objectives and language of feminism, it has always worked for feminist values: cooperation, relationship and community."[9]

Heading to California

The decade of the 1950s saw the birth of three of the Boulding children: Christine in 1951, Philip in 1953 and the last of the Boulding children, William, born in 1955. Much of Elise's speaking and writing at this time reflected her interest in and learning from her children and her parenting, and several of her articles were published. In 1955 the journal *Marriage and Family Living* published her essay on cooperative nursery schooling.[10] In that same year, Elise addressed an Indiana conference on "Christian Love in the Home," which was the beginnings of her thinking on visions of a "world family" rooted in the childhoods of individual global citizens. In 1956 she gave the William Penn Lecture at the Philadelphia Yearly Meeting of Friends, entitled "The Joy That is Set Before Us," which was later published as one of their series of pamphlets. Both Elise and Kenneth were involved in the Quaker Young Friends movement during that time, Kenneth having begun his activities with the group before he met Elise.

Wherever the Boulding family located, Elise taught Quaker Sunday School, called First Day School as, historically, Friends have eschewed using names for the days of the week as their roots lay in paganism. In 1958, Elise wrote a children's curriculum. It was put in pamphlet form by the Religious Education Committee of Philadelphia Yearly Meeting and entitled *My Part in the Quaker Adventure* and was later published by Friends General Conference.[11]

Elise believed that her mission in teaching involved more than just imparting historical facts to children:

> It should be understood that those programs were strongly political as well, strongly oriented toward producing pacifists. Our concern was to rear a generation of pacifists ... peacemakers. Not *passivists*, but pacifists. My activities revolved around creating opportunities where adults and children could be together without age barriers in the context of political action.[12]

Elise at one point mentioned that dialoguing across age barriers has been "*the* most formative thing in my life."[13]

The fall of 1954 saw the Boulding family heading to Palo Alto, California, where Kenneth took part in the inaugural year of the Center for Advanced Study of the Behavioral Sciences (CASBS) at Stanford. This was a pivotal year for both of the Bouldings, as it laid the groundwork for Kenneth's subsequent work in the founding of the interdisciplinary Center for Research on Conflict Resolution at the University of Michigan. During this time, Elise met the Dutch futurist Fred Polak, who lived near the family that year. Polak deeply influenced both Elise and Kenneth. Elise translated his work from the Dutch into English, later citing it was not too difficult, as she knew some German already and the languages were similar. She dates the process of translating as the beginning of her scholarly career. Much of the writings of both Bouldings about futures and imaging have their roots in the work of Fred Polak.

The atmosphere in Palo Alto was a "heady" one, with Elise being involved in the academic side of things as her time away from the children allowed. At this point she was pregnant with William and had four children aged eight or younger.

Participants in the academic seminar included, in addition to Kenneth, the anthropologist Clyde Kluckhohn, political scientist Harold Lasswell, and mathematical biologist Anatol Rapoport. This group led to the formation of the Society for General Systems Research of which Kenneth was the first president.[14] It was here that Kenneth received much of the grounding for his subsequent work on general systems theory, which took his scholarly work out of the realm of pure economics. Cynthia Kerman, Kenneth's biographer, writes that this group was the beginning of what would become for the next half century the peace research movement.[15] It was in Palo Alto that Kenneth wrote *The Image* in just nine days as Elise "was packing and gathering up children and goods for the trip back to Ann Arbor."[16] The *Image* established Kenneth's reputation as a futurist. The year in Palo Alto greatly influenced both Kenneth's and Elise's ideas as to the importance of interdisciplinary collaboration in the social sciences.

The Center for Research on Conflict Resolution

The origins of the modern peace research movement lie in the work of an ad hoc group that evolved out of a meeting of the Eastern Psychological Association in 1952. Entitled the Group for the Research on War and Peace, the network that was established was largely the result of the work of Arthur Gladstone and Herbert Kelman, who had been graduate students together at Yale in the 1940s. The original aim of the group was to critique the psychological assumptions underlying U.S. foreign policy and its emphasis on militarism. The first task of the group was to publish "The Bulletin of the Research Exchange on the Prevention of War," linking individuals and groups who were concerned about the future prevention of war. Later, as the focus of the group shifted to Ann Arbor, this publication evolved into the *Journal of Conflict Resolution*, begun in 1957 and published out of the University of Michigan.

Kenneth Boulding was about to leave Michigan to spend the year from 1954 to 1955 in California. Out of the year in which so many scholars from a variety of disciplines came together to discuss war, peace, and systems theory at CASBS in California grew the idea for the Center for Conflict Resolution, subsequently born in 1959 in Ann Arbor. The first of its kind in the United States, it was a university based research center with no formal academic programs but with an agenda to support and encourage the work of individual scholars. It was to provide, as Kenneth's archives note, "physical space and administrative support services" to scholars engaged in the study of the prevention of future wars.[17]

The Center was a unit of the College of Literature, Science and the Arts at Michigan, and its purpose from the beginning was interdisciplinary. As its brochure notes:

> The [CRCR] is an expression of the belief that the resources of social sciences need to be marshaled in the interest of resolving international conflicts.... Our confidence in an interdisciplinary approach to peace is based on the conviction that the conduct of nations cannot be isolated from human actions and motives in general.[18]

Among the functions of the Center were the following:

1. conferences and seminars including research and theory development, research and action programs striving for peace, and research on public opinion and governmental policy;
2. research and training specifically designed to study a world

without war and to study peacemaking possibilities between the U.S. and the Soviet Union;
3. quantifying data on international relations.

The Center also actively sought funds for graduate training in peace and conflict studies for students at the University of Michigan.[19]

It is notable that nearly all of the key academic players in the founding of the Center for Research on Conflict Resolution—and indeed in the early peace research movement—were men. When the Center was founded in 1959, Elise was serving in the capacity of a research associate for the Mental Health Research Institute at the university, a part time position that allowed her some time for her myriad WILPF and other community activities as well as some time at home with the children. Soon thereafter she became the Research Development Secretary for the Center for Conflict Resolution and her duties involved clerical work as well as running a research development seminar from 1960 until 1962. This meant facilitating meetings as well as note taking for the series of faculty meetings at which the various disciplines were represented to further the work of the Center. Her secretarial duties would prove crucial a couple of years later, as the International Peace Research newsletter was born, literally, out of the wastebasket of the Center.

Off to Jamaica

The Boulding family spent the year of 1959 to 1960 in Jamaica, where Kenneth taught at the University College of the West Indies. The warmth of Jamaican society and the beauty of the island made this a happy year for everyone, and the family fell in love with Jamaican music. The Bouldings became acquainted with the more evangelical Quaker meetings on the island, and Elise taught Quaker Sunday School. Elise served on the visitors board of a home for lepers and involved herself in starting what would become, in her words, a school library movement in Jamaica:

> It's so easy when you go to a small country to start something. Schools didn't have libraries in those days in Jamaica ... so I started a model library for the Priory school [where the Boulding children attended]. It was a private, secular school ... [T]here were Jamaican kids there but they were kids who could afford tuition. The other available school just wasn't well enough organized.... For all I know the list I made up is still circulating![20]

During that year Elise also visited different organizations and noted "the heavy colonial hand" in Jamaica. She recalled,

> You know when the Governor General of the Island came to the school that Bill attended, an ordinary Jamaican school, they had been preparing for months for his visit. And they had recitation. And these little kids were reciting *Shakespeare!* All the beautiful song and music and poetry that was Jamaican was ignored.[21]

Moving Out Into the World: International Work with the Childhood Education Committee

In the early 1960s Elise still considered herself primarily a homemaker, though certainly her life did not follow a pattern of a traditional housewife. Her involvement with WILPF and with the local chapter of the American Friends Service Committee continued to occupy a good deal of her time. In addition, she had began her part time work at the University of Michigan and its Institute for Social Research, first in a volunteer capacity and then obtaining the title of Research Associate with a small stipend.

But it was WILPF that most occupied her time during these days, providing the grounding and support for much of her subsequent peace work in the decades to follow. In November of 1961, Elise helped to host a delegation of Soviet women at Bryn Mawr College through the auspices of both WILPF and the Jane Addams Peace Fellowship. The purpose of this visit was to build bridges of understanding during a time when Cold War tensions were high. This was the first of eight such exchanges held between the two groups over the next twenty-five years.[22] There were twelve U.S. women involved in the first exchange, among them Margaret Mead, and ten from the Soviet Union. Elise took copious notes at the meetings, helping to reveal the agenda of the conference, which included the following questions and issues posed to the participants:

1. What kind of peaceful co-existence is possible?
2. How can the arms race be ended and the war system eliminated?
3. The relationship between political problems and disarmament
4. The role of the United Nations in making and keeping peace
5. The responsibility of women in promoting peace
6. Proposed projects and next steps

Recommendations from the conference were to increase exchanges between the nations of cultural and scientific knowledge. It was suggested there be established a research center devoted to peace. Elise was listed as a participant with the designation, "Sociologist with the Center for Conflict Resolution."[23]

Other projects proposed at this women's gathering were for the publication of a text book for children 11 to 15 years of age, one-half to be written by a Soviet author and the other by an American, on the history and culture of each country. In addition, a recommendation was given to the United Nations agencies working on behalf of children that they focus their attention on the psychological and physical damage being done to children by war preparations.[24] Elise took on the children's book project as her own, and, as she became more involved in the Childhood Education Committee of WILPF, this occupied a great deal of her time during the early '60s. In 1962 she began to chair the Committee.

The philosophical orientation of the Childhood Education Committee (CEC) grew out of the larger ideological conflicts between WILPF and certain aspects of the current public school curricula. In a document she wrote in 1962, entitled "A Proposal for a Working Committee to Deal with the Problems of Effective Treatment of Ideological Conflict in the Public School Curriculum," Elise wrote:

> At the present time, school systems all across the United States are confronted with a demand to prepare courses in "Communism." ... Today's children and young people are badly in need of instructional materials which will equip them to deal creatively with an international situation so fraught with impasse at the present moment that only a radical discarding of old clichés will make an intelligent problem-solving approach possible.... The current fear of being "soft" on communism ... may burden these youngsters with a fatal psychological handicap when they are placed in policy-making situations in adulthood. This is all the more tragic because so many of our leading educators are keenly aware of the importance of developing problem-solving attitudes in our children, and have made important contributions to the study of the conditions under which creativity emerges.[25]

In 1963 Elise traveled to Moscow while visiting Poland as part of a WILPF delegation meeting with women's groups and visiting schools. In the U.S.S.R. she met with various Soviet educators, following the approval of the book project by the first deputy minister of education, Alexei Ivanovitch Markouchevitch. She met with members of the Soviet Pedagogical Institute as well. Summarizing her proposal for the textbook project at the meeting, having received solid support and a rough draft from Quaker social studies educator Leonard Kenworthy, she reported at this meeting that the book would be aimed at upper elementary grades and that comparable material would be made on facing pages in each country's language.

In July of 1963 Elise traveled to London to address a conference during which she mentioned the importance of educational work in promoting world understanding. She mentioned her work on the book project, which caught the ear of James Henderson of the University of London Institute of Education. He offered to attempt to collaborate with her, as his New Education Fellowship, a international educational association committed to progressive education, was in the process of signing a contract with UNESCO for a similar kind of textbook project. The question posed at their discussion was whether the Russians would be willing to go along with their proposed ideas. Elise also sought and received some support for the project from the new Center for Conflict Resolution at Michigan as well as a foundation that *Saturday Review* editor Norman Cousins had founded. Cousins reluctantly had to turn down her financial request for legal reasons but offered continued encouragement to Elise. Elise did receive some funding from a few WILPF associates. Other sources of correspondence and feedback for her work were David Reisman of Harvard, the Fellowship of Reconciliation, AFSC, the Menninger Clinic in Kansas, and the National Education Association, in addition to education faculty at Michigan.[26]

Late in 1966, Elise was in touch with Robert Zangrando of the American Historical Association, who had written her regarding the status of the project. In a letter she summarized the project and mentioned that at the point she met with the Russian educators she realized that it was important that WILPF turn over the American part of the project to a professional educational organization in order to receive proper funding. She expressed her hopes in the letter that the project, which had not been brought to fruition, could be revived, and she offered to work with Zangrando on doing so. In the letter she explains its demise:

> The project broke down at the point of needing to call a joint conference of proposed American and Soviet authors, or at least to receive some kind of specific draft proposal from them to indicate they were seriously committed to work on this. When [we] were not able to get a specific commitment from anyone in the Ministry of Education (Mr. Markouchevitch had left and his successor simply did not have any particular interest in the project) we decided reluctantly to lay the project on the shelf, with hope of reviving it some day. We felt it would be irresponsible to commit the time of busy American scholars to something which was conceived to be a joint operation, but which had no counterpart group to work with in the Soviet Union. But I know there are some who felt we gave up too easily.[27]

The project, unfortunately, did not reach completion.

In 1962 Elise gave a talk at the World Forum on Women held in

Brussels. Her talk was entitled "Communication and Empathy: Educating Our Children for World Friendship." The essence of her message was that children must be taught world loyalty and the school curricula must be looked at closely for evidence of "demonization" of the so-called enemy (mostly referring to the Soviet Union) and that children must see the importance of negotiation as an important learning experience. Children need to have opportunities to learn about the Soviet Union:

> You see that Soviet and American children both grow up convinced that people in the other country are ruled by a small group of wicked men.... [N]ow anyone who reads the digest of the Soviet Press which is available in the United States, or who reads magazines like the Soviet review, or has spoken with Soviet citizens or visited the Soviet Union, knows very well that the Soviet Union is not controlled by a handful of men, that there is widespread local participation in all kinds of decision making, and that candidates for public office at every level from the local to the Supreme Soviet participate in extensive public debates before they are nominated. But school children do not know this, unless they are among the lucky few whose parents are better informed. So they grow up believing that the Soviet masses are an oppressed people, ruled capriciously by power-mad men.[28]

She went on to mention several excerpts from a Soviet text about America, citing its statements about the rule of "monopolistic" capitalism, that the economic and political life is controlled by the National Association of Manufacturers and the Chamber of Commerce, and that lobbyists are termed the "third party" of the USA.

Earlier that year, Elise had written to the wife of Nikita Khrushchev, ruling premier of the Soviet Union, responding to a message of reconciliation she had sent out to American women. Excerpts from this letter follow:

> Where so much divides our two countries, it becomes all the more important to find common ground where we can stand together. Soviet and American women have no difficulty in finding this common ground in their concern for their children and their families. Reading a number of articles lately by Soviet psychologists and educators has led me to realize that our aspirations for the development of our children are not so different as appears on the political surface of things.... [W]e women have a responsibility beyond that of seeing that each child can develop his fullest potential and sense of responsibility within the national society in to which he was born. We must teach our children that the berry bush blooms for

> every child in every country. This means developing in them an allegiance to something higher than their own country—allegiance to a world community.[29]

Quaker Networking

In 1961 the Kenneth and Elise founded Friends Lake Community, eighty acres of rustic woods situated on Long Lake outside of Ann Arbor, which has served since then as a place of renewal and retreat for groups and families connected with the Ann Arbor Meeting. The community's pamphlet describes it thus,

> A Quaker sponsored, inter-racial, inter-faith recreation association, more than just a place to play.... [B]usy people have found a renewed vitality in the fundamental experience of community.... [R]ecreational experiences are enjoyed across vocational specializations, diverse cultural backgrounds and challenging differences of race and creed.... [M]embers achieve together what they could not do alone.[30]

Elise continues to hold membership in Friends Lake Community and in the ensuing years there have been several Boulding family reunions there.

In 1961 Elise began one of the several Quaker newsletters she initiated, the *Lake Erie Friends Bulletin* of the Lake Erie Association of Friends (later the association would become Lake Erie Yearly Meeting). She also continued her work with the American Friends Service Committee throughout the decade, beginning with an innovative project the local area organization was launching called "conflict dialogues." According to a letter the Bouldings sent out in January of 1961 to fellow faculty members at the University of Michigan, Quakers and other friends, the purpose of this process was to:

> Consider setting up something which might be called conflict-dialogue seminars, in which individuals of sharply opposing viewpoints are brought together to consider a divisive issue, such as integration versus segregation in schools, housing or employment; military training versus conscientious objection; military preparedness versus disarmament. Our interest in bringing about such a confrontation of individuals of extremely dissimilar views stems from Kenneth Boulding's experiences last summer with the international seminar in Russia, where participating Americans quickly found that the usual friendly informal approach was completely inadequate to bridge the gap between starkly opposed ideologies.

> The motivating concern here is to develop skill in communicating across the more impenetrable of our social barriers, both at the local and the international level.[31]

There was little direct heed from the Boulding's call. Nevertheless, it gives evidence of their willingness during a time of heightened East-West conflict to take on deeply controversial issues. Radical confrontation has not always been easy for Elise, and, as the decade wore on, her turn to more intense academic work marked the beginning of the decline of these kinds of activities, as she moved more completely into the role of educator. Later, in a 1978 interview in Hanover, she admitted:

> There has always been a pull in my own thinking between a desire to be radical enough to condemn structures that clearly are not working for the human race, and a temperament inclined always to mediation and helping people to get it together where they are. My temperament wasn't harnessed to the radical thrust and that is true today. Of course, the whole business of how I was socialized as a woman is relevant, too.[32]

This quote followed her discussion of why she left the Socialist Party:

> From the time I married Kenneth, we were committed to political action, but in a Quaker context. I interpreted Norman Thomas's mandate by becoming an active Democrat.[33]

Other involvements for Elise with the American Friends Service Committee during the 1960s included giving a paper in September of 1965, at an AFSC sponsored Peace Education Retreat and being a member of the regional board of the organization. Her other Quaker activities of the early '60s included journeying to Korea in December of 1963, substituting for Kenneth who was unable to attend the Korean Yearly Meeting. The Koreans had requested that he attend, hoping to entice him from Japan where the family was residing that year, for a short visit. Initially Elise's visa was denied by the South Korean mission, as she had recently been in the Soviet Union and eastern Europe as an observer for WILPF at the World Peace Conference sponsored by the communist Women's International Democratic Federation of Russia.

Several of her publications relating to children and spirituality were published during this time.[34] In 1965, she served on the Friends Council on Education (the body representing Quaker primary and secondary schools) committee on recruitment and placement. The mid–'60s were also the time when Elise began the networking associated with the Committee on Friends Responsibilities in Higher Education and Research.[35]

THE WOMEN'S STRIKE FOR PEACE

At the 1962 Brussels conference on women, Elise spoke of the international activities of WILPF, among them the loosely organized Women's Strike for Peace movement, which had arisen out of concerns for the health of infants and children during an era of active nuclear testing. There had been a call for housewives to go out and "strike for peace" on November 1, 1961. Elise had helped to organize her local chapter of the movement in Ann Arbor and had begun editing a newsletter, entitled "The Women's Peace Movement Bulletin," to link various chapters to let each know what was going on elsewhere. She edited this newsletter from January to June of 1962. She used her correspondence list as the beginning of a project for which she sought funding from the Center for Conflict Resolution the next year to study the motivations, expectations and self-perceptions of the women who participated. The title reflects her belief that this movement represented "the new women's peace movement." The beginning query of her proposal represents the aim of her study:

> What prompted thousands of women across the United States to respond to an appeal to "strike for peace" and demand disarmament through public demonstration?

Using her bulletin mailing list, Elise sent out questionnaires to a national sample of membership, totaling nearly 2,000. The questions reflected her interest in understanding the motivations that led women, who may not previously have been activists, to become so. She also wanted to attempt to understand their visions of how peace might be possible and what in their family background or current situation might have led these women to concerns about war and nuclear testing.

Elise's findings were published in 1965 as a chapter in *Behavioral Science and Human Survival.*[36] Noting that this was, indeed, an "unaction," as there was no real national organization, she found that many of the women who participated had not previously been active in civic or political organizational affairs. Nearly half of the respondents said, as a result of the strike movement, that they now put substantially more time into working for social and civic change. A number of them seem to have given a good deal of thought to alternative visions of society. A large group of women joined the movement over a sense of urgency about the current world situation and a need to take personal responsibility for change.

The movement was largely confined to white, middle- and upper-middle-class, well educated women. Elise found that seventy-five percent of the women could pinpoint a special time in their life when they began to be concerned about war; for many of them it came in their teens (many would have been teens during World War II). Experiences ranged from reading books or seeing movies to discussing war at church or in the classroom to personal experiences of suffering and loss to giving birth, lending new insights into the value of life. Elise left open the possibility for more extensive research into the previously mentioned questions and concluded her 1963 early write-up of the study with these words, which might also be used to describe her life at that time:

> We may venture to remark ... that never has the unique combination of *individuals* with particular qualifications and *times* "ripe for change" been so auspiciously presented to a social movement as at present. At a time when most thinking people the world over are seriously questioning the adequacy of existing national rituals for preserving human security on the globe, we find released into the stream of history a large group of well educated women able to take time to participate in national and world affairs, and aroused to the necessary pitch of intensity that will help them overcome their historical preference for the quieter activities of nest building. This is something new under the sun![37]

Year in Japan

Midway through the 1960s the Bouldings took another year away from Ann Arbor, spending the academic year of 1963 to 1964 in Japan, where Kenneth taught at the International Christian University and Elise was able to continue the work she had begun on WSP. She continued her work with the International Peace Research newsletter, begun shortly before with some funding from a peace research committee of the WILPF. The family lived in Tokyo.

The annual Boulding letter to friends, dated October 9, 1963, and written from Tokyo, stated that the children were attending an American school with an international student body but few Japanese students. Elise was taking Japanese lessons from a faculty wife and studying Japanese flower arranging. As was usual in the Boulding's annual greetings, Elise found ways to insert her views, writing, "I am continually reminded of the subliminally self-assured ethnocentrism of the Christian West."[38]

Elise's father died while the family was in Japan that year, but she was unable to get back to Syracuse for the memorial service due to the distance and high cost of air fare at that time. There was a second Quaker memorial service for Josef soon after the Bouldings returned to the United States.

During the year in Japan, Elise continued the work she had begun on the Women's Strike for Peace, adapting the questionnaire she had developed for American women to study Japanese women's nongovernmental organizations. She interviewed members of thirty-two such organizations and found that the two studies, the American and Japanese, were in many ways incomparable, due to the two nation's different political environments. The study was conducted with the support of International Christian University in collaboration with one of their women faculty members, using students of the social science department as assistants. Beginning the study with the goal of studying Japanese women who were working for peace, Elise broadened her aims to study their participation in civic organizations and their perceptions of their changing roles as they moved more into the public sphere. Elise saw contrasts between what the women reported and their actual behavior, noting that fewer than one third of the women interviewed spoke of finding new roles outside of their homes and families. The Japanese study was published in 1966 in *The Japan Christian Quarterly*.[39]

The study of the roles of these women helped to give grounding to what would, in a few years, become Elise's Ph.D. work on the changing roles of women. It also clearly speaks to Elise's growing interest in the study of women's NGOs, which would find fruition later in her academic work at the University of Colorado and at Dartmouth. By the mid–1960s Elise's energies were turning again to academia and to an anticipated integration of her of scholarly and activist leanings.

Chapter 5

Return to School and the "Respite" to Run for Congress

Upon the Boulding's return to Ann Arbor in the fall of 1964, Elise was offered an adjunct position at the University teaching "The Sociology of the Family." As she was preparing to teach, at the last minute the University found someone with a doctorate to teach the course. This event together with some difficulties she had had in getting her Japan study funded convinced Elise that she would need to return to school and finish her Ph.D. if she wanted to pursue an academic career. This she did in the fall of 1965, receiving a Danforth Fellowship of $500 as one of the first class of older women to hold graduate fellowships from the organization. To Elise, the fellowship represented not only tangible support for her pursuits but also moral and psychological encouragement for her returning to school at age 45. The director of the Danforth group wrote to Elise:

> You represent precisely the kind of woman whom the authors of the program hoped to discover and that to give you encouragement in undertaking a career in teaching will be a service to the community.[1]

In an 1978 interview in Hanover, Elise reported that

> [my return to school] was like diving into a pool and holding your breath until you come up at the other end. There were a few distractions, such as being a write-in peace candidate in the 1966 campaign. I thought if I had more knowledge, I could do more effective peace campaigning. I don't have any such illusions now.[2]

Up until this time, both Elise and Kenneth had been active members of the Democratic Party. Increasingly, however, both of them had begun to see flaws in the party's stance over the war in Vietnam. Elise, for her part, believed that the party was not going far enough in denouncing the war. Because of this, she was persuaded by some co-workers in the party to create a major public debate on the war by running for the Michigan Second Congressional District as a write-in peace candidate. Citing her reasons for running, Elise said,

> I still have a hard time saying "no" to the things that need to be done.[3] My co-workers ... persuaded me that there was no other viable write-in candidate that could run. We all agreed there should be a write-in candidate, and when it came down to it, there really wasn't anyone willing and acceptable. I felt so strongly that it had to be done that I did it. Once again, Kenneth gave complete support. I guess a lot of things in my life are like that. If I see something needs to be done, the fact that it is hard is not a barrier. I just have to understand that it has to be done and then I do it. Kenneth and I have always supported each other in this "decision to do." But there are a lot of things I don't do (laughter). There are things that have seemed hard, but I've been blessed like Kenneth with an usually high level of physical energy.... We felt that there was enough public momentum for pulling out of Vietnam at that time that if we could simply make enough noise during the election, it could happen.... [T]he idea was to create a major pubic debate and to make clear the ridiculousness of continuing the war.... [T]here were an awful lot of peace candidates all over the country that year.... There was a lot of campaigning for each other.[4]

Elise's platform statement began by condemning the atrocities of the war such as the use of napalm, the support of a corrupt government in South Vietnam, and the destruction of homes and crops, all of which were taking resources away from needed social progress at home. Other things advocated were:

1. A program for the rapid withdrawal of all non–Vietnamese forces from the country and a return to the Geneva Accords of 1951, the right to self-determination by the Vietnamese people
2. The abandonment by the U.S. government of the "superpower" position and a return to a more modest role in the world community
3. A long-term program for a peaceful settlement of the existing tension, listing specific measures to be adopted, including supporting the role of China in the world community

4. A strong drive to abolish poverty and discrimination in the United States and the possibilities for each member of the world community to meet his or her potential.[5]

Elise's election pamphlet listed her as the "wife of the prominent economist Kenneth Boulding, the mother of five children of school and college age. ... She is now back in school herself, working for a Ph.D." Her other involvements with Quakers were listed, along with WILPF and IPRA. Her statement in the pamphlet read:

> To the outside world, the United States increasingly spells terror and aggression. We are a real tiger, ready to pounce and rend with our enormous sixty billion dollar claws anyone who does not see things our way. This lust for power, this utter lack of proportion between means and ends, is the essence of immorality.... [W]e have an enormous amount of unfinished business at home if the American dream is to be realized.[6]

Kenneth wrote a statement for Elise's candidacy entitled "The Effects of the Vietnam War on the Domestic Economy," citing its effect in producing a mild economic inflation considerable enough to "produce consumer discontent as reflected in housewives' strikes and so on" (referring to the Women's Strike for Peace). He went on to note that

> the present economic flurry is only a symptom of a much wider, more fundamental and more dangerous disease of the American economy which results from our obsession with being a super power and the absorption of nearly 10% of the total product of our country into the war industry. As a result of this, the technological growth of the civilian sector of our economy has been severely handicapped and many fundamental industries such as machine tools, ship-building ... and such equally fundamental activities as education ... is not keeping pace with the growth of the more rapidly developing countries such as Japan and many countries of Europe.... [This] is an even further indication of the serious long-term sickness of our whole society.... [A] further evaluation not only of our foreign policy but all of our domestic policies is strictly in order.[7]

Elise did not seriously entertain the notion that she would win the election that year. It would be several years later that the Bouldings themselves would see a shift in their fundamental agreement on the issues related to the Vietnam War.

Vietnam

In October of the same year that she ran for Congress, 1966, Elise traveled to Rome to give a paper at the International Seminar for the Participation of Women in Public Life. The essence of her paper, entitled "The Road to Parliament for Women," was that women must develop civic competence and must come to think of themselves as effective agents of change. Women have not been participating in public life to the extent which is commensurate with their voting rights, she said. Elise was representing WILPF as an observer at the gathering and was listed also as the editor of the IPRA newsletter. Her written comments at the conclusion of the conference reflected her annoyance at the lack of meaningful discussion on ideological issues, noting that she made a plea for more discussion and then was asked to preside at a subsequent session.[8]

Both Elise and Kenneth continued throughout the next few years to actively protest the U.S. involvement in Vietnam. Kenneth had helped to organize the first university teach-in on the war on the Michigan campus in March of 1965. Elise was there in the capacity of wife and "server of coffee," during the all night vigil, as she amusingly recalled.[9]

In 1967 the Bouldings were part of the Michigan delegation of Quakers who defied U.S. law by bringing money and supplies to Canada for the aid of the Vietnamese people, both in the North and in the South, in violation of the embargo under the Export Control Act. An article in the Toronto, Ontario, *Telegram* noted that the group from Detroit that brought money was part of a larger group of pacifists, mostly Quakers, who were donating cash and medical supplies for the aid program of the Canadian Friends Service Committee (the Canadian equivalent of AFSC) for distribution to three Red Cross Societies in North Vietnam, South Vietnam and the National Liberation Front (the Viet Cong). Elise, whose picture was included with other marchers, had been one of the key organizers of the Michigan delegation. The actual transmission of funds to the Canadian Quakers occurred in Detroit, but the group marched across the International Bridge to Windsor, Ontario, with a symbolic dollar bill inserted in a Bible, opened to the passage, "if your enemy is hungry, feed him, if he be thirsty, give him drink." The money was then given to the Canadian Quakers. According to Elise, the "real" money was driven across the border by Kenneth and others underground, though the *Telegram* noted that the cash was brought across the bridge.[10]

Prior to their journey across to Canada, the Bouldings had invited a group of students to their annual New Year's Eve party, which was one of the settings for the founding of what would later become the Students for a Democratic Society. Several of the students, including Tom Hayden, ended up staying with the Bouldings for the night. At that time the group still had a strong commitment to nonviolence, and as Elise remembers, "It was what happened to them later that drove them to their violence." Stating that these students were totally unprepared for the "rawness" of their treatment, Elise recalled how she needed to remember that evening to understand what drove the Weatherman faction of SDS to later resort to violence. Later in Boulder, the Bouldings would again be hosts to a group of SDS students who, in her words, were being "hassled by the police" and needed a safe place for retreat for a short time "that wasn't bugged."[11]

In 1967 Elise crossed the bridge to Canada to give funds from the Ann Arbor Friends to Canadian Quakers for relief in North Vietnam—an illegal act. The money was carried in Elise's family Bible.

The Dilemmas of Pacifism

The tension continued for Elise as the 1960s wore on, torn as she was among her understanding of hurtful, oppressive structures and the need to change them, her recognition of the need for radical reform at times, and her evolving vision of a world where peace meant people reconciling their differences in nonviolent ways. Her activism turned increasingly inward as her role as an academic educator began to absorb more of her time. Realizing that "violence is the means you turn to when you see absolutely no other recourse to defend the basis of existence itself" and that people often rationalize their use of violence, particularly in terms of societal change, she became increasingly dissatisfied with the kinds of activism that, up until that point, had continued to sustain her.[12]

While at times calling herself an "anarchist," she began to envision herself "living in a different kind of world," a world where differences would be recognized and celebrated after perhaps a breakdown in the kind of society which then existed.[13] It was as if her own journey were taking her inward into her own visioning, which would bear fruit in the development and ultimate fruition of her "Imaging for the Future" workshops, and outward into a teaching career, in which she felt called to practice her activism by helping to develop the minds and hearts of her students.

Elise began to recognize her own shortcomings in terms of her ability to take the real risks involved in a pacifist, resistive position as well as the disparities between the leftist language of oppression and the unwillingness of many in the peace movement to take the risks and consequences involved. What sustained her was her understanding that "you can't create by destroying ... you are simply postponing the work that you want by smashing the structures.... [This keeps me a] pacifist."[14] In an interview given for the *Douglas College Alumni Bulletin* in 1973, Elise summed up some of her thoughts on activism: "[It was] frustrating ... the issues were never properly focused, the analysis was scanty, the knowledge inadequate."[15]

The International Peace Research Association

The early 1960s had represented for Elise her first forays into the peace research movement, as she helped to form a peace research committee for WILPF called the International Consultative Committee on Peace Research, founded at the International Congress held in California in 1962. Her experiences in California with Fred Polak in the mid–1950s and her work at the Center for Conflict Resolution, including running the research development seminar from 1960 to 1962, together with the sharing of colleagues' interests and energy regarding peace, most notably Kenneth's, helped to continue her resolve to work in an interdisciplinary manner in her future endeavors in the social sciences. Always eschewing a solely quantitative approach, Elise's early research interests were in studying the networks and organizations by which people help to facilitate change.

While working as a secretary at the Center for Conflict Resolution, it was Elise's idea to retrieve from the wastebasket letters from peace scholars and related newsletters that the Center had received. She clipped relevant passages, pasted them, added her own comments and then sent them out as a compiled newsletter, initiating what would soon become the IPRA newsletter. Thus began Elise's reputation as the "generator of the peace research community" as she began to perfect her networking skills in those pre-computer days.[16] The newsletter was begun in 1963, predating the more formal establishment of IPRA by two years. It was keeping academic peace that researchers connected with one another, which made it relatively easy to call a meeting in 1963 in Geneva. It was followed the next year by one in London, which would eventually lead to IPRA's founding in 1965.

Funding for the initial newsletters came not from the Center for Conflict Resolution who, according to Elise were "too embarrassed to sponsor it," fearing it would not be adequately academically respectable, but from the International Consultative Committee on Peace Research of WILPF, which had just been formed. The purpose of this committee was to help national sections of WILPF as well as other NGOs to bring developments in peace research more effectively to the attention of governments, university research centers and UN representatives. In addition to Elise, committee members included Norwegian economist Johanne Gjermoe, Ingrid Galtung, a Norwegian research associate and the wife of Johan Galtung, Sushila Nayer of India (personal physician to Mahatma Gandhi), who would later serve as international vice-chair of WILPF when Elise was chair, and Fujiko Isono, an anthropologist from Japan.[17]

At the California Congress, which Elise attended, a resolution was passed which read, in part:

> The WILPF, recognizing the urgency of mobilizing the intellectual as well as the moral and psychological forces of mankind on the making of peace, advocates international cooperation in Peace Research, preferably under the auspices of the United Nations. It is important that the various institutes and organizations working in this field in different countries should be kept in contact and keep informed about each other's activities and findings. The Congress urges UNESCO as soon as possible to call an international conference of scholars working in this field, that scientists engaged in peace research may not only exchange ides but also develop a new vision of their contribution to the building of world order.[18]

Elise soon thereafter persuaded UNESCO to take over the funding for the newsletter just prior to the formation of IPRA. The first few issues of the newsletter did not include IPRA in the title, as the organization had not formally begun, but reflected WILPF 's role in subsidizing it. The first issue, sent out in the winter of 1963, made a plea for governmental and institutional support for conflict resolution. Elise also encouraged WILPF members to continue their activism in relation to issues regarding peace and war. Reflecting her belief in the importance of individual action in relation to transnational organizations, she wrote:

> [N]o individual is too small to raise his voice in the international community. As Ian Gordon-Brown points out in his article on "The NGO Movement" ... it is possible for a proposal from an ordinary man or woman living in a remote village, in an isolated part of the world, to come up for discussion in the General Assembly of the UN within two years, or its conception—through the system of NGO representation at the UN. The potentialities of this remarkable piece of machinery have not been adequately realized by even the most world-minded citizens of the international community.[19]

Later these thoughts found fruition in "Building a Global Civic Culture."[20] Elise concluded her first editorial by putting in a plea

> for communications from all parts of the world about developments, however tentative or embryonic, in the field of peace research. Scientific knowledge, to be useful, must be cumulative. At present there is no international clearing-house to which scientists can turn to find out what is happening in peace research around the world. In time this will come. In the meantime, this newsletter can provide a modest contribution to a pressing need by printing what hints can be picked up of what is going on in various countries.[21]

She requested that information be sent to her. She then described what was happening in peace research throughout the world, with apologies for the large amount of material from the western world.

A year later, Elise reported in a subsequent newsletter on the important meeting of the Conferences on Research on International Peace and Security (COROIPAS), held in Clarens, Switzerland, and the forerunner to IPRA. This meeting was called in August of 1963, just prior to the Bouldings journey to Japan, with support from UNESCO and the British and American Service Committees (Quakers), who had called it. To this gathering were invited twenty-five peace scholars from fifteen countries whose purpose was to establish a series of conferences on international peace and security. Elise wrote about the results of this conference in the next newsletter:

> Unquestionably all scholars feel the need for an all-inclusive international communications network, but individual differences lead some to prefer more informal channels, others to work for a more

> formal system of representation of bodies of scientists from different parts of the world.... [T]he very fact that scholars are meeting together to discuss each other's research will in itself bring about a recognizable international community, and the more countries that are represented at these gatherings, the better it is for the development of the necessary global frame of reference for peace research.[22]

It was decided at that Clarens conference to establish annual international gatherings with the hope of the continual involvement of UNESCO on the order of the already existing Pugwash Conferences, of which Kenneth Boulding was a member. These conferences were representative of the efforts of those engaged in the physical sciences to establish better east-west working relations. Kenneth had been one of the first social scientists to join Pugwash.[23]

The feeling among the group that convened, which was representative of the emerging movement in peace research, was that the traditional scholarly field of international relations took a too narrow view of the issues concerning peace and war, and some scholars felt this helped legitimize Cold War tensions.[24] The new movement sought to broaden its outlook on causative and prescriptive elements and, from the beginning, involved an interdisciplinary approach that rested heavily upon the newly emerging work in systems theory, of which Kenneth was a leading scholar. However, the thorny question of activism continued to raise its head throughout subsequent gatherings.

In December of 1964, the same year that UNESCO took over the funding of the newsletter, a conference in London was organized with John Burton of London University elected as Secretary General of the new Conferences on Research on International Peace and Security (COROIPAS). Elise attended as editor of the peace research newsletter. At that meeting Bert Roling of the Netherlands was elected the new Secretary-General of the formally established International Peace Research Association, which would meet the next year in Groningen, the Netherlands. Elise wrote a summary of the meeting, encapsulating the extensive debate that had little resolution and concerned about the issue of research versus advocacy:

> This group should be a research organization and should not engage in advocacy.... [O]n the other hand, research and advocacy are in some sense inseparable.[25]

How to reconcile this dichotomy was to occupy a good deal of IPRA time over the ensuing years, as well help to lead to the founding of the Consortium on Peace, Research, Education and Development (COPRED) several years later. At the COROIPAS gathering, it was decided that since Pugwash was already doing peace advocacy, any action-oriented work should be channeled through that organization and others devoted to similar work. However, possibilities were left open for some advocacy, should there be a consensus among IPRA members.

It was decided that IPRA itself would not at that time engage in any independent peace research as an institution, but that issues concerning peace should be one of its first priorities and that support should be given to those individual scholars doing peace related work. Relationships with other existing peace research organizations and journals were clarified, including Pugwash. Of the three main activities listed for the new organization, two were devoted to linking and fostering better communication among scholars in addition to advancing interdisciplinary research.

Elise attended the inaugural meeting of the new IPRA in Groningen in July 1965. There were over seventy in attendance representing twenty-three countries and nineteen scholarly disciplines.[26] Neither the Soviet Union nor China sent a representative. Most of the participants were men. Elise is listed as attending, with her title listed as editor of the newsletter. Johan Galtung of Norway's Peace Research Institute concluded the conference with these remarks:

> [W]e are scientists, most of us social scientists—our role is to make peace relevant, to make it peace research.... [O]ur research is not sufficiently issue-oriented. We have not been able to have anything significant to say on Vietnam, on Republica Dominica [*sic*].[27]

Galtung's remarks indicated that he believed that this deficit was not due to non-interest, but to a lack of adequate methodology to address the issues.

Elise continued to edit and to be the spirit behind the international IPRA newsletter until the family moved to Boulder in 1967, and again edited it in the mid–1980s after her retirement. For many years she also edited the North American section of the newsletter. Later, during her tenure as International Secretary-General from 1988 to 1991, she would begin the IPRA Foundation, the purpose of which is to help fund peace related projects for scholars in developing countries.

Move to Boulder

Kenneth accepted a job at the University of Colorado, and the family moved to Boulder in the fall of 1967 while Elise was continuing to work on her dissertation for a degree in sociology at the University of Michigan.

Kenneth requested that, as part of his accepting the job, the university attempt to find a teaching position for Elise, which it did. Kenneth had a part-time faculty position in the department of economics and a part-time one in the newly formed Institute for Behavioral Sciences, an interdisciplinary research program in the social sciences. Elise later also became associated with the Institute. Three of the Boulding children, Christy, Philip and William, came with Elise and Kenneth to Boulder. Mark stayed behind to attend the University of Michigan and Russell was attending Antioch College in Ohio at the time.

Elise divided her time among beginning her teaching career in sociology, working on her dissertation, working on the national section of the IPRA newsletter and, beginning in 1968, serving as International Chair of WILPF. In 1969 she received her doctorate from the University of Michigan, the title of her thesis being "The Effect of Industrialization on the Participation of Women in Society."[28] Beginning her dissertation with the hypothesis that women's participation would increase as modernization increased, Elise utilized a model of studying women's roles in developing countries, partly through the use of international data, and came to the conclusion that the correlation was modest at best. Part of the reason for this, as she explained in her write-up, was that "the social invisibility of women makes it difficult to document patterns of roles in any society." As she noted, "most data gatherers are men." She concluded by stating:

> In all societies, women's contribution has been auxiliary in nature; helping to get things done rather than in work which assumes direct responsibility and authority for what is done.[29]

Elise's study provided the solid grounding for her continued work on women's roles and women's contributions toward social change.

In Boulder, Elise began to teach sociology courses relating to the family, religion and social change. At the university she was soon instrumental in beginning a peace studies program, a newly emerging academic discipline that utilized cross-disciplinary faculty in the social sciences. Faculty from the Institute for Behavioral Sciences, including Kenneth, collaborated in developing and teaching the program. Elise was a popular teacher. The 1970 course catalogue listing her sociology of religion course offers the following comments, some from former students:

> "Mrs. Boulding is a well educated, active, intelligent woman who is flexible and responsive to her students and the world." Seventy-four percent [of students] strongly agreed that papers were an important learning experience. "This was one of the most inspiring, relevant

> and meaningful classes I've ever taken. For once, a class really pertained to ME, my thoughts, actions and ideas." "Mrs. Boulding is a beautiful person"[30]

Elise put a great deal of effort into her teaching while in Colorado. A former student recalled that her courses were often organized as lectures, but there was a lot of student interaction as well. He went on to say,

> I always learned an incredible amount, was exposed to all kinds of new ideas and books. Her style was not the usual write a paper, take a mid-term ... there was always a project, a group one sometimes. I remember conversations she would have with individual students, she listens, when people talk.... [S]he changed the [culture] ... she interacted with students ... she had them over to her house ... she got them involved.... It made it so easy to do service projects during the protests in the early 1970s.[31]

In 1969 Elise traveled to Santiago, Chile, representing WILPF at a UNICEF sponsored conference on NGOs. Her report on this conference was published later that year in *International Associations* and was entitled, "The Family, the NGO and Social Mapping in a Changing Society." The title was indicative of the evolution and integration of her theoretical ideas on family, NGOs and building a more peaceful world.[32] Here she recognized the family as the basic unit of society and spoke to the need for more research on families and their relationship to communities.[33]

At the time Elise was elected chair, WILPF was still heavily involved in opposition to the Vietnam War. Soon thereafter, other issues would come to the fore. In Elise's May 12, 1969, circular to international members, she mentions the Biafran-Nigerian War, the communist takeover of Czechoslovakia, and the Middle East in addition to WILPF activities connected with Vietnam.[34] Once again, using her style of prose and integrative metaphor, Elise began the circular with these words:

> This letter is written as flood waters are rising all around me in Boulder. Our house is on high ground, so we are "safe," but as I dash back and forth between the constantly ringing telephone and the typewriter, I am reminded of how symbolic of the world situation this local distress is. A minority of us in the world community are on "high ground." What are we doing about the rising flood waters? Mostly action on behalf of peace is at the sandbagging level (our children are down at Boulder Creek right now sandbagging to protect center city homes). In the WILPF our job is to create the institutions and conditions for *prevention* of the social floods which threaten mankind.[35]

As the decade came to a close, a letter to fellow WILPF member Dorothy Steffens dated February 3, 1970, gave an indication of her intense interest in the connections between locality and globalism and of her identity as an educator. After mentioning her concerns about Biafra, India, Africa and the Middle East, Elise wrote:

> The basic point is ... that we have much to learn from people whom we have defined as our "pupils"—people we thought *we* were going to teach.... [P]olitics depends on making people category-conscious, and then bargaining for rights for each category—from status internationally to the right to community control of schools in a neighborhood.... I am glad I am an educator, and don't have to either build up or tear down categories—but cut across them.... [F]urthermore an educator is in a position to redefine what education is all about—which in my terms is *listening* and *understanding*. Teaching in the talking way is *not* education. The latins [*sic*] had it in educare.[36]

The Consortium on Peace, Research, Education and Development (COPRED)

> I see us all as players of rather poorly tuned instruments trying to perform a delicate orchestration of a new symphony. We can't even read the music, let alone play in tune! The quality of our lives, and the choice of our life styles, is inextricably tied to our work as teachers, researchers and activists. It is my dream for COPRED that it will become the kind of community in which we encourage one another to a new listening and a new quality of life, which will in turn transform the quality of our work on behalf of tomorrow's world.[37]

With these words, Elise concluded her report as chairperson to the membership of COPRED on the occasion of the organization's fourth birthday in May of 1974.

The Consortium began in May of 1970, following an invited gathering, hosted by the Bouldings and Gilbert White, director of the Institute of Behavioral Sciences at the University of Colorado in Boulder. Twenty-five peace scholars were invited to the Harvest House hotel in Boulder, and to a "working conference" with dinner hosted by the Bouldings at their home. Following a lecture/discussion on peace research led by Kenneth, the group considered the topic of "how teaching and research might begin to work together."[38] Realizing that there had been a lack of communication and coordination among those involved in peace related work, the mission of the newly formed consortium was to

> foster research, education and training in the areas of peace and world security and the channeling of relevant research information to governmental and non-governmental practitioners; that the coordination function would be a primary one, and that the founding Consortium members in the United States and Canada would seek contacts with Latin American institutions on the one hand and with the International Peace Research Association and other international bodies on the other.[39]

At that initial meeting, Paul Wehr, a scholar from Haverford College and the Institute for World Order in New York (later to become the World Policy Institute), was elected chair and Elise volunteered to serve as coordinating secretary. Several years later, when the office of COPRED moved to Boulder, Paul Wehr joined the faculty of the University of Colorado to help Elise develop her peace studies program while he served half-time as the director of COPRED, a newly established position.

A six person organizing committee was formed at the Harvest House meeting, consisting of the Bouldings, Chadwick Alger, Israel Charny, Robert Hefner, and Hanna Newcomb. Soon thereafter, Hector Cappello was invited to join as a consultant on Latin America, joined by representatives from UNITAR, the UN training and development agency, the National Academy of Sciences, the U.S. Arms Control and Disarmament Agency and the Quaker International Affairs Program in Washington, D.C.[40]

From the beginning, COPRED's chief role was linkage, though specifically what form this should take was not always agreed upon by the organizers. There were those, particularly Elise, who felt that it should be considered the North American branch of IPRA, but not everyone agreed that this was appropriate, and the links between the two groups have continued to be informal, Elise playing a major role in keeping the ties strong.

During the two years following the organizing meeting in Boulder, the group met several times at a retreat and conference center in Racine, Wisconsin, under the care of the Johnson Foundation. In time, membership was opened to individual peace scholars, activists and educators. In the beginning it was institutional members that joined. As the organization developed, its mode of operation became an Executive Committee, elected annually through the membership that reported to the COPRED Council, composed of representatives from the institutional members.[41] In this way, ties were maintained between individual and institutional members.

From the beginning it was felt that the best way for COPRED to link with other organizations was through the establishment of committees devoted to various tasks. Among the ones in which Elise was involved in the early years were the Youth, Education and Training Committee and the Research Inventory Task Force, a combined attempt at integrating her interests in both research and education. The Youth, Education and Training Committee, which later evolved in 1972 into the Peace Education Network, had as its tasks the development of peace and conflict studies as a recognized academic field and the organization of peace-related seminars and workshops. In addition, it undertook the development of peace education at the primary and secondary levels.

One of the projects in which Elise was involved in the early 1970s through the Youth, Education and Training Committee was an educational project that received some funding from the Institute for World Order. This was to create a taxonomy of peace making skills, involving a questionnaire sent out to members and interested persons to attempt to understand the peacemaking skills they used. In addition, the project consisted of the dissemination of a booklet for classroom teachers as well as one for community leaders on peace education curriculum planning. Several questions drove the impetus for the project, which Elise conducted with two colleagues, Susan Carpenter and Pam Solo:

> What do children need to become peacemakers, when can they best learn these skills, and what learning modes are most appropriate to each age level? For example, at what age can a child become empathetically identified with an oppressed group of people, how can this skill of altruism be developed and at what age level is it possible for children to make the abstractions necessary for this compassion-action?[42]

This project was undertaken during the same period when IPRA's Peace Education Commission was forming and Elise had recently written her chapter, "The Child and Non-Violent Social Change," for a special IPRA newsletter addition, edited in part by Susan Carpenter.

Other peace education activities which Elise reported on in her 1974 report to the COPRED members included forming partnerships with the Detroit Center for Teaching About Peace and War, the New York Centers for War and Peace Studies and the high school program of the Institute for World Order. These projects included the beginning of the development of a peace-related curriculum. Also that year, COPRED was able to put its activities into ERIC, the national educational database.[43]

The purpose of the research inventory group with which Elise was involved was to make links between scholarly research and practitioners, particularly in terms of policy makers at governmental and nongovernmental levels. As Elise reported:

> Our first response was to set up a research inventory task force to carry out relevant research findings from the work of those who can be identified as peace researchers (we use the term loosely), as the first step toward making this information available to policy-makers and other researchers. This has turned out to be a major project indeed, and continues in full swing at the present, with member centers in North Carolina and the University of Colorado.[44]

Other activities of the research inventory group in its first few years included small conferences with national policy makers held during the first year at the Quaker International Affairs Center in Washington. Elise noted in her 1974 report to COPRED members the links with governmental agencies.[45] Another thrust was to broaden the research linkages with developing countries and with the United Nations and its agencies and to further support contacts with the emerging United Nations University, an organization with which Elise became very involved several years later.

Paralleling the development of emerging campus peace studies programs, more and more of COPRED's individual membership began to be academicians whose work revolved around developing campus programs. Elise, in her 1974 report, noted that "more members teach than do research" and mentioned the astonishment of the original founders at the growth of peace studies programs in the first year of COPRED's existence. As she stated, "[I]n my own view of teaching, every hour spent with students is an hour of experiment in the field," a statement indicative again of her ability to understand her teaching within the context itself of research. Emphasizing the important function of community she wrote:

> Our strength lies in each other, not in some mystic entity called COPRED.... Since I am currently on a year's leave from the university, I have been living for the last three months almost entirely in solitude, in a mountain hermitage (with occasional expeditions into the world for occasions like this). I am astounded to realize how inattentive, how unlistening, we become in the environments in which we ordinarily live and work. The kind of carefully tuned awareness and watchfulness which every bird and animal on "my hillside" exhibits at all times has been quite a teaching for me on the potentials for sheer aliveness that exist in us largely undeveloped. For us humans, the kind of attentiveness I speak of means a blending our intuitive and analytic skills. It can only be developed by taking some time for it, although it can be practiced at a desk,

> computer or in [a] classroom or crowded city street (but it's hard). In the absence of that attentiveness, most of our research and teaching is meaningless.[46]

How well COPRED was meeting its goals of integrating peace research, activism and education was addressed directly by Paul Wehr in his year-end report as executive director of COPRED in 1975. Beginning the report with a bit of history, he mentioned *research* as the prioritizing feature that grounded the beginnings of the organization, the aim being the advancement of peace research, the dissemination of findings to policymakers and the public, and of "sensitizing the scholarly community to peace-related issues."[47]

The statement of Wehr's was not entirely consistent with Elise's idea of why COPRED was founded, yet he directly addressed the integration issue. Stating that he believed COPRED in many ways was still in its infancy, he questioned how long the organization would/should exist, given its continual difficulties with funding, much of it having been under the care of various foundations. In addition, he mentioned his fear that the original purpose of its founding, as part of "a challenge movement against war and other forms of collective violence," would, in a sense, become too vulnerable, as "institutional structures that emerge from challenge movements often have a way of establishing themselves, to become dysfunctional as they grow." His desire was that COPRED not become vulnerable to the wishes of "vested interests."[48]

Wehr mentioned his ambivalent feelings about the need for some additional structuring of the organization, given its varied constituencies and its unique attempts at melding many disciplines and activities across the spectrum of the peace movement:

> COPRED by including in its membership researchers, educators and actionists mixes oranges, apples and bananas—they have much in common but have as well often highly divergent ways of operating and communicating. We need a model for future development that combines dynamism and productivity with the capacity to engage imagination and commitment. Perhaps a model-building contest among COPRED's membership would be appropriate. What we want is a design for getting our work done that results in a synthesis of peace related research, teaching and action—and not a fruit salad.[49]

Wehr appeared to be communicating his fear of an emerging sense of stagnation within the organization, and he was making a plea for new ways to address the continually nagging issue of the integration of the various dichotomous elements of research, education and activism. An effective integration, he believed, would help revitalize the organization.

There were other difficulties impinging upon COPRED at that time as well. In addition to chronic issues of funding, the continual shift in the geographic space for the organization's office made it difficult to make transitions from one place to another. Through the years it has been at such disparate places as the University of Colorado, Gustavus Adolphus College in Minnesota and at Manchester College in Indiana, the site of the first peace studies program begun in 1948. After a stint at George Mason University in Virginia, it is now housed at Evergreen State College in the state of Washington. In his report, Wehr wondered whether a series of regional offices might better suffice than the structure then existing for administrative tasks.[50]

In reality, it was the Bouldings who, at various times with the help of colleagues, managed to hold the organization together during times of stress in its inner workings. The mid–'70s were a time of identity questioning for COPRED and a time when Elise also was searching for her own sense of inner peace as she struggled to find her own space. Yet both Kenneth and Elise remained committed to the ongoing work of COPRED, particularly Elise, her efforts tirelessly continuing to bring together those involved in the work of research, education and activism.

By the early 1970s the focus of much of Elise's work had turned toward the study of women in their roles in peace and change. This would continue to occupy much of her energies in the decades to follow. As the 1960s came to a close, with her childrearing days essentially over, her earlier work on children and families, her activism, her Quaker involvements, and particularly her WILPF and IPRA work would all solidify and give breadth to her new and emerging ideas.

Part II

Educating Toward a Culture of Peace

Chapter 6

Philosophy of Education

Communities as Learning Spaces

Through much of her life Elise has found meaning and sustenance in the "spaces" (her term) where education and community intersect. Many were founded, either wholly or in part, by Elise, some in partnership with Kenneth. Some started as intentional spaces for learning. Others were turned into intentional spaces by Elise, in order for her to direct her own talents and energies, as well as to support those of others.

When she was a young girl, Elise's learning community was her Norwegian immigrant household and her extended family of Scandinavian-American families in eastern New Jersey. The community was insulated from the wider American culture, grounding Elise's thinking both as a Norwegian and as an American. Nature, especially water, was a teacher for her. Family swimming outings were a highlight of her childhood and swimming continued to be a delightful activity for her until chronic ear difficulties prohibited this. Until her move to North Hill Retirement Community in 2000 (she moved to the Boston area in 1996), Elise daily swam at the Wayland municipal lake, weather permitting, when she lived nearby.

The public schools Elise attended as a child, first in Hillside, New Jersey, then in Maplewood, and the prosperous suburb which represented a "move up" for the family from Hillside helped to solidify her love of learning and her musical talent. Elise played the cello in various string ensembles throughout high school and college.

Partly due to the close bonding Elise felt within her tightly-knit extended Norwegian-American "family" and, in contrast, to feeling at times estranged and outside of the mainstream American culture, particularly

Elise at her Hermitage in Lyons, Colorado (date unknown).

acute during her adolescent years, the "spaces" of Elise's early years helped to lay the grounding for her later ideas on the importance of individuals in relation to their communities and especially the relationship between solitude and connectedness. Her busy years as a young housewife and mother left her little time for the activities of the mind she so longed for, realizing, as she wrote in her journal in 1958, that

> I have made my decision that these are not the years to get deeply involved in intellectual activity—I never doubt the rightness of that decision—but I suddenly realized this morning how sad I have felt without ever consciously admitting it to myself. Sad that so much of me would die unborn. But it won't die. "it" has more patience than I.[1]

These conflicts over the need for actively engaging her mind, nurturing her growing family, and finding space for her spiritual searching played out many times over the course of her life. At times these conflicts led at times to her retreats into her "spaces of spiritual solitude," the most dramatic example being the year of 1974 when she lived in her small, one-room "hermitage" up the hill from the Waterfall, the family cabin in Lyons, Colorado.

Attending Douglas College in the late 1930s opened up new vistas for Elise, as she began to consciously understand and appreciate the power of her own mind. Marrying Kenneth at age 21, she was immediately attracted to this man who for her represented a creative genius and someone very grounded in his profound Quaker spirituality. Early in their marriage, they intended and sought to found a colony of love, which they named "One Small Plot of Heaven." Kenneth's sonnet on marriage, written for the Quaker wedding of some friends, highlights their intention to make family life a religious calling and is the source for the title for her book *One Small Plot of Heaven*:

> Put off the garb of woe, let mourning cease;
> Today we celebrate with solemn mirth
> The planting in the ravaged waste of earth
> Of one small plot of heaven, a home of peace
> Where love unfeigned shall rule, and bring, increase,
> And pure eternal joy shall come to birth
> And grow, and flower, that neither drought nor dearth
> Shall wither, till the Reaper brings release
>
> Guard the ground well, for it belongs to God;
> root out the hateful and the bitter weed,
> And from the harvest of thy Heart's good seed
> The hungry shall be fed, the naked clad,
> And love's infection, leaven-like, shall spread
> Till all creation feeds from heavenly bread.[2]

One of the first intentional learning communities that she and Kenneth began together was the Friends Student Colony in Ames, Iowa, in the 1940s, founded shortly after they moved to Iowa State College near the middle of the decade. Continuing on into the Ann Arbor days, the Bouldings made it a practice to include students in their household. In part, this helped to relieve Elise of some of the childcare duties and housework.

In her early homemaker days Elise taught Quaker Sunday School and began the practice of having Sunday night suppers at their home for "Family Sunday School," in which adults and children came together for learning. Later these ideas on "learning partnerships" would find fruition in her many lectures at Quaker gatherings through the years. Always her ideas were grounded in the "personhood" of children.

When the family relocated to Boulder and Elise began her more formal academic career, the classes that she taught became one of her intentional communities. Eschewing the formal lecture style, Elise would sometimes hold classes in her home and would periodically take her Sociology of Religion classes to the Christ in the Desert Monastery in New Mexico, where she went at times for her own personal retreats. In the mid–1970s she had discovered monastic life, and as the decade wore on and her life turned intentionally more inward, her "community" became more one of herself and her relation to God. She sought community at the several monasteries she visited both in New York and in New Mexico.

During the Boulder years and later at Dartmouth, Elise's sense of community expanded to include various collegial and spiritual networks, many of which she helped to found, including the peace research community, IPRA, COPRED, the American Sociological Association, various women's organizations, UNESCO and the UN. Though these organizations may perhaps be less obviously considered intentional communities, always Elise's capacities as a networker were operating so as to bring people together in ways which were mutually productive and educative.

During her retirement years, in addition to founding a community called 624 Pearl in downtown Boulder, she started the Friends Peace Teams movement, an outgrowth of her work uniting various faith networks throughout the world. This project began, as have most of her networking activities, with her beginning a newsletter to link like-minded academics, activists and religious leaders to learn from one another.

The 624 Pearl itself is a building just off the main street in downtown Boulder and is set back from the street. A two story structure of beige sandstone, the outside belies the simple yet elegant interior that houses several apartments inside. Founded as an intentional community for retirees, the original occupants were all academic and activist couples who had been associated in some way with the University of Colorado. Among the original founders were the Bouldings, Gilbert and Ann White, Gilbert an internationally known geographer and expert on water resources, and Dorothy and Larry Senesh, Larry a retired academic economist. Except for Elise, the women were not academics but were heavily involved with peace and activist causes both locally and internationally. Several of the founders were Quakers. According to Gilbert White, the key figure in the founding of the community was Elise.[3] In one sense, Elise's move to Boston from Boulder in 1996 freed her of the responsibilities involved in overseeing the needs of that community, whose burdens had increased, as the occupants aged and some had died.

Elise explained the intention behind the founding of the community on Pearl Street:

> We were all retirees, all "peace people," and all wanted to contribute to ongoing learning. Each of us had particular skills to bring, Kenneth and Larry as economists, me as sociologist, Ann as activist, and so forth. I was given adjunct status at the University so we were able to offer courses for credit. We used our common room at the building for classes.... [T]he chief problem we had was that we were all old and some of us died off before we could get very far![4]

Ann White died soon after the founding, and Kenneth died in 1993. Elise said, "If we were to do it over again, we would invite younger people in to join us."[5] In fact, she wondered in retrospect why they had not decided to do this. And this is surprising, given the strong belief she has in the importance of intergenerational learning spaces.

The idea of "learning spaces" is a strong theme that runs through many of Elise's writings on how to educate for peace. Some of these spaces represent physical places, such as schools, homes and community settings. Other spaces represent intangibles, such as those she calls "historical, geographical, cultural spaces and the space of the imagination."[6] Always she stresses that these spaces cannot be said to be truly effective as places for learning unless there are *connections* between the various spaces and with the individuals who reside within them. And they cannot be said to be effective unless there is the intention to view them within their historical and cultural contexts.

One of the most important educational spaces is the family, according to Elise. The importance of the family in building peace lies partly in its unique place as the interface between the local community and the larger global world. It is one of those spaces in which "over and over again the interpersonal and the local intersect with the macro and produce new futures."[7] It is in families where partnerships between the young and the old most reach fruition. And it is in families where, hopefully, children learn to love. And according to Elise, love lays the foundation for the future world. Writing from her Hermitage in her journal in March 1974, she wrote:

> [I]f the human race brings itself to a premature conclusion it will be because we failed to learn the dynamics of love. Love isn't intellectually respectable. If it were, we wouldn't be having the problems we do have.[8]

One way that Elise connected people both to the historical past and to the imagined future was through her idea of the space of the "200 year present." Developed in many of her writings and used frequently in her "imaging for the future" workshops, this concept used what she has called "focused imaging" to place an individual in a moment, looking both back one hundred years and forward one hundred years. Participants are then asked to remember historical events during this "200 year present" and also to look forward and imagine what will happen in the future during this period. The rationale for the process is that it allows for the maximum development of a sense of macro-history. Focusing too much on the present can cause a sense of despair and causes a search for solutions to conflicts to be based upon immediate needs rather than on a view based upon macro-history.

Educating for Peace

The ideas in Elise's philosophy of educating for peace include an integration of the application of her "love of the mind," which she combined together with the strong sense of herself she brought to the many learning spaces in which she found herself through the various phases of her life. Anna Spradlin, writing about Elise for a doctoral dissertation, mentioned that her life has consisted of eight distinct roles and phases. These are: child, young adult, Quaker, spouse, parent, activist, scholar and educator.[9] Wherever Elise found herself, she intentionally sought to "make sense" of her experiences. This "making sense" has found an outlet through her writings, which have usually had strong autobiographical themes running throughout. Particularly in times of spiritual crisis and exhaustion, her journals have also been an important outlet for her.

In a monograph she wrote on the occasion of a 1976 UNESCO Peace Forum, Elise cited an earlier report from the 1972 UNESCO seminar on Youth, Peace and Education and commented:

> Education for peace should ideally be a field in which there is no clear boundary between class teaching and what is called out-of-school education. This is all the more imperative because as things are at present pupils must turn to organizations and movements outside the school system if they want to take an active interest in certain important problems. The perpetuation of this state of affairs contributes to strengthening the pupil's impression that the school is isolated from life and that any action outside it is consequently more relevant to [his or her] own education as a citizen.[10]

Elise went on to note:

> There should be a strong apprenticeship component, beginning with local community apprenticeships and moving up to international organizations, in peace education. When young people are apprenticed to local community organizations to work with community members in learning to solve local conflicts, they will absorb many different kinds of learning at once. The community people they work with, given a teaching responsibility in connection with their community roles, will also become more sensitive to their own ways of working and improve their own peacemaking skills. The same is true with international organizations. Young people apprenticed to international organizations will have a salutary effect on peacemaking skills among NGOs.[11]

During Elise's days teaching college peace studies courses, she had her students "apprenticed" to local community agencies or, in the case of

Sociology of the Family students, they would be "apprenticed" to a local family and would actively engage with various family members as part of their studies.

There are some strong similarities between Elise's ideas on education and those of Maria Montessori, including the concepts that in children lies the "hope for the world" and that children inherently teach adults. Montessori did a great deal of work on educating for peace, beginning in the 1930s. Both Elise and Montessori point to love as the abiding force that should guide any curriculum, and both believe that an education imbued with love can lay the foundation for a peaceful world. Montessori believed deeply in the spirituality of every child, that each one is endowed with messianic powers. She spoke of children as "redeemers of civilization" and of the direct connection between education and world peace.[12]

Elise was familiar with the work of the Italian educator/physician. Elise, as did Maria Montessori, believed that there should be strong societal and political support for the rights of children. Montessori began a political movement to start the Party of the Child, stating, "the child can become the focus ... a sphere of action that will enable mankind to work together."[13] Where she differed from Montessori is in the importance Elise placed on education *for an interdependent world*. She believed in the necessity of preparing young people to be responsible, global citizens. Elise's theories also differed from Montessori's in that she stressed the importance of the interrelationships between local cultures and the global sphere. Elise's ideas evolved partly out of her early work with various Quaker organizations, including the American Friends Service Committee, and her developing interest in international nongovernmental organizations, beginning with her meeting Swedish sociologist Alva Myrdal, who, with her husband Gunnar, befriended the Bouldings during the early days of their marriage in Princeton, New Jersey.

Both Montessori and Boulding developed well articulated theories regarding socialization factors that predispose children to grow up to be change agents.[14] The work of Elise pertaining to this was written in the early 1970s and grew out of her work helping to form the Peace Education Commission of IPRA. The PEC was begun in 1972. In 1974 IPRA published her monograph entitled "The Child and Nonviolent Social Change," in which Elise outlined several factors that are important in guiding children into becoming nonviolent and altruistic social activists who, according to the preface, "seek to shape their society's future towards peace." In this article, Elise schematized eight interlocking sets of inputs, which she developed into a model. These inputs are both internal and external and include genetically determined behavioral programming; maturational processes;

learning processes including cognition, modeling and reinforcement; accumulative knowledge and skill stock; cultural beliefs, norms, roles and structures; situational and event "space," including family, neighborhood, peer group, school and the media; and socializing agents including family members, teachers, peers and other adult role models. She placed heavy emphasis on socialization factors, but did not discount the role of internal genetic and maturational processes.

According to Elise, those committed to non-violent social change have had the following life experiences: optimal opportunities to develop cognitive and intuitive capacities; exposure to events in the larger society; exposure to role models, both peer and adult; exposure to different social roles and opportunities for problem solving; and rewarding social feedback for these former experiences. She listed six sets of "social spaces" where opportunities for maximum socialization occur: family, neighborhood, peer group, school, other cultural institutions and the mass media. Changes occur with the amount of familial influence as the child ages, the family playing less of a role and the peer group more.[15] An overriding theme she found among the activists she studied was their sense of optimism, competence and self-esteem. While she believed in the genetic substrates for some capacities, including those of bonding, aggression, and spirituality, she placed more stock in the role of the environment and social learning in shaping human behavior.

Elise's own sense of herself as an activist was closely related to the characteristics about which she was writing. While competency and a strong sense of herself are apt descriptions of her way of being, finding optimism and looking toward the future have been an intense struggle for her at times. Working through these issues has resulted in her writings on the importance of imaging for the future and in the development of her workshops on "imaging for a world without weapons."

The 1960s Women's Strike for Peace (WSP), as one of her earliest "formal" networking functions, inspired Elise to edit a national information exchange for WSP so that local groups could communicate with one another about this loosely organized movement in which women throughout the country, many of whom had not been social activists before, marched out of their kitchens and nurseries to protest the escalation of nuclear testing. For six months, as Elise remembered, "I received from all directions the tremendous outpourings of imaginative ideas and calls to actions."[16] But she wanted to know more. What was it that got these women moving? Her study entitled "Who are These Women?" found that family and childhood experiences, especially religious experiences, influenced the women's decisions to participate. Some women noted an important book or movie which deeply affected them. Some had suffered an experience of loss such as a loved one killed in war. Many women were inspired by an important mentor, a role model, or someone they knew personally and with whom they could identify as a peacemaker.[17]

It is interesting to note the time and place of this study and to compare her findings with the characteristics used to describe the peacemakers involved. Elise conducted this study for her sociological interest in learning about others and also to help understand her own life situation and her impetus toward peacemaking. She has continually sought to make sense of whatever "life situation" in which she has found herself. In a sense, she has always tried to make intellectual sense of her life. In the early 1960s, Elise was a middle-aged housewife and mother of five, the youngest of the children at that time being six years and the oldest thirteen. The study of the women involved in WSP was her first research endeavor. She could strongly identify with the women she was studying, as she was, herself, "venturing out of house and home" to new endeavors. Always active in volunteer activities, including heavy involvement with WILPF at that time, this study mark an early beginning to her academic research career, even though it was several years before she ventured back to graduate school.

Her work on children and nonviolence in the early 1970s was a direct outgrowth of her days as a homemaker rearing five active children, who, according to her offspring, frequently "squabbled," as children who are close in age and of varying temperaments often do. Elise took very seriously her role as a parent, and her fervent wish was for her children to grow up to be peacemakers. Her guiding query during her parenting days was, "will our children choose the nonviolent path in their own lives?"[18]

Elise's thoughts on Quaker parenting came to fruition in her seminal work on families, *One Small Plot of Heaven: Reflections on Family Life as a Quaker Sociologist*. The book reflects her views on the interface between families and education, in effect two inseparable entities. Once again, early bonding and nurturing are seen as crucial. *One Small Plot of Heaven* may be seen as a valuable contribution to the theoretical literature on Quaker education, particularly her ideas on the importance of solitude for children. As in most of her writings, there are both overt and covert autobiographical sketches and references. As one of many of her writings on the importance of family in building a global civic culture and grounding individuals in peacemaking, the book attests that "the family stands as the gap between the personal spirituality and society-building." Families are the basic unit of social change, or in Elise's words, "Family life is an act of continuous creation—the creation of human beings and the society in which they live."[19] She writes also of the pain of family conflict and the potential to see opportunities for growth in this pain.

Once again making sense of her own experiences, Elise, writing in an autobiographical sketch in *One Small Plot of Heaven*, saw her later professional involvements as a direct outgrowth of her earlier home and community-based activities. As Holly Giffin, long-time Boulding family friend noted, "she grounded everything she did in terms of the basic human experience, which begins with the child and involves the family.... That's the basis of human experience and it translates into international policy and into international government."[20] Feeling somewhat isolated at times and despairing at times over the demands placed on her as primary parent, homemaker and "keeper of the peace" at home, Elise attempted to see, through "making sense of her space," her connections to the wider world. She explained,

> [B]ecause I am always aware of local-global connections myself wherever I am and whatever I am doing, I try to share that sense of connectedness in whatever setting I find myself.... [I]f we are to have more realistic and viable planning for world order, more people must see the connections between the family, the local habitat and the international sphere.[21]

One of the themes which she explored in *One Small Plot of Heaven* was the idea that children are inherently disrespected and segregated arbitrarily in age graded spaces, especially in educational settings. Children must have exposure to many different adults in addition to parents, she believes, for maximum social development. In a lecture given to the 1996 Australian Yearly Meeting of the Religious Society of Friends (Quakers), entitled *Our Children, Our Partners: A New Vision for Social Action in the 21st Century*, Elise built on this theme and upon her other previous theoretical work. Expressing concern at western society's expectation that young adults assume responsibilities without any exposure to appropriate role models, she noted that this was happening in a century that was supposed to be devoted to children's rights.[22] Reasons for this were varied, said Elise, including the fear among adults of the unexpected, which children always introduce. She explained that some adults deny facing the future that children help to shape and that "[t]he mistake adults make is to fail to appreciate the complexity of the knowledge and experience worlds of even very young children." Mentioning the work of psychiatrist Robert Coles, she indicated the proclivity adults have to ignore the deep spiritual sensitivities that some children have.[23]

In many ways, this talk was autobiographical. As the oldest of her siblings by nine years, Elise for a long time was the only child in her family, a family which had strong ties to the local Scandinavian immigrant community of which they were a part but was isolated from the larger American local culture. Elise's mother was very unhappy about the move to America. Though a tremendously strong influence on Elise, her mother's sadness at times deeply affected Elise, and it may be said that at times the roles of mother and daughter were reversed, particularly in her role as comforter to her mother. When her younger sisters came along, nine and eleven years later, Elise assumed many of the caretaking responsibilities for them.

A reading of Elise's early journals during her adolescent years reveals a young woman who in many ways was mature beyond her years, with a keen analysis of her cultural surroundings and who experienced conflicts among her roles as caregiver, housekeeper and student-learner-budding musician with not enough time to do it all. Her sense of spiritual seeking began around age nine when she sought out the local Presbyterian church and continued through her teens when she wrote of her longing to know God but realized that "no religion can quite fulfill my needs, so I will make my own."[24] Certainly at that time she was keenly aware of the capacities of her own mind, albeit at times feeling frustrated that her creativity found too few outlets.

According to Elise, all of her future work as a sociologist and academic was grounded in her days as a homemaker and teacher of Quaker Sunday School, which she began doing when her children were small. "I took a Ph.D. but my learning was really as our five kids were growing up—being around them and listening. That was my sociological training."[25] In 1958, when the youngest Boulding child was three and the oldest was eleven, Elise wrote her pamphlet, published by Friends General Conference, "My Part in the Quaker Adventure," one of several of her Quaker writings published around this time. She included children in the design of the lessons, which are a series of lessons on Quaker history, written for 12 to 14 year olds. The purpose, as outlined by Elise, was to "give children an understanding of Quakerism so that they can find a place for themselves within the Society of Friends."[26] During that time, both Elise and Kenneth were frequent lecturers at Quaker gatherings, often appearing on the podium together.

Many of Elise's ideas on educating for peace were formulated and articulated during her long tenure with WILPF, beginning with her work with the Childhood Education Committee. In the December 1961 issue of *Saturday Review* there appeared an article by Elise entitled "Toys, Tots and Terrors." Long concerned with the proliferation of war toys, Elise had made it a practice in their home that all guns and swords were to be left outside, and she explained, "for the most part, the neighborhood kids went along with this." Writing of her distress over how to distinguish between those toys which are clearly permissible and those that are not, she linked her concern with the growing arms race to the fear that

> we are habituating our children to the possibility of nuclear destruction, so that they will grow up to an unquestioning use of self-annihilating means to defend an obsolete concept of the world.... [W]hen the arms race and the toy race become synonymous, what does this mean for a country whose President has just offered world leadership in a peace race?

She went on with suggestions of what readers might do to "open the minds of the children of our time to the challenges of peace," including speaking with managers and owners of toy stores to ask that toys based on the equipment of the armed forces be removed from store fronts and that stores not order military toys for the next year. She suggested that readers refuse to purchase such toys, suggest to toy manufacturers non-war toys to order and run ads in local papers supporting efforts of stores to cooperate in removing war toys and replacing them with more constructive toys that promote mutual understanding and peace. Elise recommended "a large scale movement to demand that the toys of peace replace the toys of war in our society, that our children may grow up with a knowledge of the kinds of tools that *solve* the conflicts of men and nations, rather than with a knowledge of the tools that *destroy* men and nations."[27]

One of the best articulated pieces of Elise's educational philosophy is a booklet she prepared for the international WILPF local branches during her tenure as Chair of the CEC, a piece which presumably was written in 1961 or 1962. In this writing is evidence again of her networking skills, as she lets various branches know what others are doing. In addition, she made suggestions of what could be done to promote peace education, steering readers to thinking as activists.

In the WILPF piece, Elise outlined the history of peace education, and she credits women's groups in the 1930s with beginning its momentum. She then goes on to write of the importance of acting within the spaces with which women find themselves:

> [I]t is our task to work in whatever sphere lies open to us, whether in the home, the school, the local or state community or the nation.... [W]e must never forget that our most important contribution lies not in publicly bewailing the negative features of the current situation, but in replacing them with opportunities for positive action.... [Y]ou want to develop world mindedness in your children? How good is your own world-mindedness? Too often we

> are still talking about educating "our" children about "them." ... [T]he problem is not how American women can prepare their children to relate to the rest of the world, it is how we European, African, Asian and American women can prepare our children to relate to each other.[28]

She suggested ways of working with schools, recommending a careful approach with teachers and administrators that used humility in "approaching a field which has its professional pride, as does any other." One possibility was to offer to help teachers and librarians set up displays of materials related to international understanding. She also suggested working with PTAs to set up study groups. She wrote of her activities in Ann Arbor:

> [S]ome of the activities described in this section are being undertaken as a kind of pilot project for other communities, a teacher-librarian committee organized a series of meetings and workshops around a three-day display in the Curriculum Resources Center in the public library. Many parents as well as teachers came to look at materials which had been gathered from many sources including a complete display of UNESCO and UNICEF materials and books from the World Affairs Curriculum Materials Center in Brooklyn, New York.... Another pilot project ... is the assembling of small, well-selected displays of books and materials on various countries which are donated to the central curriculum resources library and kept in boxes ready to go out on call to the individual teacher in the system who can use a particular display in her classroom.... [I]n the pilot project the Soviet Union and Poland were the first two countries for which displays were developed and more countries from various parts of the globe will be included as we find contacts in the community who have or are willing to obtain the kinds of books and materials which will make a useful classroom resource.... [E]ach display should include books which are being read *now* by the children of the country, some in the original language, some in translation. This helps give our children a feeling for what the world's children are reading about. It is easier and less expensive to prepare these displays for elementary age children. Attention should probably be given to doing this for high school students, also, so that teenagers can have the experience of reading what their fellow teenagers are reading around the globe and not just the selected classics which appear in fragments in their world literature surveys. This kind of thing will *not* happen in most school systems unless it is offered from outside.... [W]ho else is likely to offer it [than WILPF]?[29]

She went on with suggestions for educating in the home:

> While there is a great deal written on providing love and security for children so they won't grow into hostile adults, there is nothing very much on how you raise children to be sufficiently alienated from society so they won't accept things "as they are," and sufficiently identified with it so that they will contribute in creative ways to the building of a better social order.... [W]e still don't know much about producing children who will irrepressibly dream about a better society than the one we have, and obstinately work for its realization. Most of our writing about educating children for peace is concerned with helping children to become peaceful, rather than how to spur them to the rugged, often lonely, task of peacemaking.[30]

This style of first reporting on current activities, then pointing toward future activism later found its way into her other editing endeavors, most notably when she founded the IPRA newsletter the next year. It would be ten years later that she would write her seminal article on children and nonviolent social change for IPRA.[31]

In the 1960s WILPF newsletter, on education and the community she wrote: "When a child or a nation has no feeling of being related to the larger community, no recognized role and identity, then there is complete alienation and delinquency."[32]

These writings of Elise's reflected her views on the importance of working both locally and globally to teach peace. Her early exposure to the League of Nations and later deep involvement with UNESCO, dating to the time she and Kenneth lived in Princeton in the early days of their marriage, grounded her theories of peacemaking to visions involving a better world order. Eventually this reached its fruition in *Building a Global Civic Culture*.[33] Elise was also influenced during this time by the work of Quaker educator Leonard Kenworthy and other progressive educators who believed in the importance of developing a world community and that peace, freedom and a free world were possible through education. The more formal peace education programs at that time reflected an emphasis on international understanding. Later Elise would work with Saul Mendlovitz, Betty Reardon and others to more fully develop the World Order Models Project, an outgrowth of the World Policy Institute in New York City. The Institute's original mission in 1961 was to develop curriculum materials which would teach world order values such as peace, social justice, and economic and ecological well-being. The idea was to develop "system transforming curricula," not just those which are "system maintaining," in order to educate toward a view of international relations that diminishes the role of sovereign states and enhances the role of transnational consensus.[34]

Elise's beliefs in the importance of individual-community-global linkages and the building of world community reached their fruition in her ideas related to NGOs and their role in peacemaking. Her belief in the important peacemaking functions of NGOs is what some know as her major contribution to peace education research. And "acting on" her theories, she made it a point in her classes at both the University of Colorado and at Dartmouth that students be made aware of all the NGOs to which they and their families belonged. She explained that she "would make sure that those youngsters who belonged [to those organizations] knew that the local branch they were part of was part of an international network."[35]

In *Building a Global Civic Culture*, Elise elaborated on her theories of the peacemaking capacities of NGOs and their relationship to building a peaceful world order. Distinguishing between the United Nations as a system of "nation-states" and transnationals, she wrote of the important function that the UN played in representing "both peoples and nations," especially as this related to the tremendous information-processing networks which crisscross the entire United Nations system "through the 6 major operating organs, 13 associated organs, 16 specialized agencies, 5 regional commissions and 5 peacekeeping/observer missions."[36]

It is the non-governmental organizations, however, which Elise believed most represented a relatively new visionary form of social mapping, overlaying that of the United Nations and the system of nation-states. Citing that these transnationals cover the whole range of human interests, Elise wrote:

> [T]he idea of globe-spanning associations of private citizens is scarcely a century old and is one of the most striking phenomena of the twentieth century. It is based on a new-old perception that humankind has common interests.[37]

By 1990 there were about eight thousand NGOs that had formal affiliation with the United Nations or one of its bodies such as the UN Economic and Security Council. Many more organizations are also named to be NGOs or INGOs (International NGOs) and are treated as such because they have substantial participation by private citizens and their mission is to improve the lot of humanity, though they may not have formal affiliation with the United Nations system.[38] To be listed in the *Yearbook of International Associations*, a huge book put out by the Union of International Organizations (a group with which Elise has worked closely), an affiliate must be independent of any government (they may receive grants, however), have an international headquarters and have members in at least five countries. In addition, they must have a goal of civic well-being.[39] According to

Elise, the most important thing about these organizations is that they cross national borders. Of particular import are the ones whose functions are directly related to peace education, peace research and peace action. During IPRA's early years, Elise was working closely with UNESCO to insure that the peace research association obtained formal consultative status.

A key concept related to transnational groups, according to Elise, related to their organizational structure:

> [T]he important thing to remember about INGOs is that they are organized by national sections, and national sections are organized by local branches. The networks of international people's associations thus reach directly from individual households to world forums. No other type of diplomatic activity has this capability.[40]

Thus, through this particular form of social mapping, an individual member of a household may make linkages and connections with the United Nations system and with international bodies seeking to better the welfare of society. NGOs provide an important educative function as well.[41]

Essential peacemaking grows out of early nurturing experiences, according to Elise, including opportunities for adequate bonding and also for solitude and reflection. Her early writings on these ideas reflected her own position as the primary caretaker of her children and her belief in the important peacemaking functions that women provide in their "women spaces," which, in later writings, she called the "Fifth World," a play on the terms used to name the various divisions of the world based on global wealth and technological know-how.[42] Believing in the importance of listening and connecting, Elise theorize that women's socialization has helped them to be better at problem solving and mediating. Men (and boys) must learn these skills too. Referring to the work of Belenky, Gilligan and other scholars who earlier had studied the important role of connectedness in women's psychological development, Elise wrote in *Building a Global Civic Culture*:

> [I]t can be said that women offer a nonhierarchical, listening type of culture and skills of dialogue and conflict resolution, to replace a culture based on the ability of the strong to dominate the weak.... [B]ecause women have lived at the "margins of the public sphere," they are less invested in maintaining the status quo and can visualize new ways of doing things.[43]

Again, referring to the work of Belenky and others, in a 1987 chapter published by the Royal Melbourne Institute of Technology, Elise wrote of the important contributions of feminist thinking on theories of learning and that they "stress the multi-dimensionality of learning processes and lead to a type of education that anchors theoretical knowledge in the life experience."[44]

Discussing the experiences of men and women in relation to childrearing in an interview done for the Boston Research Center for the 21st Century, Elise stated:

> I am convinced that the peaceful world of the future is going to depend on most men having the same experience that most women have with infants and small children, because the kind of things you learn by being close to a small child you don't learn any other way.[45]

Anchoring education in life experience meant, for Elise, that technological know-how must not supplant the learning that takes place from face to face, person to person interactions, involving listening and relationships. Elise's writings have reflected her deep skepticism about the passive acceptance of modern computer information technology. Using her "200 year present" language, she wrote in a chapter of a book on education and technology put out by the Royal Melbourne Institute that, in the last half century, our technological know-how has come increasingly to be used as a "shield" to protect humans from each other and from the natural environment. She wrote that this has contributed to a societal sense of despair about the future and this "insulation from human experience" can be said to have led in part to our militaristic culture.[46] In an earlier text she explained,

> What is missing from technological futurism? The long view, a recognition of the fragility of life; reverence for diversity of life, reverence for intuitive knowledge; understanding of the functions of solitude necessary to create deeper bonds among people. Eloquence about the spaceship earth and the crowded planet has on the whole not opened up new vistas of how to think, feel and behave as humans. It has not led us to an exploration of the joys of frugality, nor to a personal recognition that the earth family sits at one table and is fed from one farm—the earth farm. It has not increased our respect, to say nothing of love, for one another, nor our skill in getting along together.... And not opened up the inner space of the spirit.[47]

Elise's belief in the importance of solitude is, ironically, closely connected to her belief in the necessity of human connectedness and her idea that learning should be as experiential and as "first hand" as possible. For humans to learn to get along with each other, there must be face to face relationships imbued with the learning space of the spirit. She had bemoaned the loss of "image literacy," engendered by rising technological know-how, yet she has since realized that computers often allow those who might otherwise be unable to communicate other ways to connect with other human beings. She also has acknowledged the important functions that computers play in enhancing the connecting capacities of NGOs and in connecting "islands of cultures of peace" with one another. In *Cultures of Peace* she wrote, "It is not hard to demonstrate that computers can help make the world a better place. But like every technology, its value depends on how it is used.... [T]he overriding question is how to use them well."[48]

One of the fears Elise has had about modern information-processing technology is that it helps perpetuate the ongoing drive in Western culture to specialize: "[W]e are all on assembly lines, and the experience of completion is rare." Invoking Plato's cave analogy, she wrote in *Cultures of Peace* that "all we see are the shadows on the wall.... [W]e are protected from ... knowledge because of the immediately persuasive character of the technologies we are developing. We must recover the community base of learning." She has developed a model for such learning using, as a core, the idea of "Learning Headquarters," with linkages to many educational sites, including the home, local government, volunteer organizations, churches, parks, state, regional, national and international sites.[49]

Schools have traditionally placed a heavy emphasis on the development of verbal and analytical skills to the exclusion of other forms of learning. She explains,

> Only after a couple of years of teaching did I fully realize what a straitjacket the verbal-analytic mode imposes on the mind. After that, in my sociology classes, whatever the subject, I gave assignments that required transforming concepts and theories and fact-clusters into a series of other modes, including metaphor, music, poetry, pictures, color, mathematical equations and diagrammatic and free-form visual presentations. The increase in levels of comprehension, in ability to handle complexity, and in general creativity in dealing with the subject matter was so great that I myself was dumbfounded at the implications for general educational practice.[50]

Elise does not use electronic mail. Realizing what a networker she has been, colleagues have been amazed at this. Elise has made it clear that she is not interested, partly due to the realization, because of the extent of her contacts, that she would quickly become overwhelmed by the volume of electronic mail that she would receive. Yet she willingly uses a fax machine, receiving messages at her daughter's business. And many colleagues send her peace news and activities by snail mail or telephone. Elise is a consummate reader but finds at this point that reading too much tires her, as her eyesight has dimmed somewhat.

Educator/Researcher/Activist

Elise's career as a peace educator has been intricately bound up with her work as a researcher and activist. Indeed, in her mind any dichotomies among these concepts are false. As a consummate networker, her ideas on connecting people and organizations, from families to communities to transnational organizations, have added a new conceptual element to the idea of educating for peace: the idea that *linking* in and of itself can play an educative role.

For Elise, networking can be seen as a chief form of activism, particularly since the advent of her more formal academic career. Its role has been most evident in the parts she played in the formation of both IPRA and COPRED. These roles for her have not been without their tensions, however, as her integrative ideas about research, education and activism have not always been in agreement with those who purport to identify with either peace research or peace action.

One of the latest projects that Elise took on was writing with a group of New England area educators and activists an international peace curriculum entitled "Making Peace Where I Live." This is a project conceived by Elise that grew out of a working group whose original purpose was to envision practical contributions to the UN Decade for a Culture of Peace. MAPWIL is a curriculum for 10 to 12 year olds, involving students interviewing local peacemakers in their communities to learn more about how to become peacemakers and peacebuilders. The intention is to help young people understand the relationship between making peace and the International Decade for a Culture of Peace.

This project represented a collaborative return for Elise to her earlier years as a peace educator, when, in the 1950s and 1960s, she was writing curricula while an active member of WILPF, helping to form IPRA and COPRED and raising her family. During this time she frequently wrote about the importance of educating for peace. Though a consummate teacher, Elise, in those years when she was most involved in academic peace research, was known less as a peace educator, per se, but as a researcher, sociologist and activist. However, she never lost her roots in education and in the importance of using knowledge to make the world safe for future generations. It was in the days before she returned to finish her Ph.D. and early in her academic career that she did much of her writing on *how to* educate for peace.

Chapter 7

Quaker Educator

Becoming a Quaker in her early adulthood, Elise's spirituality has had a profound influence on her way of being as well as her theoretical ideas on peacemaking. For Elise, her marriage and her entrance into the Society of Friends, both occurring at the same time in 1941, were two events that were to transform and ground her future work.

As Quaker educator Paul Lacey noted, there is no well articulated Quaker philosophy of education, for its practice "grows out of a Quaker philosophy of life."[1] Citing the words of George Fox, Lacey reminds Friends that

> this is the word of the Lord God to you all, and a charge to you in all the presence of the Living God, be patterns, be examples, in all countries, places, islands, nations, wherever you come; that your carriage and life may preach among all sorts of people and to them. Then you will come to walk cheerfully over the world, answering that of God in every one.[2]

Thus, as Lacey points out, education grounded in Quakerism "is always leading in and drawing out.... [W]hen it is faithful to its foundations, Quaker education is neither student-centered nor discipline-centered, it is inward-centered. There is always another in a classroom, the Inward Teacher, who waits to be found in every human being.... [T]he student has an inner guide to whom he or she can be led.[3]

Elise's beliefs in the "personhood of children" and in the importance of adult-child partnering have their roots in the Quaker idea that there is that of God in every person. Two of Elise's essays in *One Small Plot of Heaven* spoke to the importance of recognizing children's contributions to family life and to spiritual awareness and capacities to nurture. One of the essays, "Children and Solitude," was an articulation of Elise's own personal experiences of solitude as a child and her desire to share these ideas with others. She wrote, "Humans will come to a spiritual dead end if they do not allow time apart and in solitude for things to happen inside."[4] She cited new psychological findings which reported the benefits of alone time and argued, "Solitude is essential because this is an experience of separating out from the world in order to integrate with it. It cannot happen if the mind is distracted by constant social stimulation."[5]

"The Personhood of Children," another chapter in *One Small Plot of Heaven*, was originally given as a lecture at the 1975 gathering of Friends General Conference, the conference of liberal, universalist and unprogrammed Quakers that meets annually. In this essay, Elise pointed to a relationship between and violence and the separation of children and adults into age graded spaces and to the need for children to have mentoring and nurturing relationships outside of the family:

> Probably in the childhood of every activist peacemaker there were one or many experiences of being trusted and attended to by an adult. Such experiences build a reservoir of competence and inner security which makes it possible to take risks on behalf of what one believes."[6]

Elise's belief in the inherent capabilities of children has its roots in her own childhood, where in many ways, as the oldest by many years of her siblings, she early on assumed adult responsibilities and, in some ways, was both a daughter and a peer to her mother. As a child, she was always deeply disappointed at their extended family gatherings when there were too many children for the main table, and she would have to sit separately from the adults at meals at a special table for the children. She was always fascinated by the adult conversations. She was deeply affected by the caring exhibited by Mrs. Northwood, the wife of the minister of the church she began attending as a child, who invited her to her house for tea and encouraged her to deepen her spiritual search.

Elise intentionally sought out opportunities to interact with children at many of the Quaker and professional gatherings she attended. During the August 1997 Yearly Meeting of New England Friends at Bowdoin College where she was the keynote speaker for the general sessions, she insisted that she also meet with each of the children's groups to give her keynote address, albeit it was scaled down. She began her talk with the children with an anecdote about youth taking the lead in activating change, mentioning several children-led peace movements world-wide of which she was aware.

While at Dartmouth in the 1980s Elise taught a course on the family. She recalled:

> I would have the students write their earliest memories of doing something that helped their mother through a crisis or their father through a crisis or whoever was the caretaker person, persons in their own families and some of the memories go back to the age of four and it was a wonderful confirmation of my point that children are much more aware of what is going on in the world than most adults realize. They were helping their parents through crises that their parents hadn't any idea that their kids were helping them.[7]

Some of Elise's ideas on education may be considered similar to those of Quaker educator Parker Palmer, who was the keynote speaker at the 1998 gathering at Wellesley College at which Elise facilitated a workshop. The general theme of the conference was "Education as Transformation." Palmer's ideas on education envision its practice within the concept of a "rich and complex network of relationships in which we must both speak and listen, make claims on others and make ourselves accessible."[8] He noted that such learning cannot happen until teachers and students are brought into relationships with one another and with the subject. This he calls "the community of learning," which is a community practicing obedience, noting as he does that the root word for obedience is the Latin *audire*, to listen.[9] Writing regarding her own inner call to obedience from her Hermitage during her year of solitude in 1974, Elise's words were, "my obedience is to be open," open to the leadings she might receive from the Holy Spirit that would lead her in and out of solitude and into the rich network of relationships that have characterized her life.[10]

History of Quaker Education

Historically, Quaker educators have seen their role as developing the whole child and educating towards obedience to an inner calling for service in the world. Quakers have not traditionally separated the secular world from that of the spiritual. This has been true of Quaker education as well. Children have historically been an integral part of Friends Meetings since the Society began. Early Quakers saw children as gifts from God and did not adhere to the doctrine of original sin, which they believed was incompatible with the Holy Spirit as being the Inner Light. Historically, a great deal of importance has been placed upon children's own experiences of God. Early Friends did, however, believe in the "divine power" of parents, that education should be grounded in the ideals of the beliefs and practices of the Religious Society of Friends, and that children should be subject to the leadings and directions of their parents. Robert Barclay, often considered the early authority on Quaker theological doctrine, established the principle for parent-child interactions based in scripture to bring up children in the "nurture and admonition of the Lord."[11] The aims of education for early Friends included helping children to integrate life as a whole and not to distinguish either work or play as being more significant. Discerning God's will was paramount. William Penn believed that education should be natural and not forced, echoing the theoretical ideas of European educators such as Rousseau.[12]

For early Friends, the Meeting served as the chief educational agency in addition to the home. Later, partly to shield their young from the "evils of the more secular world," Friends began the development of separate schools, evolving out of local Meetings. Parents who could paid for schooling, but the Meetings had a responsibility for the poorer children in their communities. Early on, Friends included girls in their education, and schools were co-educational.

The development of Friends schools provided a model as the system of public education evolved. In 1801 a group of Quaker women in New York City organized schools for the education of poor children without religious affiliation. Eventually this model was adopted by the city with the aid of the Public School Society, which had been founded mainly by Friends. With the decline in the large number of Quaker educational institutions, due partly to the growth of the public school system, some Friends schools became public schools.[13]

Since institutions of higher education had as their primary function in colonial days the education of clergy, early Friends had no need for colleges. Some Friends believed that undue emphasis on the development of the intellect prevented the full evolution of the spirit. Later several Friends colleges were formed, including Haverford, its sister institution for women, Bryn Mawr, and the coeducational Swarthmore College, founded by the Hicksite branch of the Philadelphia Friends during the theological split among the Yearly Meeting of the nineteenth century. One hundred years later, Pendle Hill was founded in 1930 on the principle that Friends needed a place where Quaker students might find spiritual solutions to the problems of the world around them, apart from purely academic pursuits. No higher degrees are bestowed. Pendle Hill was founded to be the Quaker equivalent of a theological institution, devoted to an integration of spirituality and education in a spirit of community living.[14]

Friends to this day continue to have an ambivalent relationship to state sponsored education. In part, this reflects a tension between "guarding the mind and heart" and a thrust toward activism in the world. There continue to be many private Quaker schools, many remain in the Philadelphia area. However the majority of students attending these are not Quaker. Many Friends today choose to send their pupils to public schools. In a 1958 pamphlet, Quaker historian Howard Brinton addressed this continuing struggle for Friends between the inner work and the outer relationship with the world at large. He wrote,

> Education, according to Quaker theory, ought not to be man-centered [*sic*] nor state centered. It must minister to the needs of the body, mind and spirit, it must be for time and eternity and it must partake of both the human and the divine ... not derived from society as it is at the moment, but from society as it ought to be. Quaker theory also holds that the school be a community, which prepares for a greater community outside itself by being like it.[15]

In 1939, John Lester examined the relationship between Quaker ideals and Quaker education in the conditions of that time, which he believed had evolved somewhat from earlier times, reflecting Friends movement away from seclusion and into more direct political involvement. Friends needed to value the Inner Light and respect democratic procedures in order "to help children discover that power outside themselves and what they are equipped to do."[16] Lester also advocated for all schools to provide a quiet, reflective time for students.

The important educative function of the Quaker family has been to help lead children into knowing God and finding for themselves their religious path. Harold Loukes, a British Friend, published a study of Quakers and their children in 1958 in which he noted that the guiding principle of Friends has been to make their home a place where children really matter. He wrote, "A home is not a place made by parents for their own pleasure, but a place given them to shape ... their children's growth." Thus Loukes emphasized the important educative function the family plays in Quaker households.[17]

Many ideals of Quaker education have remained the same for centuries: to educate toward respect for the individual, service to others, simplicity and honesty, and the will to do for others. In a 1951 lecture at Guilford College, Howard Brinton spoke of the the ideals of a Quaker education, including the development of both mind and heart, training in the use of the intellect and practice in the ways of virtue.[18]

Elise's Quaker Involvements

In the many Quaker meetings they joined as they moved from place to place, the Bouldings were "weighty Friends," a term Quakers reserve for those upon whom others rely for spiritual guidance. Married under the care of the Syracuse Meeting, the couple soon joined the Princeton Meeting, then Nashville, later transferring their membership to the Ames, Iowa, Meeting upon their move there in 1944. Elise recalled many visits to smaller Iowa meetings as part of her volunteer work with AFSC, the American Friends Service Committee, as she visited the institutions for the mentally ill and the disabled. She advocated for changes and improvements in the Iowa mental health system and for ongoing monitoring of the working conditions of conscientious objectors who were performing alternative service in many of the hospitals.

It was the Ann Arbor, Michigan, Meeting, which they attended from 1949 until their move to Colorado in 1967, that helped provide for Elise the spiritual base for her many volunteer activities, including AFSC, WILPF, the Women's Strike for Peace and the founding of IPRA. This was the meeting in which their children were involved during their growing years. As always, Elise taught Quaker Sunday School, giving particular regard to the program for high school aged young people as her older children entered that age group. According to Holly Giffin, a high school friend of her oldest son, Russell, Elise acted primarily as facilitator for that group, with primary guidance coming from the young people themselves.[19] Elise often wrote plays for the children to perform while she was teaching.

It was in the early days of her involvement with the Religious Society of Friends that Elise most often spoke and wrote for Quaker audiences. After her move to Boulder, with the exception of a summer spent teaching at Woodbrooke, the British Quaker study center, in 1969, much of her energies were absorbed by the demands of her academic career, her involvement with the peace research movement and her position in the late 1960s as chair of the Women's International League for Peace and Freedom.

There have been many exceptions, however, one in later years being her attendance and participation in the first Quaker Women's Theological Conference held at Woodbrooke in late July of 1990. Elise gave a paper based on the life of 17th-century Quaker Anne Downer and the concept of caring, suggesting that women, in the work of caring, need to "change the rules." Caring involves, according to Elise, a visioning of how things can be, skills in bringing about the necessary healing seen in the visioning, and the appropriation of new social spaces for this work. She is referring to the hidden "women spaces" where healing has traditionally taken place and to the necessity of continual grounding in prayer.[20]

The Boulding's were frequently on the podium together for Quaker talks. Later, as tensions in their relationship became more pronounced and their philosophical differences on some things became more obvious, this became uncomfortable for Elise. Yet they continued their practice of joint lecturing for many years. After the 1960s, Elise was more frequently speaking alone, as Kenneth's and her travel schedules were quite heavy and frequently took them in different directions.

Early Quaker writings by Elise reveal her joy at her "inner conversion" and her deep convictions as to the nature of called service to the world. In an article for the June 21, 1947, weekly *Friends Intelligencer*, she called for a renewed sense of community, a return to roots in the spirit of Meeting for Worship, and for Friends to allow themselves to be guided for their mission in the world. Reflecting her already deep involvement with the American Friends Service Committee, Elise wrote of the danger of letting the Committee do the "service work" for Friends, as Friends were wont to send money only and, therefore, risk the dangers of vitality resting with the Committee and not with the individuals. She writes,

> Let us face the fact that the Service Committee is more alive spiritually than the Society which it is supposed to represent.... [W]e must *all* share the burden of the world's suffering, all pray for forgiveness for our shortcomings as members of the human race, and for guidance to live as Children of the Light. A complete transformation and rebirth is required of every one of us.[21]

In one of her first major addresses to Quaker audiences, in a lecture she prepared in 1956 for the Young Friends Movement of Philadelphia Yearly Meeting, she talked about the joy that is a liberating gift from God and grounded in eternity, encompassing suffering and evil. Having just returned from the family sabbatical in California, where she had met and came under the influence of Fred Polak, this speech reflected the early roots of her work on futures, as she spoke of "our vision for the future providing the direction for our growth." Bemoaning what she called the loss of paradise, she asserted that Friends have allowed, partly as a result of coming under the influence of scientific and technological growth,

> the symbol of God to replace the experience of God.... God does not call most of us away from the plow, he would rather have us shift bosses, since it is after all His acre and start plowing the field for him.... [O]nly through prayer can our vision of the Kingdom come.... [I]f the call to live in the kingdom means anything, it surely

> means helping by our lives to create the conditions for the Kingdom to come into the world.[22]

Kenneth and Elise spent several summers, in the early days of their marriage and family life, facilitating and attending workshops at Pendle Hill. She became good friends with Howard and Anna Brinton, long-time directors and deeply respected for their Quaker thinking and writing. Together with Lewis Hoskins, staff member of AFSC during the 1940s, Elise credits these Quakers as some of the most influential to her during her life.[23] In July of 1965, Elise was invited to give the annual Pendle Hill lecture entitled "The Technology of the World Society and the Role of the Individual."

During the 1960s and prior to her return to graduate school to complete her Ph.D. work, Elise continued her involvement in many activities connected with the Society of Friends. Many of these related to educational issues, with particular regard to how Quaker principles could be put to work in the world. Elise write, "Friends [have] a particular responsibility to try to meet the unique educational demands of this age of transition into world community which [has] not been adequately recognized."[24]

At a conference at Pendle Hill in September of 1964 on "The Ministry of Friends to the Academic Community," a concern arose that Quakers in higher education and research should be in touch with one another. A statement presented to the conference by the discussion group calling itself the "Group on Conference Implications for the World Community," of which Elise was a part, read:

> We are concerned about the role of education in the emerging world society. We believe that Friends have a particular perspective to offer in fostering the capacity to live in a world of peace and love, with understanding, mutual concern and appreciation of persons in all nations and cultures.[25]

This led to a meeting in Ann Arbor in early 1965, hosted by the Bouldings, to explore the possibilities of setting up a committee of Friends "concerned with integrating their religious insights with their intellectual tasks in the academic community, with particular attention to the frontiers of the social sciences."[26] Elise took a leading role in this endeavor, becoming the corresponding secretary and, predictably, beginning a newsletter to link Quaker educators around the world. The intent from the beginning was to make this an international endeavor. The committee adopted the title "Committee on Friends Responsibilities in Higher Education and Research" (FRIHER) and engaged the supportive services of the American

Friends Service Committee and the mid-west office of the Friends World Committee on Consultation, the international Quaker body linking Friends around the world. Questionnaires were sent out to an unsystematically assembled list of Quaker educators, college teachers, administrators and research scholars at both Quaker and non–Quaker institutions of higher learning. The responses to the questionnaires were summarized at the end of a paper given by Elise at the Friends General Conference gathering in Traverse City in June of 1965. Her talk was entitled "The World Task of Quakerism in Higher Education," and in it she made a concerned plea that, as Friends are not "burdened with the machinery of tradition," Quakers must directly engage with the important task of systematically addressing the need for large-scale social innovations to counter traditional ways of handling world problems.[27]

The results of a round-table discussion held at the Traverse City Meeting included the beginning of an international directory and the ongoing networking and connecting of Friends in higher education and research. Plans were begun to facilitate a gathering of educators in conjunction with the Friends World Conference, scheduled for 1967 at Guilford College in North Carolina. The conference planning committee asked Elise to organize a special interest group for the gathering.[28]

In 1965 Elise had been invited by the Friends Council on Education, the association of independent and private Quaker elementary and secondary schools, to sit on their committee on recruitment and placement. This was part of a long relationship she has had with this Quaker organization, whose mission is, in part, to foster networking among Quaker schools and to offer resources for Quaker educators.

Elise's involvement with the American Friends Service Committee continued. She followed very closely AFSC's growing role in the peace education movement, particularly as it grew out of work protesting the Vietnam War. In the mid–1960s she was invited to apply for a staff position, to be based in Ann Arbor, but she declined due to her commitment to university teaching and research and because of her run for Congress. In her letter of decline, she wrote of her intention to give two years of service abroad to AFSC in the future. She considered combining AFSC work with her data gathering for her dissertation, which at that time Elise thought would be on images of alternative futures emerging in traditional societies.[29]

In 1965 Elise addressed an AFSC peace education workshop, focused on the question of "who are we trying to reach?" Reflecting the growing movement within U.S. Quakers to question the current directions of AFSC, Elise pointed out that there were many developing peace groups that could probably address the needs of war protesters better than could AFSC. What she felt AFSC could contribute was to point out that stopping the Vietnam War was only a small part of a larger problem. AFSC had, at that time, a long history of involvement in international affairs, and its expertise and "staying power" were invaluable. In addition, she advocated for AFSC to stay involved in work in civil rights and the anti-poverty movement in order to "bridge the gap between the oppressed and the poor on the one hand, and the conscientious average citizen" (she clarified this to mean middle class) on the other. She also felt AFSC could reach out to alienated students who, though idealistic, were failing to develop any constructive pattern for their personal lives. She posed the question of whether individuals involved with AFSC could "enter into" and participate in more grass-roots civic organizations and, in essence, listen to constituents in order that there might be "openings for AFSC concerns among members."[30]

In the 1970s Elise hosted at the Waterfall, their family cabin in Lyons, outside of Boulder, a group calling itself The New Society Working Party, an ad hoc association the purpose of which was, in part, to help guide the American Friends Service Committee into new ways of working within a more spiritual framework and into a more thorough study of the family and its role in socialization. As expressed in its working document of 1971, its mission was to "express an AFSC vision of a new society and to develop strategies for building it.... [There is] a basic spiritual dimension to our problem."[31] The developments and subsequent reactions by some Quakers within AFSC were part of a partial shift in its commitments away from direct service for the poor and oppressed into deepening its work for social justice that was more reflective of identification with the poor and oppressed. Elise did not subsequently pursue direct involvement with the New Society Working Party.

Kenneth was quite opposed to much of what the AFSC stood for at that point, and, as the years progressed, he became more outspoken in his views. Many influential Quakers believed that the Service Committee, whose original mission was based around service and conscientious objection during wartime, should stay true to its original purpose and not become involved in what many perceived to be radical social change and political advocacy.[32] This was a painful time for Elise, as she was very much committed to the Service Committee, understood the complexities of the issues involved, and was aware of the public nature at times of the philosophical disputes between herself and Kenneth. Elise served on the national Corporation of AFSC from 1987 until 1994.

During the third annual conference of the Friends Association for Higher Education in 1982, the group that Elise claimed to be the successor to FRIHER, she gave an address entitled "The International Dimensions of Quaker Learning." FAHE represents Quaker institutions of higher learning and Quakers who teach in colleges and universities. In this talk she regretted the demise of FRIHER, at the same time she suggested that FAHE expand their membership to include high school teachers in their membership.[33] Citing the importance of solitude for optimal educational development, Elise urged the participants to work toward developing "spiritual imagination" in their students.

Elise's interest in and long-term practice of keeping a journal led to her doing some research in the 1980s into the journals of early Quaker women. For a chapter in *The Influence of Quaker Women on American History*, she had meticulously read these journals and the spiritual struggles recorded therein, especially those centered around integrating the authors' roles as mothers and their ministerial work. In the chapter she wrote, "We see in the struggles of these women with their parenting role the foreshadowing of the struggles of today's women. The overarching concept of a divine love which could transform and encompassed the natural affections was ever present as both a goad to the struggle and a solution to it."[34]

As time went on, Elise further developed her strong interest and involvement in ecumenical concerns, particularly those related to religion and peace. This culminated in her work during the mid–1990s with the Interfaith Peace Council, an ecumenical group of international religious leaders. This group was an offshoot of the World Parliament of Religions, which had been held in Chicago in 1993 at the 100th anniversary of the original conference. Elise was asked to represent Quakers for the Peace Council. This is the group with whom she traveled to Chiapas, just prior to her relocating to Wayland, Massachusetts, in 1996. In the fall of 2000 she attended the gathering for the last time, held at the Thomas Merton Center in Kentucky.

In June 1994 Elise gave the lecture at the 15th annual conference of the Friends Association for Higher Education at William Penn College in Oskaloosa, Iowa. Her talk was titled "Coming Down to Earth in Peace Education." Beginning her talk with a tribute to Kenneth, recently deceased, this speech resonated with many of the ideas found in her earlier writings, which culminated in the writing of *Cultures of Peace*. Citing that every religion has a holy war doctrine, she pointed out that also in every religion is a doctrine of holy peace, or peaceable kingdom. The task of peace educators is to be open to and to strengthen those islands of peace culture which may not always be visible, but which account for perhaps 70 percent of human interactions. Articulating some conceptual dimensions of peace education, she stated that the work of such educators has been grounded in the

> empirical reality of community conflict, in the first-hand awareness of the structural violence that steers resources and opportunities away from the poorer members of each society. They [peace educators] have preached—and practiced—that research, education and action are inseparable.[35]

This refusal to dichotomize between peace research, education and action is reflective of Elise's lifelong journey to make sense of and integrate the various parts of her life and work and is the grounding of her continued active spiritual seeking.

Chapter 8

The Culture of Peace

At the 1998 Wellesley Conference on education and transformation, Elise spoke of her experiences as a faculty wife and mother at the University of Michigan beginning in the late 1940s and continuing into the 1960s. Much of what she spoke about at the conference was an encapsulation of her theoretical ideas on education as well as thoughts on her personal journey toward peace. Her talk included many of the experiences in Ann Arbor that gave her insights into the creative potential of partnering in peacebuilding, as she spoke lovingly of how Kenneth had so greatly influenced her in their work together. She indicated that peace studies and "spiritual awakening" were closely related and that much of her work in beginning peace studies programs at both the University of Colorado and at Dartmouth had involved working with campus spiritual and religious organizations.

Elise noted that peace studies programs, as they came to be developed in the late 1960s and 1970s on college campuses, were largely interdisciplinary and were the result of many different partnering arrangements between various campus departments, faculty, and students. More importantly, Elise stated, they would not have developed were it not for the student-led movements on college campuses in the 1960s to protest both the Vietnam War and the involvement of the U.S. government in war research.

Tensions between academics and activists over the role that research should play in promoting peace activities had been in evidence since the beginning of the development of the peace studies movement in the late 1950s and early 1960s, particularly exacerbated by the chronic funding problems that many peace research centers faced. Initially, universities were reluctant to fund programs. Some of the early centers, such as the Lentz Institute in St. Louis, the first of its kind in this country when it began in

1945, became free-standing sites, not connected with universities but remaining in working contact with local academics.

Peace researchers had not been able, as a group, to clarify for themselves what their role should be in promoting peace action. Part of this confusion has stemmed from problems of definition. Historically, it was difficult to reach consensus on what is meant by peace education and its conceptual relationship to research, peace studies and activism. Adding to this mix is that, historically, the concepts themselves have been characterized by fluidity. As both peace research and education for peace developed as fields of specialization in their own right, a more transformative, integrative and holistic approach took place, in good part due to feminists within the field such as Elise. Some current scholars view this as healthy. However, some, especially those associated with academic institutions, view this as moving away from the kinds of analytic thinking needed to further peace work. Elise has spent much of her life's work attempting to link and integrate peace research, education and activism. Indeed, her life may be seen as a stage enacting the drama of such integration.

At the Wellesley workshop, Elise spoke about the first American campus teach-in, held at the University of Michigan to protest the involvement of the university in military research. "And guess what we were doing there?" she joked, "I and the other faculty wives were serving coffee as the nights wore on!"[1] Then she laughed heartily with the rest of the audience at the conference. Other teach-ins, held on the Michigan campus and across the country to protest the Vietnam War, soon followed. What made these teach-ins true partnerships, Elise stated, was the *listening and dialoguing* that occurred between faculty and students. These two ingredients, she believes, are key components of peace cultures.

Elise spoke at Wellesley of the importance of her own spiritual journey as it has related to all of her other endeavors. At each of her academic settings she was involved with a group of like-minded seekers (not always Quakers) who met regularly for meditation and contemplation. One group she started was called "Contemplation and Social justice." "It was always clear it was a spiritual journey," she said, "it was not *only* social justice, because peace involves social justice.... [W]e understood that but not everyone does."[2] These groups almost always included both students and faculty as full participants.

The importance of community and acting within communities has been central to Elise's conceptions of educating for peace. She explained, "Service learning means you go into that world you want to change while you are learning to collect the data about that world and learning by doing.... [P]ractice generates theory." She elaborated during the workshop upon the importance of apprenticeships as an educational concept. While teaching various sociology courses at the University of Colorado and at Dartmouth, she often involved her students in experiential learning. Her Sociology of the Family students would apprentice to families, and her Introductory Peace Studies students would intern with NGOs that were local branches of international agencies such as the YWCA and the Red Cross. She helped her students to see the links that transcended national boundaries. Her belief was that *anything* that can be taught can have a service component:

> [T]he kind of research I am talking about involves developing an intimate, intuitive relationship with the family, group or organization. You can't just keep taking notes sitting at the dinner table, about what people are saying, you *have* to relate differently. And you learn to listen, so for any community, peacemaking is about listening. If I had to put the whole of peacebuilding into two words, one of them would be *listening*.... [T]he other would be *relationship*.... [Y]ou can't have one without the other.

Just prior to the workshop, which ended with a question and answer period, Elise led the participants on an imaginary inward journey, using their bodies as a metaphor for the earth. She told them,

> Our body is the envelope for this extraordinary biosphere, the soil and the rocks ... they are in us.... [T]he one billion households on earth, the 185 nation states spread around the planet, the twenty thousand peoples associations and transnational networks weaving in and out ... those intergovernmental treaties, the UN itself ... lumbering, hurting, but trying hard, the heart of that ... is in us.[3]

The Concept of the Culture of Peace

The idea of a Culture of Peace has its roots in work done by UNESCO (the United Nations Educational, Scientific and Cultural Organization) beginning in the late 1980s. A monograph published by the organization in 1995 stated that such a culture consists of "values, attitudes and modes of behavior based on nonviolence and respect for the fundamental rights and freedom of all people."[4] These rights were recognized in the Declaration of Human Rights adopted by the United Nations in 1948. In 1989, an International Congress was held entitled "Peace in the Minds of Men" in Yamoussoukro, Cote d'Ivoire, Africa. Elise Boulding, as part of her long association with UNESCO, attended that conference.

From the beginning, Elise was involved in the UNESCO Culture of Peace program, which was a continuation of her long association with the organization. At that meeting, the congress was urged by its international representatives to further elaborate on the initial ideas generated. In 1992, the Culture of Peace Program was first formally proposed by UNESCO at the first of many international forums that subsequently elaborated upon similar themes. The Director General, then Federico Mayor of Spain, was invited to consult leading experts in the field of peace and conflict resolution and to submit an action program. Through the many conferences in the ensuing years, it became evident that the role of education, both formal and informal, was integral to any working program on the Culture of Peace.

In 1992, Mayor established a unit for a Program on the Culture of Peace, appointing David Adams of Wesleyan University in Connecticut, as director. A 1995 statement by then Secretary-General of the United Nations Boutros Boutros-Ghali read as follows: a Culture of Peace "is at the heart of the great historical enterprise of the United Nations.... [Our goal is] to foster integrity of cultures and to promote information, dialogue, understanding and cooperation among peoples of the world's diverse cultures."[5]

Elise's associations with UNESCO and the United Nations go back to the 1940s, to the early days of her marriage to Kenneth when they lived in Princeton and he was with the League of Nations Economic Section. It was there that Elise first learned, with the help of sociologist Alva Myrdal, of the importance of the work of nongovernmental associations, particularly as these transnationals relate to the ongoing work of the United Nations. Later, her own ideas on the importance of these organizations in connecting individuals in local communities to the larger world were conceptualized and elaborated upon in her most important work on the educating for global citizenship, *Building a Global Civic Culture*, written shortly after she retired from Dartmouth.[6]

Elise's involvement with the Women's International League for Peace and Freedom, her work studying nongovernmental organizations while the family was on sabbatical in Japan in the early 1960s and UNESCO's role in helping her start IPRA in the mid–1960s all contributed to deepening her understanding of the important connecting, peacemaking role that NGOs provide in linking citizens locally and globally.

The 1995 UNESCO monograph noted the increasing role that NGOs were having in energizing the United Nations system. UNESCO's recognition of this important role is found in these words: "[C]itizens, if supported by international networking, can play a key role in peace-building."[7] These words echoed the important work Elise had been doing with the agency since the 1960s. Beginning with her involvement with WILPF and continuing through the founding of IPRA and the Consortium on Peace, Research, Education and Development (COPRED), these organizations, all of which link activism with research and education, have as part of their mission the promotion of the ideas which are included in the action plan of the Culture of Peace. They also all have consultative status with UNESCO as nongovernmental associations. In 1994, IPRA formally took up the Culture of Peace program at its biannual meeting in Malta.

The central role that education, both formal and informal, must play, according to UNESCO, is evident in the following statement made by Federico Mayor at a forum held in Moscow in May of 1999: "Education, a fundamental right of citizens, is one of the essential keys to a construction of a culture of peace." The action program as it has developed has educational concepts woven throughout. In one sense, educating toward a culture of peace was not a new UNESCO initiative. Words found in the original constitution of the organization indicate that "since wars begin in the minds of men, it is in the minds of men that the defenses of peace must be constructed."[8]

The UNESCO role in helping to shape the emerging field of peace education in the 1970s was an important one and one in which Elise was a key player. In 1972, UNESCO gathered a group of international youth together to elicit from them their ideas on peace education. The resulting synopsis of these ideas, which was published and distributed, provided the basis of a December 1975 letter that Elise wrote to UNESCO just prior to a Paris conference the agency sponsored on peace education. She wrote of the importance of young people obtaining "new maps" of the world in order to look beyond mere geographical boundaries and the importance of looking through the lens of "non-territorial boundaries" such as non-governmental organizations. Echoing the words of the students, she proclaimed, "[M]ethods of peace education must shift away from lectures and classroom based teaching.... [E]ducation for peace should ideally be a field in which there is no clear boundary between class teaching and what is called out-of-school education.... [Otherwise, a] pupil's impression is that school is isolated from life." She argued strongly for community-based apprenticeship programs to link youth to local NGOs and noted the importance of the *processes* of peace and the behavioral skills needed to make peace, including negotiation, cooperation and mediation.[9]

Though UNESCO originated the idea of the Culture of Peace Program in the 1980s, enthusiasm for the concept soon spread to other UN agencies. In November of 1998, partly at the urging of all of the living Nobel Peace laureates, the UN General Assembly adopted at its fifty-fifth plenary meeting a resolution naming the decade of 2001 to 2010 the International Decade for a Culture of Peace and Nonviolence for the Children of the World. Key items contained in the resolution are the following: the recognition of the role the UN plays in saving future generations from the scourge of war and the necessity of transformation towards a culture of peace; the recognition of the role of education in constructing a culture of peace; and nonviolence and the importance of its teachings to children. Included is an invitation to the Secretary-General to work in cooperation with UN agencies such as UNICEF and UNESCO and with nongovernmental organizations to draft action plans to promote implementation at local, national and international levels. Also included is an invitation to member states to take the necessary steps to ensure that the practice of peace is taught at all levels of their societies, including educational institutions.

The appeal of the living Nobel laureates to the heads of states read in part as follows: "[W]e can offer hope, not only to the children of the world, but to all of humanity, by beginning to create and build, a new Culture of Nonviolence.... [F]or this reason, we address this ... appeal to declare that the first decade of the new millennium be declared the 'Decade for a Culture of Nonviolence.'" They also suggested "that at the start of the decade the year 2000 be declared the 'Year of Education for Nonviolence' [and] that nonviolence be taught at every level in our societies to make the children of the world aware of the real, practical meaning and benefits of nonviolence in their daily lives." Signatures included those of Joseph Rotblat, Jose Ramos-Horta, Shimon Peres, Aung San Suu Kyi, Elie Weisel, the Dalai Lama and Oscar Arias Sanchez.[10]

The UNESCO program included several important ideas within the concept of a Culture of Peace. These were:

1. power defined as active nonviolence.
2. people being mobilized not against an enemy, but to build understanding, tolerance and solidarity. This can liberate oppressors as well as the oppressed.
3. democratic processes replace vertical and hierarchical power structures and authority.
4. secrecy by those in power is replaced by the free flow of information.
5. male dominated cultures are replaced by cultures based on power sharing among women, men and children.
6. women as empowered and women's cultures as centers of peacebuilding replace structures which glorify those activities traditionally associated with men, war making and preparation for war.

Elise with the present author at a book signing for *Cultures of Peace* at the Boston Research Center for the 21st Century, 1999.

7. exploitation of the environment, closely associated with warfare, is replaced by cooperative sustainability.

Peace was seen not as static but as an active concept.

CULTURES OF PEACE: THE HIDDEN SIDE OF HISTORY

The aim of Elise's book *Cultures of Peace: The Hidden Side of History*, published in 2000 by Syracuse Press, was to point out that there are and have historically been places where peace cultures may be found both locally and globally and that the central tasks of peacemakers are to make these known, celebrate them and learn from them.[11] To build peace we must learn, as a beginning, what these "hidden spaces" can teach us about making connections. Elise changed her original title of the book, which used the singular *peace culture*, in order to use the term *peace cultures* because she realized in writing the book that there were many places, so called "islands," where peace may be found, even in the midst of the larger world culture that is dominated by a paradigm of competitive, male-dominated, hierarchical institutions, in-short, attributes, values and behaviors which promote and glorify war.

The title of the book reflected the importance she placed on these sometimes "hidden places." In her words, "[T]his book can be thought of as a story of human potentials for peaceableness."[12] The title also was a play on the words from the title of her earlier book, *The Underside of History: A View of Women Through Time*, written in the 1970s while she was spending a year in solitude in her Hermitage outside of Boulder.[13] Both titles were statements of the importance she placed on seeking out and finding people and places that have traditionally been marginalized by the larger culture. Finding them, uncovering them and celebrating them provide important peacebuilding opportunities. Elise wrote the book, in part, as a celebration of UNESCO's Culture of Peace Program.

Part I of the book is an historical overview of peace and war, concentrating on historians' preoccupation with documenting war and outlining how the world's religions have historically promoted a "holy war doctrine." Elise discussed religious traditions in which the main teachings espouse peace. She considered these groups peace cultures. She discussed historical utopian communities and the important work of these groups to "think, dream, sometimes actually design social orders that will correct the evils of a violent and unjust present."[14]

Part II is a description and analysis of identified peace cultures and of the peacemaking which goes on in everyday life in families, schools, communities. The important work of women in peacemaking and the necessity of finding and nurturing partnerships in this work between women and men as well as children and adults was dealt with in depth, echoing her earlier written work in this area.[15] Her ideas on the capacities that children bring to peacemaking was a recapitulation of the writing she did throughout the 1970s, reflecting her long-held belief in the innate capabilities of youth that most often go unrecognized. Children have often been *protected* but have not been given the authority to decide on matters which concern them, leading, as Elise believed, to a tremendous underestimation of what they can do, which directly impinges on what and how they learn.

Elise's belief continued to be that there are virtually no activities in which children should not participate fully as equals, with the exception of warmaking. She believed, while writing her many articles, chapters and pamphlets on children, that they were thought to be weak and ill-informed and that they were taught that society is so complex that they must be segregated in age-demarcated spaces. This, she believed, robs both children and adults of the chance to learn from one another.[16]

Because of the importance Elise placed on women and women's cultures, a great deal of her writing in *Peace Cultures* dealt either directly or indirectly with women and peacemaking. Women have been in the forefront of peace education, she wrote, beginning in the last century. As she noted, "[P]eace education to a large degree is a product of many different women's groups—teachers, social workers, peace activists." These such groups helped to lay the foundation for UNESCO.[17]

It was women in the peace research movement who insisted that it move beyond its association with international relations and who came to realize that peace studies must be inclusive of social, economic, environmental and human rights issues. Elise explained,

> It was a combination of vision, theory and practice that brought peace educators into a leadership role with the new discipline of peace research that developed in the 1960's. Peace educators insisted that peace research should not only undertake general systems analysis of intergovernmental relations but should conceptualize the interrelationships of peace, security and economic and social development, environmental issues, human rights and the participation of women and minorities as the central problematique of human learning.[18]

Women were able to envision peace because historically they had been marginalized, which allowed them, as "outsiders," to develop new approaches to world order. The same is historically true of children, said Elise.

Identifying herself strongly with the so-called "social feminists" of the late 19th and early 20th centuries, including Jane Addams, Elise has been unapologetic in celebrating the importance to peacemaking of the traditional work done by women, such as nurturing, caring for children and the elderly, mediating and negotiating. She credits the feminist movement with creating a more public space for the practice of peace culture and with legitimizing the networking skills that women have long practiced in private spaces. If her ideas on education might be summed up in one word, that word would be *networking*. To quote from an interview she did with the editors of *Peaceworks*, published by the American Friends Service Committee, "I have probably started more networking newsletters than anything else in my life."[19]

Part III of *Peace Cultures* concentrated on institutional patterns of behavior and societal values that promote violence. Here, Elise discussed the roles of governments, global capitalism and international monetary systems. She wrote of how modern global technology was at times diminishing our capacity to image and vision for a better world. She emphasized the importance of community learning, noting that such sites will mean "a substantial redeployment of school personnel and a redefinition of the relationship between schools and the community and between adults and children." Her ideas on learning as inherently related to community and on communities of learning as places for risk taking, partnering between old and young, and creative play and visioning amount to a somewhat radical reconceptualization of traditional ideas of education. These ideas have at least part of their roots in how Quakers have traditionally educated their youth.

Central to Elise's *Peace Cultures*, as she wrote it, is the idea that to promote peacefulness it is important in order to recognize and capitalize upon the peaceful behaviors that go on all the time in most societies. Most human life revolves around the work of feeding families, organizing the work of production and solving the problems of meeting human needs. Celebrations and rituals are interspersed throughout as well. Though every society is a blend of peaceable and warrior cultural themes, for the most part our everyday behavior involves negotiating, dialogue and listening. Much of this is learned in families. The work of socializing children to learn these skills has largely fallen to women. Elise argued for the importance of partnering in parenting. Men have much to learn from women. Elise explained, "Raising children and shaping attitudes and behaviors determines how peacefully or violently individuals handle behavior."[20]

Conflict is ubiquitous, as it is the partial result of the tension between the two universal human needs for bonding, including the need for nurturance, and for autonomy. Peace is not the absence of conflict. The success of peace cultures is based on how these differences are managed. Conflict resolution does not necessarily mean a reduction in emotive content but rather a transformation to a greater awareness of how these two needs interplay in creative ways. We find peace behaviors in families, in human celebrations, in reproductive cycles of bonding such as birth, and in dying. We find it in human play, in places where we can find and create new realities, and sometimes in having fun.

Cultures of Peace was the culmination of Elise's lifework. Readers find themes and ideas from her earlier writings elaborated upon within this new paradigm for peace culture. Yet a review of most of her earlier work gives strong evidence of the roots and evolution of these ideas, beginning with her most early writing on Quakers and families in the 1950s and 1960s and continuing through her academic years and beyond.

This book was difficult for Elise to finish. She knew while writing it that it would probably be her last full-length book. Poignantly, it so eloquently speaks of much of her life's work. She subsequently soon confined herself to articles and introductory chapters for the works of others. She is now doing very little academic writing, though still keeping up with book and journal reading and hand-written correspondence. Elise, at times, found the energy required for the discipline of writing *Cultures of Peace* quite difficult. During this time of her life she was turning inward, actively journaling as she entered "the country of the old."

This tension between the discipline of writing and her inward spiritual seeking was not a new one. It had manifested itself throughout much of her academic life, most notably coming to a head in the mid–1970s when she retreated to her Hermitage, fully expecting to spend a year in solitude and reflection. As it turned out, there she wrote *The Underside of History: A View of Women Through Time*, her major treatise on women, reflecting in the preface how difficult she found it at times to discipline herself to write: "The tension between the activist, the sociologist, and the inwardly inclined Quaker ... has been almost unbearable."[21] Yet she felt spiritually called to the work. "It is necessary for women to be willing to stick out their necks when an unprecedented task presents itself," as she wrote in the introduction. The tension was of itself a form of spiritual discipline for her for the two years it took to finish it. And her solitude gave her the space to actually envision her chronologies and maps and, as she noted, "to unroll in my head to write the history.... [F]or two years the Hermitage was bursting with images."

This "sticking her neck out" to perform necessary tasks is a characteristic aptly describing Elise's activism throughout her life. Colleagues have admired this about her. As Ann Levinger, long-time friend and Quaker activist, said,

> Elise would look around the table [of colleagues] and think, "I am not sure anybody else would do as good a job as I could do it." ... It wouldn't be an ego thing, but a perfectly rational thing.... [S]he would be able to do it well and she could and would do it, she would know that it was going to get done ... and so she would volunteer to do things.[22]

Most often these tasks that Elise performed involved networking and usually taking copious notes during meetings and transcribing them into minutes, which she then would send out, or have her secretary do so, to those who had attended the meetings and to others she believed could benefit from hearing about what went on. She often included short notes to individuals, reminding them of ways in which their skills were useful to the endeavor, thus giving one-on-one encouragement, particularly to young activists and scholars. Recipients were made to feel affirmed in the recognition of their particular gifts. Russell Boulding noted that "one of my mother's great skills is the ability to, in a sense, get other people to do things without them really realizing they are doing it because she has inspired them to do it.... [S]he is there making the connections."[23] This ability made it easy for Elise to find administrative help wherever she lived and worked.

Having had excellent secretarial help was essential to Elise. From the time she was elected to the International Chair of the WILPF in 1967 while beginning her academic teaching in Colorado, continuing on into her teaching at Dartmouth and assumption of her duties as the international Secretary-General of IPRA in 1988, and through the time she became president of the IPRA Foundation in 1989, she relied upon both student-helpers and university and free-lance administrative help. Often Elise paid for extra help herself when university funds were scarce for her needs. She was grateful to those who had assisted her, and she formed deep bonds of friendship with several of these former associates. Anna Spradlin, who became acquainted with Elise when she took a course on peace studies that Elise taught after she retired, later wrote her dissertation as a study of Elise's leadership rhetoric style. Anna was instrumental in organizing Elise's archives, located in the library at the Boulder campus, and in helping her get her files in order prior to her move east.[24] Another graduate student, though she did not take a course from Elise, was Marty Gonzales, who was hired by Elise upon her retirement to help organize the IPRA files and to manage the work of the IPRA foundation.

It is women who have most often helped Elise in these endeavors. Elise's sense of her own power to make change is central to her ideas on the importance of women's cultures in building peace. She has recognized the importance to women of acknowledging their own contributions and gifts in whatever endeavor they undertake, even at the same time the larger culture may malign them. Sociologist Robert Irwin noted:

> I think it is interesting that, like every single one of us does when we look at the world, we project ourselves into what we see.... *So when Elise looks at women, she sees a lot of power.*[25]

Elise's intentionality combined with her networking skills were a strong force for mobilizing those engaged in the tasks related to peacebuilding.[26]

Not all of Elise's associates agreed that her leadership style was helpful. She was thought to be bossy in meetings, with firm insistence that things be done in certain ways. As one fellow member of the Boulder Quaker Meeting noted, when Elise came into a meeting where discussions around a particular topic were being held, "She would then tell us what she thought we should do, and sometimes I don't think she really knew what she was talking about!" Others, however, were grateful that she usually kept meetings on task. "We need[ed] the rules," as one said, but "I am afraid of her ... afraid of her 'eldering,'" a play on a term used for an ancient Quaker practice of correcting behavior which seems "out of line."[27] Some colleagues described a certain brusqueness in her interactions with them. Most recognized, however, the singularity of her purpose when she embarked on a project. This intense focus has, at times, been a barrier to Elise's developing more light-hearted and intimate relationships with friends and colleagues. A long-time member of the Boulder Meeting noted, feeling a bit put-off by Elise when they first met, that "I don't think any of us knew her very well. Upon our first meeting she said to me, 'I don't go in for card parties, only an occasional pot luck. My work is my life.'"

The Culture of Peace in Action

In the Spring of 1999, the Boston Research Center for the 21st Century hosted a conference, consisting of three week-end sessions, entitled "From War Culture to Cultures of Peace." The BRC is a Boston organization founded in 1993 by Daisaku Ikeda, a Japanese Buddhist peace activist and president of Soka Gakkai International (SGI), a world-wide association of peace-related lay Buddhist organizations. Elise was a co-convener of the series and was a featured speaker at the first gathering, "Creating Cultures of Peace: Family Life and Education." In her talk that evening there were few remarks directly relating to families and peace. Yet her ideas on the importance of relationship building, listening to one another and dealing with differences were well articulated.

At the gathering she said, "A listening culture is any group of people who are really listening with the heart to each other. They are practicing peace culture. Whenever there are two human together, there will be differences." She spoke of the important work of women's groups and adults partnering with children in learning. She spoke of the importance of faith communities. It was as if the listeners were to understand that families, where relationships find their foundation and where listening and dialogue have the opportunity to occur so often, are so central to the concept of peace culture that no formal mention of them was needed.

One of the things that happened at that first session was that several participants responded to Elise's descriptions of peace cultures by raising the question of why young people were not included in the conference series. By the following session a month later, Elise and the other organizers had put together a "children's peace camp," which included the children of participants as well as other young people and was held concurrently with the remaining two conference sessions. Elise spent a good share of her time during the rest of the conference interacting with the young people, whose meetings were held concurrently with the remaining adult sessions.

The essence of Elise Boulding's views on educating toward a culture of peace may be summed up in two statements of hers, as noted by Robert Irwin[28]:

> Human life even at its best is so full of contradictions, paradoxes, and conflicting needs that surplus energy for loving is absolutely necessary to keep human relationships from deteriorating.
>
> Human goodness I will define ... as a quality of inner security and well-being involving the possession of vast reservoirs of surplus emotional energy for listening to, loving, and caring for others, linked to a discerning intellect that will utilize that reservoir wisely.

Education cannot be separated from the action concepts of listening to, caring for and loving others. Elise Boulding's ideas on educating for peace are rooted in her Quaker faith, a faith which celebrates the divinity within each person and the power of love to transform the world. Reworked and grounded through her many life experiences, these ideas, as they have evolved, represent the culmination, the weaving of the threads of her life and work into a patterned whole.

Chapter 9

Women, Futures and Peace

The three major intellectual strands of peace, women's studies and futures have all played out in Elise's life and in her theoretical work. She was on the cusp, as each of these movements developed during the latter half of the 20th century. Her deeply felt passion for the contributions of women to peace and social change have their roots in her early childhood and, in particular, in her relationship with her mother. She gained an appreciation for the many roles of women, particularly in the developing world, through her dissertation work. Her theoretical ideas continued to evolve through the 1970s and 1980s and into the 1990s with the writing of *Cultures of Peace*. Elise's in futures work was a natural outgrowth and integration of her scholarly work on women.

In the years following the founding of COPRED in 1970, Elise and other female colleagues in the organization consistently argued for the inclusion of the contributions from women in peace research. Elise was criticized by the more militant feminists for her arguments in favor of men and women forming partnerships to work for peace in families, in communities and in the world. Some feminists pointed to inherent contradictions in feminist ideas and peacemaking. Elise's ideas on the important roles women have historically played in "keeping the world going" and in working for peace have their grounding in her identification with the social feminists of the nineteenth century, including Jane Addams, and in her being mentored by both Alva Myrdal and Margaret Mead.

Elise's work in futures had its roots in her childhood daydreams. Her ideas were brought to fruition in part by the dramatic meeting and the subsequent influence of the futurist Fred Polak, when the family was in California in the mid–1950s. Translating Polak's work into English, learning Dutch to do so, is remembered by Elise as one of the first "heavy-duty" academic activities she undertook, all the while enjoying the challenge. For her, learning Dutch proved not too arduous, as it helped that she was fluent in Norwegian.[1] Later Elise worked with Warren Ziegler of the World Order Models Project, and together they developed a training manual and curriculum to teach visioning skills. Together, the two Bouldings authored a book, *The Future: Images and Processes*, published posthumously for Kenneth in 1995.[2] Kenneth's interest in futures was also greatly inspired by the work of Polak and by the interactions of colleagues during the sabbatical in Palo Alto.

Women and Peacemaking

An analysis of Elise's ideas on women and peacemaking reveals how closely related are the concepts of educating for peace, networking and connectedness and the social processes of human development found in women's cultures all over the world. These factors are related to women's superior capacities for peacebuilding. They have played a significant role in Elise's own life. It is the multiplicity of women's roles through the work of "breeding, feeding" and productive labor, done mostly "out of sight and mind," which have helped to provide women with the skills necessary to build peace and to envision healthy futures.[3]

Elise's research revealed that women have primarily been responsible for the process of human development throughout history. Education, so necessary for passing on cultural values to subsequent generations, has primarily been a woman's profession, both in formal and in informal settings. Women's socialization has taught them the skills needed to build a peaceful world, skills such as mediating, negotiating, listening and dialoguing. Men have much to learn from women. Because of societal pressures and patriarchal structures, women have not always valued themselves or been given affirmation for these skills, which are essential for the maintenance of society and for contributing to new visions of a different world.

Elise's writings affirm the power that women possess, a power which women themselves do not always recognize nor appreciate. Feminine power is "power with" rather than "power over." It is found in connections rather than in the competitive clamoring to possess and to rule over others, so characteristic of male dominated cultures. In *Cultures of Peace* and in many of her other publications, this kind of power is discussed, which is power "in relationship," not in hierarchy.[4]

Personal use of her own power and her sense of self-efficacy has given Elise the ability to shape and mold the projects in which she has been involved. While she believed feminine power ideally describes that which is shared, she was not averse to the use of her own assertiveness and had a strong ability to contradict those with whom she disagreed. Sociologist Robert Irwin, who worked with Elise in the 1980s on a project entitled "The Exploratory Project on Conditions of Peace," recalled a time during a meeting when Elise became incensed that some male members of the group were espousing a policy that went counter to what she perceived was the group's mission, the study of ways to promote non-violent solutions to conflict. And, in Irwin's words, Elise just "shut these male members up, those who could flippantly espouse killing without getting really upset about it," with these words:

> I really think the premise for this group has to be that we reject violent solutions because if this is a group that says that maybe this other way is equally good, if we put that on equal footing, well, then that is not the kind of group that I want to be part of.[5]

Both Elise and her daughter Christine have spoken with warmth of the memory of Kenneth Boulding's description of the power of a "determined woman," no doubt referring to his feelings about Elise:

> If you have a determined woman, it is important that she be right because determined women are an irresistible force and they can lead you really down the wrong path!

According to Christine, Elise "is a very determined woman," and by all accounts, Kenneth agreed.[6]

Social Reform and Feminism

Elise has identified herself strongly with the social feminists, whose ideas found fruition in the 19th-century social reform movements.[7] These early feminists, including Jane Addams, who helped to found the Women's International League for Peace and Freedom, were not only interested in gaining the vote for women, but in improving the lot of the underclass and in contributing to the development of society, albeit molded to their own middle-class standards. This was to be achieved chiefly through the process of education.[8] Addams is best known for the founding of Hull House in

1889 in Chicago, the mission of which was no less than the transformation of American society, beginning on the local level. Addams was deeply influenced by her Christian faith and believed that love could be a cosmic force for social change.[9]

According to Charlene Haddock Seigfried, who wrote the introduction to a 2002 edition of Jane Addam's *Democracy and Social Ethics*, Addam's life and work were deeply intertwined. Addams was part of a long line of feminists, of which Simone de Beauvoir is the most conspicuous contemporary example, whose lives provided the material for the testing of their theories against their life experiences. Much ahead of her time in her inclusive political thinking, Addams believed that if women's particular issues could be raised to full consciousness, then they could be tapped as revolutionary material for social change. She wrote of the necessity that political action concern itself with human needs and of the imperative of women having a stake in the political process for the sake of a better world for their children.[10]

In her 1922 book, *Peace and Bread in Time of War*, Addams wrote of the founding of the Women's Peace Party in 1915, a pre-cursor to WILPF, with feminist colleague Carrie Chapman Catt. The eleven tenets in their platform emphasized the necessity of morality in relationships between nations. Platform statements included educating youth in the ideals of peace and the extension of suffrage to women. As Addams wrote, "[W]e hoped for a great spiritual awakening in international affairs."[11] Speaking as a visionary, Addams noted that "we [have] fail[ed] to bring about the end of war simply because our imaginations are feeble."[12]

During the latter part of feminism's second wave, in the 1970s and 1980s, the ideas of such psychologists and social thinkers as Carol Gilligan, Mary Belenky, Jean Baker Miller and Sara Ruddick helped to identify as theoretically important the process of human growth and gave credence to the role of "connectedness" in women's lives, both for women's own development and for their part in the physical, moral and cultural development of others.[13] Elise's ideas resonate with those of these thinkers, predating much of their later scholarly work.

According to Sara Ruddick, mothers are responsible for the "preservation, growth, social acceptability and the nurture of children's developing spirit." This process, according to Ruddick, describes and defines the work of mothering (Ruddick does not exclude men from the role of mothering), and, if done well, this can contribute to the ongoing work of making peace. Ruddick acknowledges (as does Elise) that women have not been and are not always peaceful. There have been many women warriors throughout history. Women also carry the double burden of birthing and nurturing men, who often must go off to war. If this notion of sending their sons off is resisted by women, it can be a source for peace and social change, according to both Ruddick and Elise.[14]

The writings of Belenky, Gilligan, Miller, Ruddick, Boulding and others during the 1970s and 1980s marked an important step toward a recognition among scholars that women's cultural, moral and psychological "ways of being" were different from those of men and, in some ways, were arguably superior. Shortly thereafter came some backlash that these ideas were "essentializing" women, placing them within a paradigm of caretaking, which many feminists believed devalued women.[15] Elise vehemently denies being an essentialist.

According to Elise, it is precisely being part of the "underside of history" that has allowed women to possess their unique capabilities as peacemakers and as visionaries for change.[16] Because women (and children) have historically been marginalized, they are and have been less invested in the status quo and are, therefore, in a unique position to envision and work for change. Women have not always taken advantage of these opportunities for growth. Patriarchal structures have greatly impeded this process.

Beginning her formal teaching career in Colorado in the late 1960s, just prior to receiving her doctorate, Elise's dissertation work on women helped poise her to be on the cusp of the emerging movement establishing women's studies, which now is an academic discipline in its own right. The terms "women's studies" and "feminist studies" were first used in 1970.[17] They began with two or three courses on several college campuses. Elise's growing interest in women's studies progressed through the 1970s and 1980s as she began to become more involved in academic life at the University of Colorado. Merging her scholarly pursuits in sociology and women's studies, she helped to firmly establish the place of women within the governing structures of both the American Sociological Association and the International Sociological Association, beginning in the early 1970s.

The Hermitage

During this time came a year of solitude. By the end of 1973 Elise was experiencing physical and emotional exhaustion, as her hectic, non-stop pace of teaching, travel, IPRA and COPRED activities, and growing involvement in peace, women's and futures studies were taking up more and more of her time. 1974 was a year in which Elise gave up most of her outside activities and retreated to her one room mountain Hermitage near Lyons, Colorado, which a friend had newly built for her. The cabin was up a mountain from the Waterfall, the family cabin to which the Bouldings escaped from the pressures of academic and activist life in Boulder.

This was the year in which Elise began writing *The Underside of History: A View of Women Through Time.* This was time in which she came to identify her own struggles in the so-called "underside" of her own history and a time when she was able to give up many of the demands that had been placed on her by the multiple roles she had been playing since the beginning of her married life.[18] A quote from the preface of *The Underside,* written by Elise, aptly describes her own situation at that time:

> [A] woman activist in the twentieth century cannot avoid identity struggles because society gives her little ground on which to stand.... [W]omen for centuries have had to work for the public good from privatized spaces."[19]

Elise felt, as 1973 drew to a close, that she had little choice but to retreat from her exhausting work schedule and from the demands she was experiencing in her marriage. Her childrearing days were drawing to a close at that time, as the youngest Boulding child, William, was off to college that year. By 1973, the chronic mastoid problems plaguing Elise in her earlier life had become acute, which necessitated surgery and left her head spinning for days at a time. It was not until relatively late in 1973 that Elise decided to take this year off. Earlier she had planned on a different sort of sabbatical from the university.

Beginning in January of 1974, she took a year's leave from her duties at the University. During the next few years she was to return often to the Hermitage, sometimes for a week-end, sometimes for longer periods, but never for as long as the year she spent there. This was a place where she felt she could spend time in prayer and reflection, write in her journal, create poetry and connect with the natural environment of the cliffs, animals and plants around her. During the year she was there, she often came down to the Waterfall to be with Kenneth and occasionally came into Boulder for errands. She attended a few professional meetings which involved travel, but this was a time when she was essentially alone with her thoughts and with her God. This withdrawal, though seemingly drastic at the time, was part of a lifelong pattern for Elise, escalating in the years to come, of intense activism followed by prayerful retreat, sometimes dictated by her overexertion in activities.

Excerpts from her journals at that time reveal the joy she experienced at beginning this year away and the relief that she felt in getting a faculty fellowship so that Kenneth would not have to subsidize her. She also recognized that "all along I have known that the one thing that mustn't happen is that I develop a compulsion about 'something to show' for this year."[20] An early dream, about which she wrote in her journal, can be said to describe some of the conflicts she was experiencing over her choice to retreat from the overwhelming responsibilities which had been weighing her down:

> Feb. 2, 1974: woke up to a familiar patterned dream. I was responsible for some sort of gathering, everybody came and I wasn't there! Terrible remorse when I found out![21]

The decision to withdraw was not without ambivalence for Elise.

Elise had not originally planned on writing a book during this time, but thought she would spend the time in prayer, contemplation and reading. The book idea came to her as she prayed, and, as she states in the preface to *The Underside*, she came to understand in a metaphorical sense the "weight of women's history" as she literally carried the hundreds of books needed for the project up the mountain to the cabin. The cabin had very few amenities. There was no running water, and she cooked on a hot plate and slept on a mat on the floor. She wrote in her introductory remarks in *The Underside* of the difficulties involved in disciplining her mind to writing when she was called at that time much more toward inward seeking. This struggle was one that occupied her at many times through her life.

The Underside of History, now in two volumes, is a social record of women from the dawn of recorded history, with particular emphasis on the importance of the multiple roles that women have played. Contradicting some social historians who believe that the cultural constraints placed on women have been limiting, Elise, while not discounting this, wrote that women's contributions, because of their placement in the "underside of history," have given them unique opportunities for building toward and envisioning social change. The book seeks out and celebrates these hidden "spaces" and urges both men and women to recognize and affirm them and to celebrate the creativity found in this multiplicity of roles. Women's socialization and their assumed tasks as nurturers and caretakers have taught them valuable survival and envisioning skills, which men need to learn as well. Elise believes women must teach these to men, and men must be open to learning. Much more partnering needs to go on between women and men.

WOMEN'S ROLES AND SOCIAL INVOLVEMENT

Elise's interest in women's roles began to be articulated as she adapted to her marriage and duties as a young housewife. Earlier in her life she became aware of the difficulties associated with responsibilities toward others and finding time to nurture her mind. Entries from her early journal as a teen-ager note the conflicts she was experiencing then, as a fifteen year old with multiple household duties, glad to be moving to Maplewood from Hillside, New Jersey, where she hoped she would feel less encumbered with household tasks. The family's increasing prosperity, partly due to Elise's mother's growing clientele as a masseuse, allowed them, following their move, to hire part-time household help.[22]

In an article written for the journal *Marriage and Family Living* in 1955, Elise wrote of the role conflicts "entrapping" the American mother, particularly acute during years of raising pre-school children. In what well may have been an articulation of her own conflicts with regard to roles (at this time there were been five Boulding children, ranging in age from eight to an infant) and her wish for some freedom from the tasks she felt encumbered her, Elise characteristically ended the article on an upbeat note. She offered suggestions as to how to resolve this conflict, namely involvement in a cooperative nursery movement, which would allow a mother time away from as well as time with her children. Citing the importance of using the nursery as an outlet for "unused professional training," Elise ended the article by saying:

> [O]ne answer to the problem of many activities outside the home allowing too little time for the family to build up a needed feeling of togetherness is to plan family-style participation in outside activities. [This] widens social relationships that family members can have with each other, and cuts down on the fractions that develop if family relationships are based entirely on emotional and security needs. The cooperative nursery is especially valuable ... because at its best it emphasizes the contributions that fathers, grandparents and older siblings can make.... [T]he fact that the whole family thinks the pre-schooler is important enough to warrant their undertaking a joint project in the cooperative nursery solely on his behalf increases the small child's sense of worth.[23]

Elise's dissertation work, completed in 1969, was a continuation of her interest in the study of women's roles, begun during her years of involvement with WILPF and continuing with her study of Japanese women while the family was on sabbatical in 1963 in Japan. She began her dissertation work in sociology with the idea that there was a direct correlation between women's participation in the labor force and the rise of global modernization and industrialization, but concluded that any correlation was modest at best, sometimes going in the opposite direction from the one expected.[24] Perhaps more importantly, what she discovered through her dissertation work was that the historic social invisibility of women has made it difficult to accurately document patterns of roles.[25]

The evolution of Elise's ideas on the importance of NGOs has its grounding in her direct experience of understanding her own place in history as a woman. During the years of her growing family, as a mother and homemaker involved as she was in peace work in her own community, Elise began to see that even though her work was local, she was contributing to world peace through the connections of the organizations in which she was involved. This was a kind of "connected knowing," similar to the idea promoted by Belenky and others, which builds on the "subjectivist" conviction that the most trustworthy knowledge comes from personal experience rather than the pronouncements of authorities."[26] Miller also discusses the importance of women's individual experiences in forming the foundations of their connections to others.[27] It is women's experiences which primarily have shaped their ability to be peacemakers, according to Elise. These ideas are very similar to those of Jane Addams.

Mentors

Elise began to understand, through her own life, that peace work done locally is equally as important as that done globally and that both are integrally linked. Her mentor during her young adult years, Swedish sociologist Alva Myrdal, whose life pattern of working for change in the roles in which she found herself Elise has emulated and who befriended Elise while she and Kenneth were living in Princeton, had an important influence on Elise's ideas. Myrdal, a Swedish family sociologist, child development specialist and leading disarmament expert, began her work in sociology while her children were in nursery school, writing on families and children, and concluded her career as an international disarmament expert. She utilized her own experiences with her small children, struggling as she did with the demands of rearing three while married to internationally known economist Gunnar Myrdal. As she researched, she helped to create local institutions with the aim of producing citizens able to make peace in an increasingly armed world, thus contributing, in a sense, to the transformation of society from "the inside out."

Margaret Mead also provided Elise with another role model. Elise identified Mead as a "peace educator and promoter of the idea of women as 'housekeepers of the world'" (an idea which many would not easily associate with Mead).[28] This "housewives project" later evolved into the U.N International Cooperation Year in 1965. This was originally conceived as a project for women to visit other women around the world to see how nurturing families and communities was carried out. International Cooperation Year was, according to Elise, the precursor to the International Women's Year (1975), and Elise attributes much of its success to the earlier work of Mead:

> There is hardly a social movement of the post World War II decades that she did not personally touch. She was always enthusiastically nurturant but also penetratingly critical when such discernment was needed.[29]

Margaret Mead and Elise worked together in the 1960s during the Soviet-American women's exchanges sponsored by WILPF and maintained intermittent contact through the following years. Elise learned from Mead the importance of systems modeling, which Mead developed, using the tools of the anthropologist, beginning with "micro-societies." Mead also studied human development in various global societies, with a particular emphasis on patterning, which influenced Elise's later work as a sociologist. Elise also considered Mead a futurist, as her research was longitudinal in nature, studying human life cycles "and the phenomenon of continuities and discontinuities between generations as technological developments keep speeding up rates of change."[30] Her classic book, *Cooperation and Competition Among Primitive Peoples,* was an early contribution to the new field of peace research developing after World War II, and she was tireless in urging colleagues to do more for peace.[31] Mead also worked for the inclusion of peace education in school curricula.

Networking

As Elise moved more "out into the world" from her days as a young housewife and mother, she never lost the footing she had gained by involvement in local activities. She began to realize, beginning with her work in Princeton shortly after her marriage, that transnational associations represent a civic culture of peace which goes beyond nationalist borders, such organizations all having in common the purpose of improving the human condition. Women, who have traditionally done the work of development of the human species, have been at the forefront of the evolution of NGOs because, according to Elise, historically men would not give priority to decentralism and non-violence and refused to see women as individuals.[32] Citing the phenomenal growth in the number of transnationals from less than two hundred at the beginning of the century to nearly twenty thousand at this time, Elise believed these groups and organizations represent a new way of "mapping the world," outside the confines of nation-states, whose cultures are invested in the status quo and in patriarchal, war-like structures.[33]

Non-governmental organizations now deliver more aid than the entire United Nations system. The citizens' groups are gaining political and social leverage as international institutions such as the World Trade Organization and the World Bank are losing their base of power and influence.[34]

Elise believed that the beginning of the peace education movement can be traced to the development of women's NGOs during the last century. The social feminists of the late 19th and early 20th centuries, the women who helped to found such organizations as the YWCA and the Women's International League for Peace and Freedom, helped to invent the concept of NGOs, a new social form which grew out of the "historical reality that women's work ... [has] produced skills ... critical to human *development*."[35] Women's groups, social workers, teachers and peace activists developed the use of "the oldest tool of human sisterhood, networking," and began curriculum projects, started studying child development, and developed a vision of what a peaceful society might look like, eventually leading to the founding of UNESCO in 1945.[36]

For Elise, networking has been both a way for her to teach and to learn, involving knowledge and resources and linking people who are working toward common goals. Her role has most often been as a catalyst, fueled by her sense of the importance of what she is doing and her confidence and willingness to take a leadership role. LeRoy Moore, Director of the Rocky Mountain Peace and Justice Center in Boulder, summed up his thoughts on Elise and networking with these words (speaking in the past tense, as he had worked with Elise when she lived in Colorado):

> It's almost as if the word networking was invented for Elise. She was as good at it as anybody on the planet, probably.... [S]he was an incredible resource person, but she knew who all the other resource people were in the area and she was trying to find who she [had] missed ... get all these people in touch with each other.[37]

A major form of networking for Elise has been starting and editing various newsletters. These include[38]:

1. South Central Friends newsletter, during the Boulding's time in Nashville
2. Lake Erie Friends Bulletin—Predecessor of Lake Erie Yearly Meeting of Friends

3. Women's Strike for Peace newsletter
4. IPRA newsletter
5. Research Committee for Women's Sociology, out of the international Sociological Association Meeting, 1970
6. Sociology of Religion Newsletter of the International Studies Association
7. Futures newsletters, out of a meeting in Finland, out of which grew a 1987 conference on women and the military
8. Peace Teams newsletter

Two of these newsletters were Quaker (1,2), two were primarily devoted to peace (4,8), three involved women (3,5,7) and one involved religion and social change (6). Elise's concept of the importance of these newsletters is that they have served at least three purposes. These are: community building, discovering new thinking and creating an action body for social change.[39]

Closely related to the concepts of networking and connecting is "midwifery," which is not something Elise might readily identify with herself but something some colleagues feel has been one of her major contributions to the peace research movement and to Quaker history. People who have worked with her have spoken of her ability to launch a project and then remove herself at an appropriate time, a skill her son Russell believes she has perfected.[40] As Mary Garman, feminist theologian at Earlham College's School of Religion remarked:

> Any of us who do Quaker history think of her as our intellectual mother.... [S]he is the one who kind of blazed the trail in doing Quaker [women's] history.

And Garman went on to note how Elise "opened up new rooms" for Quaker women and that what she admired about Elise is that she has never had to "clear other's viewpoints away so that she could stand."[41]

Writing so often on the importance of listening, relationship and dialoguing, it is as if on some level Elise has realized the importance to herself of continuing to work on these skills, so often associated with women. One former student at Dartmouth remarked that Elise became more endeared to her as she realized her struggles to juggle so many activities and still try to create a space for listening:

> [Listening] was something she wanted to be her strength and so she could project that, but [at times] her energy wasn't in it ... particularly for women who have been socialized to be empathetic, that energy isn't available as much for the kind of work [they do] because of how much goes out into the lives of other people ... enormous caring.[42]

Of the many honors and awards Elise received, several relate to her work for and on behalf of women. In 1980 she received the Woman of Conscience Award from the National Council on Women. In 1981 she was the recipient of the Jessie Bernard Award of the American Sociological Association. Part of this recognition was for her work during the 1970s helping to establish women's networking within that organization, including starting a committee on the status of women in the profession. In 1985 she received the Woman Who Made a Difference Award from the National Women's Forum. Earlier she had been the founder of the Colorado Women's Forum, a network of women leaders in business and academia. In 1985 she received recognition from the convent order the Sisters of Loretto, to whom she later bequeathed her Hermitage, now used as a retreat center by the order. In 1996 she was inducted into the Colorado Women's Hall of Fame.

Futures

"Peace cultures thrive on and are nourished by visions of how things might be, in a world where sharing and caring are part of the accepted lifeways for everyone. The very ability to imagine something different and better than what currently exists is critical for the possibility of social change."

These words of Elise begin chapter two in *Cultures of Peace* on utopias. Early in this chapter she cited the work of Polak, whose work in the 1950s so influenced that of both Elise and Kenneth. Fred Polak's *Image of the Future* was written a few years after World War II. It represented his attempts to both make sense of the horrors of war and to find ways of preventing it in the future.

Polak's theories revolve around the idea that people cannot work for things that they cannot imagine. His research rested on the assumption that societies throughout history that have embraced positive images of the future have been empowered by these visions to bring them to fruition. Elise, in translating his book into English from the Dutch in the 1950s, hoped to bring the message of empowerment to peace scholars and activists and helped to set in motion those processes that can help to realize a more hopeful and interdependent world. "That put me in the middle of the new futures movement," as she said many years later.[43]

That futures movement, with its roots in the 1950s, took off in the early 1970s with the founding of the World Futures Studies Federation by the Italian feminist Eleonora Masini. Subsequently there evolved a growing contingency of American futures scholars, among them Elise and other women academicians. Of women's involvement in the futures movement she wrote, "Women, outside the centers of power, [have] envisioned creative egalitarian futures in which people [have] lived at peace with one another and with nature, in contrast to the high-tech futures more often described by men."[44]

Elise continued her scholarly work in futures throughout the next two decades. Seeking to dispel the notion held nearly universally that war is inevitable, Elise hoped to show that every civilization has the capacity to envision a human condition of peacefulness. During the 1980s, visions of nuclear Armageddon began to proliferate, as scholars and educators, as well as average citizens, became aware of the very real possibility of planetary annihilation. Elise criticized peace scholars for perpetuating fear by failing to encapsulate imagery and imaginings of a more peaceful world and too often playing up the drama of nuclear holocaust, real though the threat was and continues to be.[45]

Both of the Bouldings were highly influenced by the work of Fred Polak. Kenneth Boulding's book *The Image*, written in a little over a week as the family was packing to leave California in 1955, was inspired by his collegial interaction with Polak during the year at Stanford. "Imaging," according to Kenneth, Elise and other scholars is closely associated with memories, both recent and in the past. It can and does go beyond mere remembering and rests on the assumption that visions of the future are essential to working for social change. Important to the concept of imaging, according to Elise, is the idea that the visionary must imagine minute details of a healthy society. "Humans construct social reality in their minds prior to the sociophysical task of constructing the external reality," she wrote.[46]

During the 1980s, Elise, together with futurist Warren Ziegler, began holding a series of experimental workshops combining the theories of Polak with practical problem-solving techniques developed by Ziegler. Participants were asked to discover a viable future social order that was devoid of weapons. Since that time, Elise has at various times, alone and with others, continued to conduct these workshops.

Elise's best known concept from her imaging workshops is the idea of "stepping into the future" through a series of exercises after which the participants would report back their observations of society. Workshops typically ran for an entire weekend, and, as Elise wrote, "were very demanding, drawing on both fantasy and analytical thinking and requiring suspension of pessimism and disbelief."[47] Participants drew up a wish list for the future, recalled a childhood memory and then stepped into the future, most often 30 years earlier. As Elise noted, this time frame was chosen because most participants would still be alive, yet there was time for real changes to take place.

General themes of the future emerged from the many workshops she conducted. The world is non hierarchical. Locality is important. There is a strong sense of space, with community gardens and a prevalent sense of "greenness." Personal needs are taken care of, such as food, shelter and clothing, within community settings. Central to the workshop process is the final activity in which participants analyze steps needed to realize their visions.

As an immigrant child, Elise's vision of America was tempered by the views of her mother, Birgit, who saw Americans as crass and materialistic. Nevertheless Elise shared the view of many immigrants that America was a land of promise. She also held the utopian view that Norway was a safe and secure place, until the Nazi invasion of World War II, when her vision was crushed.

Elise's early Quaker speaking and writing, begun around the time of her early work in futures, which included the importance of spiritual visioning. In the William Penn lecture she delivered in 1956 for the Young Friends of the Philadelphia Yearly Meeting, her words were, "[O]ur vision for the future provides the direction for our growth," citing the need for prayer in order for the visions to reach fruition.[48]

Elise believes she became a futurist through the years of raising her five children, spending time with other Quaker children in Ann Arbor and in Colorado, and in her teaching students at both the University of Colorado and at Dartmouth. It was her experience with families, her own and others, that most convinced her of the important functions they play in creating spaces for imaging. Families, according to Elise, contribute greatly to futures-creating capacities. This is particularly true in times of rapid social change. Instead of the prevailing notion of families as preservers of the social status-quo, Elise has long espoused the view that families, historically, have pointed the way to the future.[49] The visioning capacities of children can be shared, if adults will allow this to happen. Every new family is also a new social invention.

Women are better at imaging than men because of their socialization and because they have traditionally been marginal to social decision-making, hence there are fewer vested interests to protect. Women's cultures have developed ways of working together and connecting, and they possess energy and skills can be tapped to look toward the future.

It was the visioning of women peace scholars and educators, during the early days of peace research in the 1960s and 1970s, that brought new life into the field, long dominated by men. These educators insisted that the notion of peace include more than the absence of war and the relations between nations. Peace activists should also conceptualize a more total view of world peace, emphasizing wholeness, integrity, the environment and the inclusiveness of marginalized peoples, including women and children.

Part III

Teacher, Preacher and Heavenbound Reacher: The Later Years

Chapter 10

Sociologist and Traveler for International Peace: The 1970s and Early 1980s

The 1970s through the mid–1980s were years in which Elise solidified her reputation as an academic sociologist and became a leading expert in the emerging field of peace studies. Beginning her teaching career when the family moved to Colorado in 1967 and soon thereafter starting a peace studies program at the university, Elise's interest in women and social roles, begun with her dissertation work, continued. She became active in several professional associations, most notably the American Sociological Association and the International Sociological Association. She went on the editorial board of the journal *Peace and Change* in 1971 and was appointed to the board of the Institute for World Order in 1973, remaining on the board for the next fifteen years as the organization became the World Policy Institute. She became active in several committees of the American Association for the Advancement of Science. By the time of her retirement in 1985, she had moved to Dartmouth and become an international advocate for peace research and for the integration of research, activism and education. Throughout this time her work in futures studies continued. And she began to receive national and international recognition for her work in peace.

In 1968 Elise was elected International Chair of the Women's International League for Peace and Freedom at their seventeenth triennial gathering, held in Nyborg Strand, Denmark. Her tenure of three years would mark the end of her intense involvement with this organization, begun so long ago during her "stay-at-home" days as a housewife and young mother. Elise's vice co-chairs, elected in 1968, were Ellen Holmgaard of Denmark and Sushila Nayar of India. At that meeting, Dorothy Hutchinson was elected the U.S. Chair.

The 1971 eighteenth WILPF triennial, held in New Delhi, the first ever in what was then a developing country, marked the end of Elise's tenure as international chair, a post she was all too happy to relinquish, believing that the job in its latter days had sapped her energy and left her with not enough time for the kinds of activities she felt best equipped to do. Elise's address at that gathering, the last of hers as chair, was entitled "NGOs and the Search for Economic and Social Justice," which was later published in *Associations Internationale*.[1] In this address, Elise pleaded for the WILPF membership to overcome "our stato-centrism." She called for a truly international focus, taking into account the needs and experiences of women from developing countries. In this address she also was explicit that the efforts of WILPF needed to be directed, as they were in earlier days, to the identification of the skills and strengths of women in all societies and all countries in order to work for peace and world development.[2] She identified the need for women's NGOs to partner particularly with those sectors of women's society that have traditionally been excluded, not only in developing countries but in western European nations as well.

The platform statement of the New Delhi WILPF Congress included new approaches to disarmament, the abolition of all military bases, the seating of the People's Republic of China at the United Nations, the withdrawal of all foreign troops from Vietnam, and the urging of UNESCO to promote "ethical principals in education" worldwide. Within a few years these ideas would be fruitfully explored in more depth in Elise's books on women and society, *The Underside of History* and *Women in the Twentieth Century World*.[3]

Theoretical Work in Peace Education

Elise continued her theoretical work on children during the 1970s. "The Child and Nonviolent Social Change" was published in 1974 by IPRA, which outlined contributing factors in childrearing for developing future peacemakers.[4] In this article, Elise gave recognition to her belief that it is not only women who are marginalized in most societies, but children as well, and both groups have a unique contribution to make toward peace by virtue of their position as standing outside the mainstream. Later that year she spent her own year outside the mainstream, at her hermitage in

Colorado, where she put down in writing her thoughts on women's contribution to world history, culminating in the publication of *The Underside of History*.

Elise's work with IPRA continued through the 1970s and 1980s. In 1971 she attended the organization's conference that was held in Bled, Yugoslavia, one of the many meetings she subsequently attended over the following decades. COPRED had been founded the year prior, in 1970, and she was representing that organization at the gathering. At that meeting, Elise was elected to the newly established Peace Education Commission of IPRA. Other members serving were Betty Reardon of the U.S. and Johan Galtung of Norway.[5] In a memo written later to committee members, Asbjorn Eide of Oslo, then IPRA Secretary-General, listed the functions of the PEC:

> 1. collection and dissemination of information on peace education activities carried out in various parts of the world, by national and international institutions
> 2. the formation of transnational curricula for conflict, peace and development studies
> 3. the initiation of education programs by IPRA itself. An example proposed is a summer school for peace researchers and activists, in order to examine what the two can contribute to one another.[6]

And Eide asked:

> [E]ducation—for what? We know ... that what we aim at is both to increase awareness of present conditions and trends and various alternatives for a peaceful future. We know also that the aim of education is to make the individual more qualified and more courageous in his or her participation in the formation of the new society.... [B]ut we need also to become much more concrete on the following points: *who* should do what ... who should be involved in the education process (as far as peace is concerned), *how* should it be done ... and *when* should it be done?[7]

Until that point, it had not been IPRA's intention to become involved in the more formal aspects of peace education. With the formation of the PEC, this would change.

Elise replied to Eide's memo, stating that COPRED had recently put together an annotated list of peace studies programs on college campuses in the U.S. and that soon she would circulate a questionnaire among members to ascertain who was doing peace education work in primary and secondary schools, an outgrowth of her work with the Science Education

Commission of the American Association of the Advancement of Science.[8] During this time Elise had developed her own interdisciplinary peace studies program at the University of Colorado.

Teacher and Professional Sociologist

Elise continued her busy schedule of teaching during the early and mid–1970s, as she also began intensive involvement in two major professional sociological associations, the ASA (American Sociological Association) and the ISA (International Sociological Association). Courses she taught at the university included the Sociology of Religion, Sociology of the Family, Sociology of Peacemaking, Sociology of Global Systems, Problems and Prospects of Peace, and a course she co-taught with Kenneth, the Social System of the Planet Earth, using readings from science fiction, a passion of hers. In 1980, *The Social System of the Planet Earth* was published as a book, adding an additional author, Guy Burgess.[9]

In 1970 Elise was elected secretary of the Working Group on the Study of Sex Roles in Society of the International Sociological Association, serving in that role for the next three years. Between 1973 and 1977 she co-chaired the research committee of ISA on the study of sex roles in society.

Elise's interests in the issues associated with women and the profession were partly an outgrowth of her dissertation work on women in the developing world, piqued also by her own internal struggles around the multiple roles she recognized that she and women in general play as professionals, partners and parents. Many of her published work during this time dealt with these issues, in addition to her work on children. These reached fruition in the publication of *The Underside of History* in 1976.

Elise began her association with the American Sociological Association through chairing the Committee on the Status of Women in the Profession from 1970 to 1972. She was elected to the general Council of ASA in 1976, serving until 1979. Earlier, between 1972 and 1974, she served as chair of the Committee on the Sociology of World Conflict. In 1974 this committee, with Elise as one of the signers, petitioned Executive Officer Otto Larsen of the ASA to create a regular section. The purposes of the section were:

> To foster the development of the application of sociological theories and methods for the understanding of those conflicts which are wide enough in scope and involve a large number of participants to be regarded as a property of the sociosphere, or the total world system.[10]

The wording is indicative of Elise's influence. Their petition was successful. In 1980 Elise was elected section chair, later to serve on the Committee on World Sociology of the ASA for a year, ending in 1984.

As the 1970s progressed, though she continued her work on women, increasingly Elise was turning to issues relating to global peace, security and the environment. As well, her interest in futures studies continued. She, along with Kenneth, had joined the American Association for the Advancement of Science when she began her career as a sociologist. She served on several committees of the association, most of the time separately from Kenneth. Looking back on those years, Elise recalled that "I had more fun—I really enjoyed it. We were doing such 'cutting edge' stuff."[11]

She served on the AAAS Commission on Science Education for two years, beginning in 1972. Between 1979 and 1981 Elise convened the AAAS Working Group on Climate Change Project and out of this work a book was produced of which she was co-editor, *Social Science Research and Climate: An Interdisciplinary Appraisal.*[12] Always mindful of the strong attractions of interdisciplinary work, much of the work Elise did with the AAAS afforded her much appreciated contacts with colleagues in other scientific fields. Elise recalled, "It was such fun realizing we *all* live with climate change, especially in our temperate zone where there are four seasons.... [H]ow we do adapt to climate change!"[13] Between 1981 and 1984, in addition to serving on the Nominating Committee of AAAS, Elise was a member of the Committee on Arms Control and National Security and then served on the Committee on Populations, Resources and the Environment until 1989. The committees each met several times a year and also at the annual AAAS meeting. Research papers were given, with an eye, particularly when Elise was in leadership positions, to interdisciplinary sharing.

Between the late 1960s and the early 1970s Elise was among a handful of scholars and activists who founded the World Futures Studies Federation. The Federation is comprised of member institutes and individuals from around the world and "strives to be a forum where the stimulation, exchange and examination of ideas, visions and plans for alternative and long-term futures can take place."[14] The mission includes the promotion of interdisciplinary futures studies with a view toward analysis and critical thinking. Elise continued her regular contacts with futures scholars, including Eleonora Masini, the Italian futurist who greatly influenced her ideas, throughout the 1980s and 1990s.

Personal Struggles

The years prior to her move to Dartmouth had proved stressful for Elise in many ways. Following her year of solitude in 1974, she had returned to her hectic schedule of teaching, research and travel, with the increasing realization of some powerlessness in controlling her overworked schedule. By 1975, her journal entries revealed a need to slow down. For Elise, her Hermitage was her place of retreat, where she felt embraced by the solitude. She was spending increasing time there as the 1970s came to an end. Following her year of retreat, she had had some intentions to continue to live out in Lyons, Colorado, dividing her time between the Waterfall, their family cabin, and her Hermitage up the hill, because she felt overburdened by the demands of keeping up the house in Boulder. She had wanted to sell the house, citing it as too much of a burden in many ways, but Kenneth resisted. Journal entries reveal Elise's poignant struggles:

> [Kenneth] gets lonely at the Waterfall, he said. He needs to be near people. It tugs at my heartstrings to realize how different our directions are. But so be it. I will need god's continual guidance to find ways to give enough companionship to Kenneth and yet be faithful to my own leadings. I need other anchors ... (Kenneth never wanting things to change, the house is his anchor). While the hermitage is a very important anchor, there is a profound sense in which Kenneth and I will always be anchors for each other.[15]

The 1970s were stressful years for Kenneth as well. Nearing the end of his tenure at the University of Colorado, after being hired ten years earlier as one of the highest paid faculty, he was increasingly feeling isolated and under-appreciated by the university community. Elise was realizing that much of his continued criticism of her, some in public, which would profoundly embarrass her, was due to his own insecurities. She realized that Kenneth was threatened by, as she noted, "my choice to travel a different spiritual path." She explained,

> He sees it as a denial of the reality of his life and that is why he is continually accusing me of putting him down.... Lord help me to work out the basis of our togetherness so that his bitterness may go away. We do love each other, and that is a precious reality to build on.[16]

It had not always been that easy. Among differing temperaments and differing life views on many things, it was their deep love and commitment to their relationship and their mutual love for God which kept them anchored for each other through the years. Though some would see Elise as an extrovert, at her core she had a deep need for solitude, which Kenneth never totally understood. As one colleague noted, "Kenneth even surrounded by people was able to retreat into the cabins of his mind and still find some solitude."[17] But for Elise, solitude meant experiences away from people. In the end, Elise agreed, it was grace which ultimately was their redemption, that which saved their marriage. As a journal entry for Elise noted in 1975, "[T]he tension between [us] has been resolved.... [D]oing things [such as accepting invitations to jointly speak at Quaker gatherings] even when they are painful, represents a kind of testimony of love and acceptance in the face of differences."

No one would deny, least of all Elise, that her marriage to Kenneth ultimately shaped the woman she became. But as Christine Boulding acknowledged, "[I]t had to be hard being married to my father." Russell Boulding recalled being awakened at night by Elise and Kenneth arguing over some philosophical strategy of peacemaking. Russell believed their differences lay in their differing upbringings, Kenneth coming from a background of suffering as a member of the lower class in a very classist society in Britain. Russell explained, "It made him much less critical of the things that were wrong in American society ... and my mother coming from a Norwegian egalitarian background saw those much more clearly than my father."[18]

For two avid peacemakers, personal conflict was difficult for them. Daughter Christine Boulding said:

> When you think about the amount of time both of them spent in developing theories of conflict resolution, the thing they did least well at home was learning how to resolve conflicts between themselves and the family.... [W]e don't resolve conflicts, we ignore them and hope they will go away.[19]

She agreed it was easier for them to argue publicly, but much more so for Kenneth. Other family members cited that often this was painful for Elise. Particularly difficult were the times they publicly disagreed before Quaker audiences. For the Bouldings, the personal, the public and the political were conflated. A long time friend noted, "I always felt the Gods were playing nine pins when they argued—the philosophical and the state of the world *was* personal."[20]

Though it was their mutual love of God and their devotion to each other that grounded their marriage, at times Elise experienced spiritual "erosion" around Kenneth, particularly acute during the 1970s when she was suffering health difficulties and emotional exhaustion. It was during this time that she returned to Catholic worship, for the first time since her early adult years, and actively sought out monastic experiences. Many of her journal entries during this time reflect her deep longing to remain connected to Kenneth physically and spiritually and yet to find her own inner space, feeling at times she had lost her sense of the grace of God.

> March 9, 1974—isn't it time that my own spirituality should begin to mediate my relationship with Kenneth.... [T]he old signs of spiritual erosion are beginning to show in me.... [W]hy can't I just accept this fantastic ivy plant of a man who sends shoots off in all directions and is crowned with many flowers? Growth, productivity are good, not hurtful. What is there that is hurtful to me? And ... why can't love deal with it?

Ten years later, in a letter that she wrote but never sent to Kenneth from Dartmouth, she acknowledged some of the roots of those hurts:

> From time to time I felt crowded by your creativity. There was so much and it never stopped! But that was a churlishness on my part of which I was ashamed ... and it passed away.... [O]ur differing temperaments led me to ask questions differently and I began to discover that you sometimes didn't like the way I addressed social issues. [Author note: She goes on to describe a Quaker gathering in Michigan where she was giving a talk.] You were [both] with me and in the audience. You started interrupting and contradicting me while I was still speaking. I can still feel the intense burning shame I felt that you should treat me like that before old friends who had "honored" me.... I realized that you meant nothing hostile by your criticism, you didn't realize you had done anything inappropriate and were distressed when I disappeared after the session for a few minutes to regain my equanimity. But the others knew! ... [M]y only reason for writing this is to try to explain that there was a certain amount of stress involved for me in establishing my own separate identity as a scholar. Further I still had many domestic responsibilities and never enough time for writing once teaching and various project responsibilities were taken care of.... [Y]ou were working every bit as hard as I was, but you had so much more to show for it! ... [S]ometimes I felt smothered by it [his outpouring of creativity]. I could no longer live up to the role of nurturing your creativity ... given to me so many years ago.[21]

And in the letter that she did send to Kenneth, dated February 20, 1985, she acknowledged that since the year she had spent at the Hermitage she had, "in a sense felt 'on loan' to more worldly activity." Having had a mastectomy in 1978, following her mastoid surgery just prior to her entering the Hermitage, she revealed that these "approaches to death" had intensified this feeling. She acknowledged the pain of realizing she had hurt Kenneth by not being able to nurture his creative energies. But she realized that at that time her "calling" was to repattern her life. The letter continues,

> I know I am not to become a hermit, but I am to be available to God in a different way than I am now. I sense so much wrong in how we pursue knowledge and human and social well being, so many barriers to the simple response of Stop! Listen! The faint signals that rise to the surface of public life from the desperation, misery, anger, deprivation, helplessness, of so many of the world's peoples, be they minorities or "successful" mainstream carriers of the achievements of science and industrialism, are a loud and insistent cacophony to my inner ear. I sometimes become physically ill when reading the current issue of science [*sic*], and experiencing the gap between the activities of science, the flower of our civilization, and human well-being. Our age is so full of paradoxes, contradictions, ambiguities, and there is so much good intertwined with evil. For you these conditions are the challenge which are leading you to the heights of productivity you are now experiencing. For me these conditions are calling for retreat time, reflection time, prayer, and inner reworking of understandings of what is at work in the creations. To repattern for more reflection time doesn't mean inaction, only a quieter rhythm. It certainly doesn't mean questioning your calling. In fact, I will be able to be more supportive of your calling when my own frantic pace has slowed.

Elise's journals of the year she spent in solitude reflect some of the deep struggles she was experiencing during the turbulence of the mid–1970s. As has often happened to her, she created useful metaphors that helped guide her and give clarity to her difficulties:

> April 29, 1974—I thought of a good simile this morning. This year Kenneth carefully dug a special trench to channel the water away from the tree [at the Waterfall cabin near her Hermitage]. I am like that tree and Kenneth like a perpetual spring stream at full flood. The water in his stream is pure and sparkling but it can kill my roots if I am inundated too long at a time. My hermitage diverts the stream and protects my roots, while still keeping me near the beautiful sparkling waters.

Many of the Boulding's social and political differences reached a head around their differing evolving views over the Vietnam War. In 1970 Kenneth had registered as a Republican, much to the consternation of Elise and many of their associates. His main reason for switching party allegiance was over his disputes with the Democrats over their views on the war, which he believed refused to take into account the violence he thought was being perpetuated by the North Vietnamese. The Boulding's views on the Vietnam War become widely divergent, as Kenneth in May of 1975 suffered greatly over the fall of Saigon, and Elise was jubilant that the North Vietnamese took over the South, celebrating with others in Boulder the attempts to rebuild the country. Kenneth broke with many Quakers over issues related to the war and picketed a meeting of the American Friends Service Committee being held in Philadelphia, where discussions were being held on this subject in the mid–1970s. Elise recalled that

> Kenneth thought the student protests were violent and leading to support for the North Vietnamese. But our Quaker Meeting in Ann Arbor was bringing money to Canada for Vietnam. Kenneth and I were a part of this and he volunteered to drive the car with the money through the tunnel to Canada.[22]

As Kenneth's biographer, Cynthia Kerman, noted, "Kenneth was a heretic, even among radicals."[23]

Elise's Move to Dartmouth

A pivitol year of change for Elise was 1978. In that year the Boulding's youngest child, William, was married. The wedding was in Princeton, New Jersey, and very soon thereafter Elise was on her way to New Hampshire, to a new life, away from the University of Colorado. Upon the eve of his wedding, as her last child was "emptying the nest," Elise had a dream in which she received the following words, which she believed were given to her to be the trajectory of the rest of her life. The words were, "nine years teaching, nine years practice preaching, and nine years heaven reaching." It was a powerful moment for her, as she interpreted these words to mean she would continue teaching into the 1980s, then retire to a more contemplative and spiritual life, then enter her journey into old age.

In the fall of 1978, Elise and Kenneth were offered joint Montgomery visiting professorships at Dartmouth College, each in their respective fields. Kenneth was nearing retirement from the University of Colorado but was continuing his association with the university, despite his heavy schedule of international travel. By the end of that academic year, Elise had been offered the position of chair of the sociology department at Dartmouth with a full-time ongoing teaching post. Kenneth, while enjoying some aspects of his teaching during the visiting year, did not wish to remain on the Dartmouth campus and returned to Boulder.

For the next six years Elise and Kenneth saw each other as their academic and traveling schedules allowed, frequently meeting in airports, as she subsequently humorously noted, on their way to various peace research meetings and en route to family gatherings. For Kenneth, Dartmouth could not offer him the kind of teaching and research he desired. In a letter written later to Elise, he expressed surprise that she had had some expectations that he would stay with her in Hanover:

> [I]t never occurred to me that you really wanted me to do that, and after a gulp or two, I accepted our "commuter marriage" and I don't regret it for a minute. I joke about how Dartmouth fell in love with you and didn't fall in love with me, when I try to explain to people who may seem puzzled about the arrangement.... [T]here was never the slightest indication they [the Economics Department] wanted me to teach there. You are enough of a feminist to know that a spouse needs to be much more than a house spouse, though there is nothing wrong with a dash of that (I always say the only time I am sure I am doing good is when I am clearing or washing dishes).[24]

Tireless Traveler

The Dartmouth years were important ones for Elise in many ways. Her energy during those years was invested in her international work and in her teaching. She maintained a heavy travel schedule, teaching on Tuesdays through Thursdays so that she could leave early, often around four or five A.M. on Fridays to catch the bus to Boston for her overseas flight. She would then return Monday to return to teaching on Tuesday. Occasionally she took a small commuter plane to Boston, but most of the time she traveled by bus, or by car, for the two-hour drive, chauffeured by one of her office assistants who often was a Dartmouth student. Elise did not have a car during her years in Hanover.

Elise taught several courses at Dartmouth, including Women and Work, Human Relations, War and Peace Studies and Global Systems. She became chair of the department of sociology in 1979 and developed and chaired the Dartmouth interdisciplinary peace studies program.

The years at Dartmouth were important as Elise was able to establish herself as an international scholar in her own right, away from and out of the shadow of Kenneth. Most of the work with which she was involved

On her 60th birthday, 1980, Elise met in Hawaii with other commissioners for the establishment of the National Academy of Peace and Conflict, later the U.S. Institute of Peace. Jim Laue (left) was commission co-chair, and Senator Daniel Inoue, a fellow commissioner.

during the Dartmouth years concerned international peace. Many of her activities revolved around increasing consultative work with UNESCO, culminating with her appointment in 1978 to the National Commission, serving as an advisor. In addition she was elected to the Council of the United Nations University in Tokyo and was appointed by President Jimmy Carter to the Commission on Proposals for a National Academy of Peace and Conflict, now known as the U.S. Institute of Peace. She also helped to found the Academic Council of the United Nations Systems (ACUNS), just prior to her retirement. Though Elise continued to integrate her ideas on women's roles and women and peace, the focus of her work during those years turned increasingly to the work of building a global society and to the world structures which would help support this. She continued to serve on the Board of Directors of the World Policy Institute in New York, her term having begun in Boulder before she left for Dartmouth, and she continued on the board until 1987.

Prior to her appointment to UNESCO's U.S. National Commission, Elise had been active in consulting with the agency since the early 1960s when she was involved with peace education projects, in particular work with the Women's International League for Peace and Freedom through their consultative status with UNESCO. UNESCO had provided start-up funds in the early 1960s for the establishment of what would later become the IPRA newsletter, and the agency was a co-sponsor of the conference in 1963 in Clarens, Switzerland, which led two years later to the founding of IPRA. Through the many organizations with which she was involved throughout the 1960s, 1970s and 1980s, Elise facilitated the connections between the work of those groups and UNESCO, and, as she stated, "every time [UNESCO] had a consultation on peace research, I was there."[25]

The UNESCO National Commission was established by a joint resolution of Congress in 1946. Its established role was to serve as the prime advisor to the U.S. government on the program and budgetary aspects of UNESCO. There have been typically over 100 members, individuals and representatives from NGOs and governmental bodies. Advisors are appointed by the Secretary of State. Elise described her role as a member of the UNESCO National Commission:

> We met once a year, the Social Science Committee ... and then of course we [the U.S.] left UNESCO ... because [of] its new information order work which said that information should flow equally from east to west and west to east, north to south and south to north, and the U.S. said, "Oh, that must mean giving in to third world dictatorships." England left too, but England came back. We have never rejoined. So what we used to do was to meet once a year at least ... to examine the different social science programs in UNESCO and make suggestions about things that we thought they should be doing that they weren't and praising things we liked and would like to see more of, kind of the input of the social science community in the U.S....There is an international social science committee for UNESCO that has member representatives from NGOs, so for example in that role I served as IPRA's representative to the social science division of UNESCO and there we would meet at UNESCO and ... it was quite a lot of input from various NGOs.[26] [Author note: The U.S. voted to rejoin UNESCO in 2003. Her files indicate that Elise actually represented COPRED on the U.S. National Commission.[27]]

In the mid–1980s, Elise sat on the jury for the international UNESCO Peace Prize.

Prior to the U.S. withdrawal from UNESCO in the mid–1980s, there had been controversy about its membership in the 1970s. Between 1975 and 1976 the U.S. withheld, by Congressional action, its payment of dues to the agency because of issues surrounding Israel's exclusion from the European Regional Group of UNESCO and problems over the funding of excavation sites in Jerusalem. Of the five sectors of UNESCO, communications, education, natural sciences, culture and the social sciences, communications has consistently been the area where politics and culture have collided. Criticism of western media by developing countries ostensibly was one of the reasons the U.S. withdrew. It was feared that some UNESCO programs provided a platform for ideas "inimical to a free press," including licensing of journalists and governmental censorship. The Cold War during these years was played out through UNESCO.[28] As a member of the social science committee of the National Commission, Elise was part of the group that recommended that UNESCO support the development of interdisciplinary studies devoted to peace and that the agency continue its work in developing countries in training and in building social science infrastructures.

From 1982 until 1985, Elise served on the International Jury of the UNESCO Peace Prize for Peace Education. She described her work as follows:

> [We] were appointed by UNESCO and the jury met once a year to go through all the nominations for the peace prize. IPRA received the prize after I went off so we have both been the recipient of it and I served on it.... I think I was appointed because I had served on the council of the UN University and that was a prestigious enough position to make me eligible to be on the UNESCO Commission and what we did, it took 3–4 days to go through hundreds of applications.... I think IPRA got $5,000.... [E]verybody said it was really me that was getting it [for IPRA].[29]

The United Nations University and the ACUNS

Elise was appointed a Council Member of the United Nations University in 1980. Prior to that time she had served as an advisor to the university's Human and Social Development Program and, in 1982, began the Household and Gender Age Project out of her concern that women were underrepresented in the research projects of the UNU and that women's experiences were not adequately taken into account. Her hope was that the UNU could "develop criteria and indicators that will be indicative of progress in regard to women's participation in development."[30]

Elise thought that the reason that she was appointed to the UNU Council was partly because of her association with IPRA.

> I served a six-year term, and that was a fascinating chapter in my life, we [had] one meeting in Japan each year and one in some other part of the world, that's how I came to go to the United Arab Emirates, which I never otherwise would have visited.[31]

The roots of the UNU, according to Elise, went back to the student movements of the 1960s, particularly to a group on the campus of the University of Michigan, when, according to Elise,

> I was a homemaker and started the IPRA newsletter and was volunteering at the Center [for Conflict Resolution]. I had a lot of interaction with [the students].... [T]here was a spin-off group which was responsible for the work which got the Peace Corps started, I mean there were other groups, but they took a very important role, there is a plaque in the University Union. This is where candidate

> Kennedy, before he was elected president, met the delegation of students who formally asked him to establish the U.S. Peace Corps. And I was there ... it was 4:00 in the morning.... The other group wanted to form a UN University, a world university that would be a UN University and I helped raise money for them to go to Paris to get support from UNESCO for a world university, now that did not lead like this at all, but it was the first initiative and then.... [There were] spin-offs, but the idea of a UN University that would be based in the UN took longer and it finally came to the General Assembly and it was authorized there should be a UN university and Japan really took the lead and offered to put money into it and that is why its headquarters are in Japan.[32]

The actual founding of the United Nations University occurred in 1974, following its approval the year before by the General Assembly. The original mission of the university was to contribute, through research and capacity building, to efforts to resolve the pressing global problems that are the concern of the United Nations, its peoples and its Member States.[33] There are four key roles for the UNU listed in its charter:

1. to be an international community of scholars
2. to form a bridge between the United Nations and the international academic community
3. to serve as a think tank for the United Nations system
4. to contribute to capacity building, particularly in developing countries[34]

From the beginning, it has been a "university without walls" in that there is no central campus other than an office building in Tokyo. In 1979, the UN General Assembly established plans to found another United Nations University in Costa Rica, with land for a campus deeded from the Costa Rican government, whose ties to the Tokyo university have remained elusive and somewhat tenuous.[35] In essence the original UNU is a consortium of international scholars and institutions throughout the world, each devoted to the advancement of research for world betterment.[36] According to Elise, the fact that there is no central campus has been significant in reducing the overall ability of the institution to advance the cause of peace and world problem solving. She explained,

> The whole time I was on the board I worked to get them to establish a policy that whatever associate university they have, they would offer courses that would be labeled UNU courses.... I couldn't ... never got that through, was trying the whole time I was on the board, but they do have graduate students and they have research projects and research fellows but the campus ... the nearest

> thing to a campus ... they do actually give courses at the headquarters in Tokyo.... They have a section where they have classes, a special spin off program for Japanese university students but it is a research university ... meant to serve as a research resource for every UN agency. And they do an impressive amount of work.[37]

Her statement reflects her deeply felt belief that interactions between scholars and students are central to peacebuilding. According to one UN scholar, the establishment of the UNU reflects the theme, explicit in the founding of the United Nations itself, that "education is central to the goal of ending the 'scourge of war.'"[38]

In total, Elise had a ten year relationship with the UNU, from when she served as an advisor with their Human and Social Development Program in the late 1970s until she ended her tenure on the Council at the time of her retirement from Dartmouth in 1985. As early as 1980, Elise had been concerned about the UNU, in particular regarding its lack of interface between the production of knowledge and of policymaking. She also recognized the particular need for research on and support of the roles of women.[39]

The writing of *Children's Rights and the Wheel of Life* in the late 1970s had also given her the sense that the world's children are underrepresented in the kinds of policy-making decisions undertaken by the United Nations.[40] The founding of the Project on Household Gender and Age in 1982 was an outgrowth of her work with the Social Development Program, the gender project having as its predecessor a committee formed by Elise in 1980, the Interprogram Advisory Panel on Aspects of Gender and Age. The starting of these groups had its grounding in her long-held interest in the differing meanings and consequences of development in the world, as experienced by different categories of individuals and social groups. This interest had begun with the writing of her dissertation in 1969. In a written report following discussions on the proposal, citing the need for the Program on Gender and Age, Elise wrote:

> [A] whole new conceptual framework for viewing human activity is required.... [T]his framework must not be limited by conceptions of age and gender-based social roles.[41]

In the formal proposal for the committee put before the UNU, entitled "Interprogram Advisory Panel of Women Scholars," Elise's words were:

> Developmental processes cannot be adequately understood without a consideration of the differential meanings of these processes for women and men. A specific focus on the condition of women and

> the structural and psychological constraints on their participation in development is therefore necessary. However, we find that frequently the condition of women is not sufficiently considered in UNU program and project formulation. This is a problem extending far beyond the UNU, reflecting a general failure of insight into the nature of sex roles in the modern world.[42]

Elise itemized specific things the UNU could do, including examining all research projects for evidence of their relevance to and enhancement of women. In addition, she called for there to be an examination of existing research approaches and their underlying assumptions. Elise, in a 1986 interview with the *Denver Post*, shared her pleasure that, by 1985, research on the lives of women was no longer considered separately but had become integrated into the university's larger development research process. She said,

> Previously the attitude was "now we are going to pay attention to women, so we'll stop the important work and do a little something for women, and then we can get back to the important work. Like all other major institutions, the United Nations is male-dominated, and as a result, the information gathered for its development projects has been flawed by leaving out women's knowledge. For example, if you want to increase agricultural production and you never talk to women, you never are going to do much about agricultural productivity, because in many parts of the world, women do most of the farming.[43]

Just prior to her retirement, Elise helped to found another academic network associated with the United Nations, the Academic Council on the United Nations System. This group, founded in 1987 at a conference at Dartmouth, had as its purpose the formation of a new organization devoted to the stimulation and support of research and teaching on the role of the UN system. A year earlier, at a conference sponsored by the New York office of the UNU and the Dickey Center, scholars had discussed their concern about the gap between the UN and academia. According to Gene Lyons, with whom Elise worked closely at Dartmouth, she "took the first step" in establishing ACUNS. He also acknowledged that she "had to move the operation forward if anything was to be done."[44]

At that time, Elise had recently completed her term on the UNU Council. She had a keen sense that the activities of the UNU and those throughout the UN were not connecting with the research and teaching taking place in outside universities and research centers. The original group who began ACUNS agreed that its purpose should be "to encourage and support new initiatives in teaching and research that are designed to increase our understanding of the role of the UN system in international relations." In addition, reflecting Elise's long-held interest in peace education and its integration with research, the group hoped to encourage the establishment of working relationships with other organizations such as secondary schools and adult education programs.[45]

Elise left Dartmouth shortly after the ACUNS was formed but maintained connections with Gene Lyons and others. The group has become more international and included scholars from Mexico and Canada. But Elise's consistent concern with ACUNS has been that ongoing and direct operational connections between scholars world-wide and the UNU have failed to evolve on any substantial scale. She explained,

> My original idea was to connect scholars who were interested in the UN with the UNU.... The ACUNS people are the ones who are doing the kind of conflict and peace research work that UNU needs, they [UNU] have some, but do more with the environment and development issues and technology and don't do that much on conflict and peace so ACUNS ... they really need.[46]

In a letter Elise wrote to Tom Weiss, an active ACUNS member and an associate with the Ralph Bunche Institute on the United Nations at the City University of New York, she mentioned again that the original goal of the ACUNS is to help the academic community connect with the workings of the UN system and expressed her dismay, saying, "[T]he UNU needs more contact with the peace studies international relations field that ACUNS represents."[47] She inquired, "What happened to ACUNS? ... I planned on writing to the rector of the UNU and ask the same question, but I ran out of steam that day."[48]

The National Academy of Peace and Conflict

The other large peace project with which Elise was involved during her time at Dartmouth was the proposal for the establishment of the United States Academy of Peace. In 1979, President Jimmy Carter set up, under House Bill 5088 and Senate Bill 1839, a commission which spent the next two years with their mission as the following: to hold nation-wide public hearings; to survey the conflict resolution competencies available to the federal government; and to make available state-of-the-art evaluations of research and training in conflict resolution and related fields.[49] Elise served on the commission with several U.S. Senators, including Mark Hatfield of Oregon and Jennings Randolph of West Virginia.

The idea of a peace academy, analogous to the U.S. military academies, dates back to the time of George Washington. There were bills introducing the idea in 1935 and again in 1945, the latter one a direct ancestor of the legislation that eventually established the U.S. Institute of Peace.[50]

The commission process had three main components: research, public outreach and deliberation of findings, and conclusions and recommendations. A total of fifty public meetings were held with educators, practitioners and various community groups. The commission report to the President, the Senate, and the House of Representatives in 1981 listed its principal recommendation as the establishment of a United States Academy of Peace, the aim of which should be the promoting of peace by developing knowledge of the processes of peace, education in conflict resolution and advancing cooperation among peoples. Three major functions recommended for the academy were research, education and training, as well as informational services on international peace and peacemaking. The academy was to "build upon the fundamental peace principles and experiences in our nation's heritage to expand the analytic and problem-solving competence that is necessary to promote and serve international peace."[51]

The report mentioned that the findings of the commission were not to be seen as recommending a reduction in military and diplomatic power. These were viewed as assets. But the purpose of the Academy would be to "go beyond the military" and offer a range of options, including reliance on lower-level interactive mechanisms to resolve conflicts. Elise's influence on the commission's findings may be seen in the wording of the report that establishes that peace studies is a legitimate field of the learning process because:

1. it has literature, courses of study and professional organizations
2. there are well-defined assumptions within the field
3. there are a variety of research methodologies
4. there is a strong applied component

The report also mentioned that many outside observers confuse peace activities with peace research. Elise was quoted as saying, "[M]ost researchers are international researchers with a focus on disarmament and nonmilitary solutions to conflict." The report went on to note that peace learning encompasses more than just the absence of war, though that is an important component of peace studies. Echoing her words, the commission in the report recognized "peace as social justice" as a useful way of looking at peacemaking, though not as analytically available or as useful as looking at peace as the absence of war.[52]

The Report on the Commission on Proposals for the National Academy of Peace and Conflict may be read in part as a treatise paying tribute to the emerging field of academic peace studies. In addition, peacemaking was seen to encompass more than research; that is, it may be made practical and might continue to be practiced in the ways discovered through the commission.

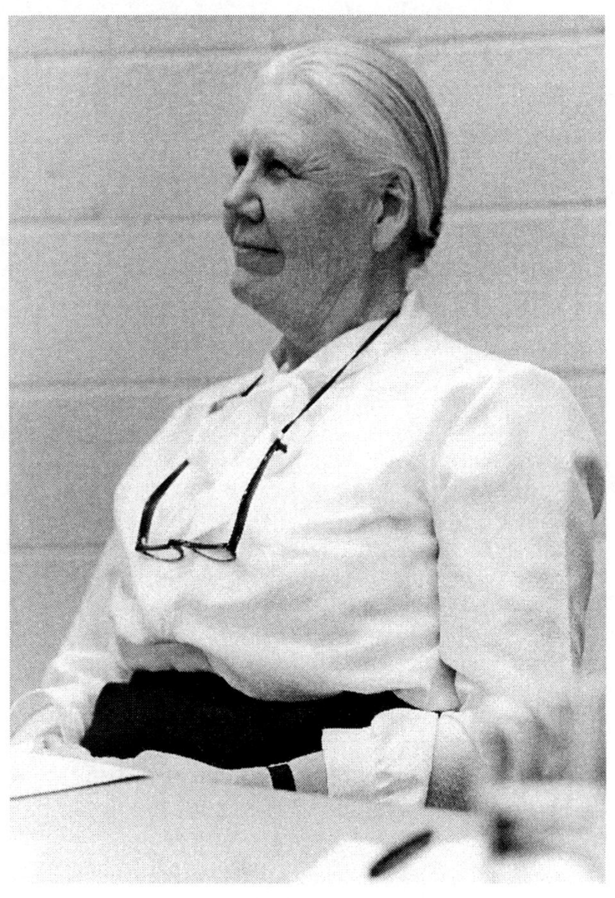

Elise at Dartmouth College in the early 1980s.

The academy, as recommended, was not to have policy or intervention authority. It was to be primarily a graduate academy with a focus on international concerns. Recognized as a central tenet was that the skills of conflict resolution, negotiation, mediation and arbitration can be taught. It was hoped that the academy would rectify the gap between research and peacemaking.

Elise believed that her appointment to the commission had something to do with her being active in the Democratic Party, though in the years prior to her appointment she had also been engaged with a group campaigning for the academy. This group made recommendations to President Carter for appointments to the commission, and Elise believed some other members may have put her name in. There was an attempt for political balance on the commission, as Elise explained:

> [B]ut you see Carter appointed the commission but Ronald Reagan appointed the actual staff of the Institute and my name went in

> repeatedly to serve on the Board of the USIP but my name never made it to the top. By then I probably had a big FBI file (laughs), and I didn't do dangerous things, but from some perspectives I may have looked dangerous.[53]

Elise was never appointed to the final board of what is now known as the U.S. Institute of Peace, the mission of which encompasses some but not all of what was originally recommended by the commission. She did serve for two years, from 1984 to 1986, on the board of the National Peace Institute Foundation, an organization not formally affiliated with the USIP but that provided support, education and fundraising for projects closely related to the work of the USIP. She has maintained close relations with many who continue to be associated with the USIP and, in a recent letter to Richard Solomon, the president, expressed her

> joy over how USIP has developed since that day in 1981 when we signed the recommendation and proposal to create USIP, though called the U.S. Academy of Peace at the time. It would be interesting if those of us who are left could reconvene ... to review the years and directions and reconsider actually setting up a Peace Academy, to be comparable to the military academies. We have the know-how for that kind of training now, much more than in 1981.[54]

Looking Toward Retirement

By 1985, Elise was ready to retire from Dartmouth and return to Boulder to rejoin Kenneth. Her years at Dartmouth had been for her a continuation of her very busy work life, and she was looking forward to a return to more local work in Boulder and the hoped for slower pace of retirement. Elise recalled happy memories of her teaching at Dartmouth, yet a former student who worked closely with her there mentioned conversations with Elise in which she confessed how difficult it was for her at times. Most of her close associations were with only one or two faculty members in other departments, not in sociology, though she was chair of that department. There was some bickering among members of her department. Her heavy travel schedule combined with her teaching load also often crowded her schedule.

Correspondence between Kenneth and Elise during that time revealed their frank discussion of the options for their living arrangements upon

***Opposite:* Elise retired from Dartmouth and came home to Boulder and to Kenneth in the mid–1980s.**

Elise's return. Prior to this time, the couple had helped to found 624 Pearl, the intentional community in Boulder of mostly retired academics and peace activists. Kenneth wished to continue to live in their house in Boulder, but Elise did not. Kenneth very much wanted to remain in their large home with views of the Boulder mountains from his study where he could keep his large collection of scholarly books. Elise wanted to "downsize" and move. As she wrote to Kenneth:

> I share happy memories of that house, but feel the need to leave it. Let's say its all a part of the difference in our temperaments. It has nothing to do with our love for each other.... [T]he message that has come so clear to me is one of repatterning. Maybe I have five years, maybe 25, but they are to be spent in a different kind of learning-teaching about the human condition than I have been engaged in since 1965. [T]he call is clear.... I would not want a grumpy, deprived-feeling Kenneth to abandon his beloved Willowbrook house! Nor do I want you to expect me to stay there. I would rather be together than separate, but not at the cost of violence to our individual sense of rightness. We must support each other in our differences.... We will spend lots of time together even if we sleep under different roofs.[55]

Kenneth, who had always handled the family finances, was experiencing intense conflict with the University of Colorado over some monetary terms of his retirement. The university had withdrawn its support of his office, and he had lost a grant from the Ford Foundation, which had helped him continue his work. Concern over the financial implications of their investment in the condominium was partly responsible for his wish to remain in their Willowbrook home. The FIR experiment, as they called it (Friends for Interdependent Retirement), was a risky endeavor at that time and he was urging Elise to consider selling their share in it. Kenneth was concerned about their ability to leave a financial legacy to their children. As Russell pointed out, "[W]hen my Dad died, I taught my mother how to balance a checkbook,"[56] as Elise had never handled any of this side of their marital and family life, even during her years away at Dartmouth.

Elise was very determined to move into the apartment, realizing that this meant that she and Kenneth might have to continue to live separately, as they had since 1978 when she moved to Hanover. She offered to sell the Waterfall, their family cabin, and the Hermitage as well, so that he could continue his work. The Boulding children suggested that Elise go ahead and move into the apartment, suggesting that Kenneth would follow. And this is what happened. In the end, Kenneth and Elise both moved into 624

Pearl and remained there together until his death early in 1993. In a letter to Elise early in 1985 he stated his reasons for acquiescing to her wishes:

> As Edward Hicks [a Quaker] says in his journal "when you have a determined woman it is very important that she be right," and I sure hope you are right in spite of all my misgivings. And as I love my wife more than I love my house or anything in it, I'm prepared to make this sacrifice and condone this folly. And if it doesn't work out as you expect I promise I will refrain from saying "I told you so." And if it does work out [I'll] admit it. You can't ask for more than that![57]

Elise later recalled, with a laugh, how happy Kenneth was that he had moved.

Chapter 11

Journey to the "Country of Old Age"

Upon her return to Boulder in 1985, Elise picked up some threads of activist work she had begun earlier and engaged in some new projects, reflecting an intentional wish on her part to do more local work. However, she was still heavily involved in international work, culminating in her 1988 election as Secretary-General of IPRA at the general conference in Rio de Janeiro, Brazil.

Elise continued her work with the World Policy Institute (formerly known as the Institute for World Order), working closely with Saul Mendlovitz, Professor of Peace and World Orders Studies at Rutgers University. Elise was elected to the board of directors of the organization beginning in 1973, serving until 1987 with the Reverend William Sloan Coffin, Richard Falk of Princeton and Father Theodore Hesburgh, the president of Notre Dame University as other members of the board.

Saul Mendlovitz became co-director of an international consortium of scholars and political figures known as the World Orders Models Project, of which Elise was a vital member. WOMP was based at the World Policy Institute in New York. Other affiliate organizations included the Centre for the Study of Developing Societies in India and the World Orders Studies Project in Tokyo. The aim of the group was using interdisciplinary research, education, dialogue and action to create conditions for world peace. WOMP first met in Delhi in 1968. The ultimate goal was transformative education. Participants actively promoted ideas relating to shared global values based on equality, justice and ecological sustainability. As the group evolved, the idea of a global civilization became their hallmark.

Elise was involved in several of the major projects of WOMP, the work of these became major focus of the group in the mid–1980s. One of the projects in which she was involved was WOMP's Committee for a Just Peace, organized in 1985 in support of the UN International Year of Peace (1986). The committee's purpose was to encourage those in civil society and political decision makers to participate in processes designed to create world conditions for a just peace. In the early 1990s, WOMP developed a working program with the United Nations, hiring an executive consultant and engaging scholars, UN officials and "engaged citizens from civil society" in seminars whose central features included "the exploration of 'geogovernance as a counter to the geopolitics especially as it relates to a politics promoting humane governance.'"[1] In 1990, WOMP received the UNESCO prize for Peace Education, awarded in Paris.

Another project with which Elise was engaged, beginning in the mid–1980s, was EXPRO (Exploratory Project on the Conditions of Peace). Meeting every few months for the next five years and using Elise's wide network to engage ever more scholars, the group published a book in 1991 entitled *Conditions of Peace: An Inquiry*.[2] Their purpose was to "break through the strictures that the Cold War had placed upon political imagination" and try to figure out what a *real* new order would look like.[3] The group included, true to the aim of Elise, peace researchers, social scientists and activists. Elise helped to distribute the book but did not contribute directly to its writing. Publications of hers at this time reflect the influence of the work of EXPRO.

True to her intention of reengaging in local work upon her return to Boulder, Elise went on the board of the local parenting center in Boulder, an agency devoted to networking, educating and advocating on issues related to children and childrearing. She also became an active member of a contemplation group which met regularly at the Rocky Mountain Peace and Justice Center in Boulder, directed by LeRoy Moore, who described their meetings:

> [A] campus minister [and a few more] of us got together and decided we would meet every Monday afternoon and we would create a contemplation and social justice group, the Monday Group. I knew her [Elise] by reputation and I was attracted to the idea. We got so big we split.... [W]e would meet one and one half hours and the first half in silence.... We would spend the last forty-five minutes in conversation and that's how I got to know her. We met from [19]85 to [19]93, every Monday afternoon for all those years. She was busy but this was a high priority for her. We focused on our personal lives, on social justice issues, we sometimes did

Elise in the late 1980s.

projects to help the homeless ... in that first year we took on a project of having a series of speakers talk abut nonviolence. Elise was one, Daniel Berrigan and Matthew Fox were others.[4]

Elise also reengaged her work with the Colorado Women's Forum, an organization she had founded earlier with Ann White, a fellow Boulder Quaker who had also helped the Bouldings to found the 624 Pearl community, shortly before Elise left for Dartmouth. The Women's Forum was, as Elise's 1977 president's report indicates, a "New Girl's Network" (a play on the words "old boys' network"). Launched in 1976, its purpose was to bring together women of diverse accomplishments and to provide them with a forum for the exchange of ideas. The founding was assisted by the chapter in New York, and, at the time of its founding, the Colorado group was the only other forum besides the New York one and a chapter in North Carolina. In her report, Elise urged the group to speak out on issues and to take positions in accordance with the original mission.

The reason for the forum's founding lay partly in the writing and speaking Elise was doing at that time on issues related to women and their roles in society and her recognition of the need for affirmation of their accomplishments. The organization continued after her move to Dartmouth, yet the activist component her legacy left did not continue during her absence. According to Ruth Correll, former mayor of Boulder and a friend of Elise's who became acquainted with her through their involvement in the Women's Forum in the late 1980s and who remains a member, though not active,

> [This was] not a typical Elise thing to do ... a national women's organization [that] is an exclusive group.... [I]t picks people to be members who have done something of note ... [and are] chosen to get in.... [It is] kind of elite, and another friend and I wonder if this

is what Elise meant for it to be when she got it started, and I doubt it is ... something which recognized and elevated and excluded by virtue of what someone had done.... I think she wanted recognition for capable women.[5]

Quaker Connections

Elise reconnected with her local Boulder Quaker Meeting upon her return from Dartmouth, though she was never as involved in that group as she had been in previous meetings in other places the family had lived. Her chief involvement in Boulder was to continue to teach Quaker Sunday School, called First Day School as a term used by Friends. One member of the meeting remarked that Elise had managed to revitalize a flagging program. Elise became clerk (Quaker term for chair) of the committee in 1988.

Other Quaker activities for Elise during that time included consultation with the Denver office of the American Friends Service Committee, a return to her local AFSC work that had begun years before in Ann Arbor. The controversies surrounding AFSC and its mission soon reached the Inter-Mountain Yearly Meeting of Friends, which included the local Boulder Meeting within its constituency. In 1987, a proposal circulated among Quakers asking that the Inter-Mountain Yearly Meeting withdraw from AFSC, as the organization was "not sufficiently representative of the Friends Testimonies."[6] A committee of concern of the Yearly Meeting was established on which Elise continued to serve until the 1990s, even as the formal committee was laid down in 1989. Because of the concern that AFSC had laid down much of its historical service work, the committee evolved into one entitled IMYM-AFSC Joint Service Projects and was designed to bring life back into the AFSC and in its mission toward service. Because of her active involvement, Elise was nominated to represent the Yearly Meeting on the AFSC Corporation in Philadelphia beginning in 1987, and she served until the mid–1990s. Shortly thereafter, in 1996, the Boulder Meeting appointed a committee devoted to issues around the AFSC, and Elise served on this, though not as clerk.

In 1995, shortly before her move to Boston, Elise joined the Committee for the Quaker United Nations office. QUNO, located in New York next to the UN, as an organization has ties to the AFSC and the Friends World Committee for Consultation, the world body of Friends. Its mission is be a resource for the peacebuilding efforts of the United Nations, and it offers, in addition to educational programming and information dissemination, opportunities for informal meetings of emissaries from disputing countries away from the public space of the UN building. Elise ended her tenure on the QUNO board in 1998.

Elise later reflected on her varied experiences in working with the AFSC, beginning with her helping to start the local office in Ann Arbor, when the family was living there, and with other Quaker groups:

> Dayton, Ohio, was the regional office then, and so I would fly in in the morning and fly back at night because I had kids at home, babies at home, and so they [these activities] were important in the sense of policy decisions but never any substantive project involved in doing, always just a committee of support and information and ideas, but neither [with] the AFSC nor the QUNO board or the regional board did I ever feel I was *making* something.[7]

Elise was being modest in her statements of her work with the organization. In 1990, AFSC, as a group that had formerly won the prize in 1947 for their peace and service work in post–World War I Germany, nominated her for the Nobel Peace Prize. The three page nominating letter to then Director of the Nobel Institute Jakob Sverdrup was written by Asia Bennett, serving as the AFSC Executive Secretary. Elise was at that time the Secretary-General of IPRA. Major accomplishments of IPRA were cited in the letter, with a special tribute to Elise's work in stimulating and drawing upon the work of scholars in developing countries. Elise's work in peace education, consultative work with UNESCO and UNITAR (UN Institute on Training and Research), her work in futures and her advocating for the contributions of women were noted. The letter concluded with two statements previously written by Elise:

> Even more important is to acknowledge the core fact that peace has continually been made, moment by moment, in the course of the daily affairs of women, men and states. Peace never exists as a condition, only as a process.

The nomination committee's letter concluded with these words:

> On the strength of her record as a champion of international peace research, of peace education, and her work for the human rights of women and children, the American Friends Service Committee takes satisfaction in submitting the nomination of Dr. Elise Boulding for the Nobel Prize in 1990.[8]

Elise was not given the award that year. The recipient was Mikhail Gorbachev.

In July 1990, Elise was invited to play a special role in the first International Conference for Quaker Women, held at the Woodbrooke Conference Center in England. She was invited, according to her letter of invitation, to become part of a conference "with all participants encouraged to contribute their insights, gifts and leadership."[9] Elise gave a major address at this meeting, and devoted her talk to the story of the life of Anne Downer, an early Friend and a member of the group known in England as the Publishers of the Truth. In the 1660s, Anne Downer, along with other English Quakers, ministered in English prisons. Elise wove in her story the themes of caring and nurturing. Her words included the statement that we have to "change the rules" for such work to include visioning and new social skills and spaces.[10] During her trip to England, Elise also was invited to speak with a group convened by the British counterpart to AFSC, Quaker Peace and Service (co-recipients of the 1947 Nobel Prize), and the London Diplomat group to speak on futures studies.

International Peace Research Association

The fall of 1989 saw Elise and Kenneth serving together as Visiting Professors at George Mason University in Virginia, just outside Washington, D.C., in their Center for Conflict Analysis and Resolution. But the project which probably took up more time for Elise than any other during the years between her move back to Boulder and Kenneth's death in early 1993 was the assumption of the International Secretariat of IPRA. She was elected in 1988 and held the post until 1991.

Elise was able to get office space for her work with the organization from the University of Colorado and hired Marty Gonzales, a sociology graduate student, as her office assistant, with help also from Anna Spradlin, who later wrote her doctoral dissertation on Elise's leadership rhetoric style.[11] Several others helped her on a part-time basis. According to Marty, much of the job of administrative assistant involved updating archaic address files of IPRA's current and former members, computerizing them, and keeping track of IPRA's voluminous correspondence among international peace researchers. Marty discussed the reasons she believed Elise was elected to be chair:

> There was some discussion that it wasn't right for Elise to have that secretariat in that time period, because the concern [was that] it was being run by Americans. But the only reason it went to her was because they knew she wouldn't do that. Other people might ... have taken over.[12]

In 1990, the World Order Models Project had sponsored an international conference in Cairo, Egypt. Out of that conference arose concerns about the growing crisis in the Middle East. At the urging of Saul Mendlovitz, Palestinian activist Mubarak Awad, and peace scholars including Elise, Paul Smoker and Louis Kriesberg and spurred on by the outbreak of the Gulf War, IPRA formed a 26 person Middle East Commission, with Elise elected Secretary and Project Chair, to devote substantial scholarly pursuit to the "identification of the most productive role for the United Nations in the future and to encourage governments and NGOs in the region and in the West to strengthen problem-solving."[13] The understanding was that the Gulf War represented to the scholars of peace studies "an application of out-moded national security paradigms/principles that rest on the immediate exercise of superior military force."[14] The commission included nine representatives from the Middle East, eight from developing countries outside the Middle East and nine from Euro-America. The idea was to stimulate new visions of social and structural arrangements, taking into account not only regional needs but global ones as well, based on shared values of a new world order based on law and human rights.

The commission was launched in January 1991 and laid down its work in 1994. Elise edited its series of papers, which eventually became *Building Peace in the Middle East: Challenges from States and Civil Societies.*[15] In her editor's introduction, Elise made reference to the dependence on the world to access to the region's oil reserves and asked whether the peace research community had any concepts that could be used in this or future conflicts. Models were offered utilizing newer, more inclusive definitions of peace and taking into account sustainability and democratization with the goal of working in solidarity with the people of the region. She concluded her report with the aims of the project being peacemaking and peacebuilding in addition to peacekeeping, borrowing these terms from the vocabulary of the emerging peace education field, and presented the spectrum of approaches to understanding peace as a concept, from a view meaning the absence of conflict to a more tranformative approach linking peace to healing and social justice.[16]

In an address to the Peace Studies Association meeting at the University of Colorado in 1992, Elise spoke of the progress of the commission. Sixty papers had been prepared up that point in time, forty of which were coming from scholars outside the West and Europe. In an eerily prophetic of the following decade, Elise maintained that, in the perceptions of people of the developing world, states in the Middle East were "fellow victims of a typical pattern of U.S. imperialism."[17] The commission called for the active participation and empowerment of local institutions in the region, both governmental and nongovernmental, to devote themselves to new visions for problem-solving and away from militarization. It also urged groups to work together across state and regional boundaries, including a slowing of the regional and world arms trade. A role for the UN as an interface between various civil groups working for peace in the region and governments was suggested. Elise argued for the UN to regain its neutrality in creating conditions for Iraq's long-term reintegration into the community of nations and stated that this should include Israel's role in the international community as well. The importance of globally re-legitimizing the UN was stressed. Elise argued for the importance of tapping the creative energies of Arab-Muslim and Israeli colleagues to envision a different future. She spoke of her own visions as an "outsider," listing her hopes for events to unfold in the early decades of the next century:

> A demilitarized Middle East in a demilitarized world with highly developed regionalism and localism, and with a strong family-community base for social and economic development. In the long run, the West needs the diversity of cultures the Middle East has to offer, just as the Middle East needs the diversity of cultures the West and the rest of the two-thirds World have to offer. In the sustainable society of the future, diversity, mutual respect and an openness to new learnings will be the keys to continuing human development.[18]

In 1989, during her tenure as International Secretary, Elise founded the IPRA Foundation, an outgrowth of her concerns for the lag between peace research in the West and that of the developing world, particularly acute for women. The foundation offers stipends and scholarships, upon application, for research and to enable participants, especially from globally impoverished areas, to attend international IPRA gatherings. Elise served as the foundation's first president, a post now held by Ian Harris of the University of Wisconsin at Milwaukee.

Early on, Elise's approach differed somewhat from others within the peace research movement, many of whom were men whose aim was to quantify the study of the prevention of war. In a 1981 publication for the *UNESCO Yearbook on Peace and Conflict Studies*, she wrote of the completion of her recent survey of women peace researchers revealing that gender had played a major role in the setting of priorities among peace researchers. Women believed that too much of the focus within the peace movement was on the technical aspects of disarmament and not enough on the social aspects of violence. Two years later, at an IPRA meeting, a delegation of women, led by Elise, read a statement to the plenary session addressing the failure of the male leadership in addressing the more complex structural issues surrounding violence, including the oppression of women.[19] Peace efforts must take into account, the group espoused, the issues of freedom from want as well as freedom from war. In an address to COPRED soon after in 1987 in Milwaukee, Elise spoke of peace education as "pioneering" much of the recent peace research. Her talk reflected her fervent wish for an integrative, nondichotomized view if the relationship among research, education and action. Indirectly citing the work of Columbia University peace educator Betty Reardon, Elise noted that peace education "is not a step-child between research and action, but the critical interface between them."[20] Later in a book chapter written in 1992, Elise wrote of the marginalization of women within the peace research movement. Peace education, as she noted, has conceptually been relegated to the "women's sphere," a view that Elise believed contributed also to the marginalization of educational efforts in peace.

Friends Peace Team

Always connecting the local and the global, Elise began a newsletter in the early 1990s to network between international groups doing peace teams work. She believed that those called to serve as peacekeepers in international areas of tension needed the support and training that Friends could offer. Grasping a need, visioning and then creating the network for it, Elise connected those interested in serving with those who supported the idea in order to better understand the concept of nonviolent peacemaking and its application in various settings, given the new world order since the end of the Cold War. In one early newsletter, she advocated for active networking among NGOs, those connected not only with peace and disarmament but scientific organizations, health and welfare groups and religious transnationals as well.[21]

The first meeting of the Coordinating Council of the Friends Peace Team Project was held in 1993. It included forty Friends from around the U.S. Quaker Yearly Meetings that were asked to send representatives. The FPT project was designed, as Elise wrote later, to be a "practical application of our [Quaker] Peace Testimony."[22] It represented an active effort to connect Friends who found themselves called to serve in areas of tension both at home and abroad with opportunities for training and linking of availability of service opportunities. Though there was not total consensus among the founding national council members, of which Elise was a part, on the exact nature of the concept of the FPT, as Elise wrote, Peace Teams were groups

> formed in ... local Meetings for training in the skills of nonviolent action and peacebuilding, in order to work in partnership with local residents in areas of violence and deprivation. After "apprenticing" themselves locally, some Friends might feel called to work in teams of situations of violence abroad, but only after they had learned to cope with violence close to home.[23]

According to Elise, locals doing peacework do not always see the connections between the work they are doing and global peacemaking, and therefore networking can result in peacemakers feeling less isolated.

From the beginning, the FPT project was not designed to become a new global peace service but to partner with other groups doing international peace work, some of them Quaker, some not. In addition, early on, the FPT coordinating council decided to support a newly emerging program in Quaker volunteer service, as it was seeing humanitarian work as another aspect of active peacemaking with the view that the AFSC's service opportunities had markedly declined. As Elise concluded in an article written for a publication put out by the New England office of AFSC, "the intention [of FPT was] to bring Friends into more active relationships with their surrounding communities, in a process of mutual learning."[24]

Back to Japan and Beyond

The summer of 1992 saw both Kenneth and Elise heading to Japan and the Aoyama Gakuin University's School of International Politics, Economics and Business to co-teach a course. Elise facilitated an imaging workshop and lectured on futures and on peace cultures. Her recent writings at that time showed the development of her ideas that would later bear fruit in *Cultures of Peace.* Elise continued to do imaging workshops with Warren Ziegler of the Futures Invention Associates in Denver whenever asked, as the work the two began in the 1980s continued well into the next decade.

During the year 1995, Elise was nominated as the Judith Weller Harvey Quaker scholar at Guildford College in North Carolina. She spent two days there, giving lectures and meeting with students and faculty, sharing her life's work and her spiritual journey.

In 1995 Elise attempted to revive the Peace Studies Network of the Friends Association for Higher Education, the organization representing

Quaker institutions of higher education and Quakers who teach in universities and colleges. Attending the annual gathering, she was hopeful that this might serve as a resource for the Friends Peace Teams. This did not bear fruit to the extent of which she had hoped.

In 1997, Elise gave a workshop at the annual gathering of the Yearly Meeting of New England Quakers at Bowdoin College in Maine. Her workshop was on imaging a world at peace, a continuation of the facilitation of futures imaging she had begun many years before. In addition, the focus of her work at that gathering was to begin a network of people who were interested in continuing to dialogue and interact on issues related to the mission of the Friends Peace Teams project. Out of that initial meeting, a network of over seventy participants began to meet and correspond. The network was maintained for over two years, kept mostly active by the work of Elise until she left the national coordinating council as the New England representative. In the meantime, the national FPT project had involved itself in a major peacemaking effort in the Great Lakes region of Africa, culminating in the sending in 1999 of an international team to join with locals to rebuild churches and residences destroyed during the civil war in Burundi. Several months later a team of facilitators trained in the Alternatives to Violence Program, a nonviolence training program for prisons started by Quakers, partnered with local trainers in Uganda, to facilitate a series of workshops in local prisons and community based organizations.

Grief and Loss

Kenneth became ill in the early 1990s. As his health declined, Elise gave up virtually all of her outside activities to care for him during the last year of his life. It was in the last years of their life together that their relationship reached its ripe flowering. This became evident to family members and to those who surrounded them, the fruition of "their love made visible." To Elise, these were special and precious years. Family members described his dying as a beautiful time of togetherness, one in which Kenneth was able to be open and vulnerable, to show his love in ways he had not been able to in the long course of his life. Kenneth died in the spring of 1993, and, in the fall, the thought came to Elise that "I am what is left of us," as she realized she must carry on the work that they had initiated together over fifty years previously. For years afterward, Elise was not able to speak of him without tears. Though she had put off any active involvements during her care for Kenneth, she continued as a Senior Fellow of

Elise and Russell Boulding at the opening of the Kenneth Boulding Memorial Library, Antioch College, 1994.

the Dickey Center for International Understanding at Dartmouth, her tenure having begun in 1992 and ending in 1996.

Peace Council

In 1995 Elise was invited to sit on the Interfaith Peace Council as a Quaker participant, the council being an offshoot of the 1993 World Parliament of Religions. The council's first meeting was at Windsor Castle in England, in November of that year. The original mission of the council, which included a core membership of the world's religious and spiritual leaders as an interfaith collaborative, including the promotion of peace and social justice, environmental sustainability, the overcoming of interreligious misunderstanding, together with the vision of shared responsibility for the people of the world.[25] Writing in her journal at the time of the initial meeting, Elise wrote of her hope that in sitting on the council she could help with local and global connections as "most religious leaders do not know how to do local peace work."[26] In 1996 the group met in Chiapas, Mexico. Her journal entry from Chiapas read:

> [H]owever inadequate, it [the council] represents an effort to translate our deepest spiritual awareness into an interfaith presence that represents love and caring that transcends the institutional hierarchies of each religion.... God knows the world needs this. Where is the love going to come from to transform human violence into peaceful societies, if not from a more developed human spirituality?[27]

Issues at the forefront of the 1996 meeting included dialogue between China and Tibet, facilitated by the presence of the Dalai Lama, and interfaith efforts toward the reunification of Korea, as well as the abolition of land mines, Elise being aware that this was the only interfaith group working on this latter issue. The Earth Charter as a paradigm for ecological sustainability was endorsed as well.

The third annual meeting of the Council was held in 1997 in Victoria, British Columbia. Elise continued her involvement with the Council for the next few years but then told the group that she could only attend meetings if they were held in the United States, as she stopped foreign travel as the century waned. She later joked that "they wouldn't take me off of it, even though I couldn't make all the meetings!" The meeting in 2000, which Elise attended, took place at the Thomas Merton Center in Kentucky.

Move East

Elise had originally planned on staying indefinitely in Boulder, keeping up her active networks in Colorado and engaging in the local and international projects of which she was an integral part. Yet her family in the early 1990s was urging her to consider moving closer to Christine, her daughter, who lived in Wayland, outside of Boston. In addition, Elise was continuing to grieve the recent death of Kenneth and felt a need to be nearer to family members.

In 1996, she made the decision to move to the Boston area. Her son-in-law built an addition on to their home as her living quarters. Elise agreed to move, realizing that she needed to do it while she was still in reasonably good health. In November of 1996, following a week of spiritual retreat at the Sisters of Transfiguration Monastery as well as the trip to Chiapas with the Interfaith Peace Council, she settled in her new home, intending to stay there indefinitely. She began putting down roots and rebuilding her all-important networks. In retrospect, she realized the move was harder on her than she thought it would be. However, she quickly involved herself with many activities, mostly local, as she intentionally began doing less traveling.

Much of Elise's activity in the Boston area was facilitated by her involvement with the Boston Research Center for the 21st Century, an organization founded by Soka Gakkai International, a Japanese Buddhist organization devoted to dialoguing and education in faith-based peacemaking. She was honored by the BRC with their first Global Citizens Award in 1995. The BRC and its director, Virginia Straus, have offered her numerous speaking and writing opportunities and have facilitated her connecting with other peace academics and activists throughout the region.

Her Quaker contacts have been valuable, as she has involved herself in the activities of the Wellesley Friends Meeting, including attending a monthly worship group at the nearby Norfolk prison and serving on the peace committee of the Meeting. Other local networking has included speaking engagements and ongoing consultations at several local colleges, including Wellesley, Harvard and Brandeis University. She is delighted when invited by various women's and church groups to give talks on peace. Each year Elise is asked by Professor Gordon Fellman to address his classes in peace studies at Brandeis, which she greatly enjoys.

Elise helped to begin another contemplation group, the members of which come mainly from the academic communities with which she has been involved in the Boston area. This group began meeting at the Cambridge Friends Meeting and now meets regularly in Elise's apartment at North Hill.

Elise has become increasingly interested in the concept of restorative justice, having been energized by ongoing involvement with the Boston Theological Institute, which is engaged in research and teaching on the subject. As she wrote in *Cultures of Peace*, the creation of Truth and Reconciliation commissions in countries such as South Africa and other community-based activities have

> led to a realization of how much violence [has been] generated by the criminal justice system, the celebrated "rule of law" imposed by western occupying powers on national and local communities

> during the period of colonial expansion from the 1500's on.... [Such a movement as restorative justice draws on] the most humane of discarded traditional systems of justice, systems and practices oriented to the well-being of both victims and victimizers and answering to the need for healing and restoration of broken relationships.[28]

Home at North Hill, Needham, Massachusetts, in 2003.

Elise believes that the western judicial system has much to learn from the traditional practices of indigenous societies, located throughout the world.

Two other local initiatives in which Elise involved herself soon after she arrived in Massachusetts were serving on the Wayland Council on Aging, culminating in a local celebration of the accomplishments of area senior citizens at the public library, and serving on the board of the local historical society. In addition, during 1999, she was appointed to the town's Y2K committee. As a member, she took it upon herself to engage local residents, particularly the elderly, in an educational and networking effort around potential problems related to Y2K, hoping as a result that neighbors would reach out to each other in assistance should there be utility and water shortages as a result of computer breakdowns. As it turned out, the anticipated problems did not occur, but Elise believes her efforts were worthwhile.

By mid–year 2000, Elise was becoming increasingly concerned about her growing deafness. She had recently had additional ear surgery and had had a pacemaker inserted for continuing heart difficulties. In addition, she was feeling increased isolation due to her declining energy and concomitant difficulties with local travel, having confined herself to driving mostly within an immediate radius of her apartment during the day. By the summer, she had decided to move into North Hill, a local life-time care facility, located in Needham, about twenty minutes from her former home in Wayland. A group of Quaker residents, who are also members of the Wellesley Friends Meeting, hold regular meetings for worship at the facility. The existence of this group made it easier for her to make the transition. In August, she moved and began yet again to put down roots. And she gave up driving.

Elise has kept up her contacts with the Women's International League for Peace and Freedom, attending local chapter meetings when she is given a ride. In addition, she has been working with colleague Nancy Wrenn with the Coalition for a Strong UN, a Boston based group and with WAND, Women's Action for New Directions. Nancy Wrenn interviewed Elise for a video based on her life that recently aired on a local Boston public television station.

Ever involved in ongoing dialoguing, Elise is currently participating, in addition to the contemplation group meeting monthly in her apartment, with a Friday night "Free Flow Discussion" group at North Hill, composed partly of residents and a group of women Friends from the Wellesley Meeting, which meets two times a month at North Hill. Elise has consciously eschewed, to her own surprise given her history, any continued responsibility for "making things happen," stating that "it makes me all uptight and nervous at this time of my life."[29] However, if asked and it is convenient, Elise readily agrees to do imaging workshops and to talk about a culture of peace. She joins local peace activists, among them many Quakers, for a weekly peace vigil on the town green in Needham.

Continuing her long history of active involve involvement in peace research, Elise recently engaged a Brandeis graduate student to help her find sources on NGO involvement in the country of Iraq. She sits on the board of the Peace Abbey, the organization hosting the New England Peace Studies Association, which Elise helped to re-invigorate with the help of Brandeis and Tufts scholars. The Peace Abbey periodically invites neighbors, students, activists and scholars to "tea with Elise." This has proved a popular pastime, usually involving about twenty participants.

Family continues to be of paramount importance to Elise. She keeps up voluminous correspondence with her sixteen grandchildren, their spouses and the growing cadre of great-grandchildren, and she eagerly looks forward to the Boulding clan gathering in 2004 on Cape Cod.

Recently Elise, reflecting on her long life, queried, "[H]ow did I do all of that? I am puzzled," looking back at her own life dispassionately, true to her vocation as a sociologist. As her physical activities have markedly declined, her spiritual endeavors have kept pace, as she keeps to the vision given to her some twenty-five years earlier as the trajectory for her life. Elise has often spoke of her "journey into old age" and of her "entering the country of the old" as an "exciting venture." As always, she continues to make sense out of her experiences and to impart them with meaning. Just prior to her last move into North Hill in the spring of 2000, Elise wrote in her journal:

> This is what the "heavenward reaching" of my message back in 1978 was all about! To clear and cleanse the mind of all its turbulence and rise to a new level of awareness of our relationship with all creation. We are such an unevenly developed species—so far to go—and the culture of peace decade gives real opportunities to deal with our individual and social turbulences and come to a new place. I love the image of each apparently solid object constantly changing molecules with its surroundings especially that every 2 years the human body has replaced all its molecules—how evanescent [*sic*] is solidity![30]

Epilogue

It has been an honor and a great privilege for me to be able to work closely with Elise Boulding since our initial contacts in early 1997. Many biographers do not have the opportunity of direct engagement with their subjects, as they are often long deceased when their life stories are published. I have benefited from innumerable hours of delightful formal interviews and quite informal contacts with Elise over the course of the research and writing of this book. I have had ample opportunity to, in the words of Leon Edel, try and understand the "figure under the carpet," so important in biographical work so that the subject becomes more real. My deepening friendship with Elise, whom I had not met prior to beginning my research, has been a continual source of joy for me.

Studying and writing about a living subject has not been without its challenges, however. Though I do believe, as does biographer Catherine Bowen, that "being a little in love with your subject" is a good thing, difficulties ensue as to how to sensitively portray conflicts within the life of the individual, so necessary for a true picture, yet at times so painful for the people involved. Conflict is essential to any biography. Without it a subject's life story either becomes so dry as to be of little interest or too full of adulation by the biographer as to be unbelievable.

One major challenge of this work was to do justice to the life of Elise Boulding with its many facets: academic, family, Quaker, wife, activist and feminist. My challenge was to integrate these facets, to make the story into that which could be seen holistically, yet also portray its distinct phases. Though certain things have, regrettably, been left out, it is true that any biography leaves in its legacy more stories untold.

I was intrigued during the course of my research on Elise's life to understand how she was able to accomplish so many things. What factors contributed to her extraordinary ability to get things done? My work has led me to the conclusion that several things have helped in this. As a former student of Elise's told me, "she took big strides," both physically and metaphorically. Her steps have been long and purposeful, with nary a wasted moment. This continues to be true, even as her steps have slowed. Blessed with a great deal of self-confidence and a high energy level, she has, throughout her life, overextended herself and yet rarely failed to meet her commitments. She is highly organized, and her promptness is a virtue and an expectation.

One of her sons told me that he believes that certain qualities of impatience and a quickness to judge are related to Elise's Norwegian heritage and that she has fought to keep these under control all of her life. He remarked that she has had the ability to get things "up and running" and then disengage herself at appropriate times. Elise was willing to take on jobs that others might eschew, if she believed that in the long run the projects were worthwhile. Her outstanding legacy is her commitment to intentional connectedness. A colleague remarked to me that her most important book is her address book.

Along with Elise's strength of character is a certain vulnerability, a need to be needed. Despite her charisma and her international reputation, she is easily approachable. I saw often how young people would gather around her at conferences and speaking events, particularly young adult women. She has enjoyed very much the honors and acclaim bestowed upon her, yet has maintained an almost childlike sense of humility and wonder at being so singled out.

"Her gift is her ability to integrate everyday life and scholarship.... [S]he applies her intelligence and imagination to everything within view. A feminist to the marrow of her bone, she refuses to dichotomize, as some recent 'feminists' do. She is a presence, not just a rhetorical statement as is the case with so many people committed to a cause." This statement, by fellow peace activist and academic Michael True, may be said to sum up the qualities that describe Elise.

Yet, as with any attempt to depict a life, there is more. This book has enumerated the highlights of a long and rich life devoted to educating for a better world. Its limitations are in the necessity to make linear what essentially needs to be seen as a hologram. For if we metaphorically slice any part of the life of Elise Boulding, we inevitably see it all before us. The themes and patterns of her life weave and interweave into a rich tapestry, grounded in her constant sense of the importance of working to make connections between people, between the local and the global and between what is now and what will be possible in the years to come.

Chapter Notes

Introduction

1. Giffin, Holly. Personal interview, July 15, 1999.

2. See Harris, Ian M. "Editor's introduction to issue." *Peace Education in a Postmodern World* 71, no. 71 (1996): 1–12; Harris, Ian M. *Peace Education*. Jefferson, NC: McFarland, 1988; Kreidler, William. *Creative Conflict Resolution: More than 200 Activities for Keeping Peace in the Classroom*. Glenview, IL: Good Year Books, 1984; Lantieri, Linda and Janet Patti. *Waging Peace in Our Schools*. Boston: Beacon Press, 1996; Prutzman, Priscilla, Lee Stern, Burger M. Leonard, and Gretchen Bodenhamer. *The Friendly Classroom for a Small Planet*. Philadelphia: New Society Publishers, 1988; Reardon, Betty A. *Comprehensive Peace Education*. New York and London: Teachers College, 1988. Stomfay-Stitz, Aline. *Peace Education in America, 1828–1990: Sourcebook for Education and Research*. Metuchen, NJ: Scarecrow Press, 1993.

3. Peace Education Commission of the International Peace Research Association. "Peace Education Miniprints." Malmo, Sweden: R and D Group, School of Education, 1997.

4. See Galtung, J. *Peace: Research-Education-Action: Essays in Peace Research*. Vol. 1. Copenhagen: Christian Ejlers, 1975; Harle, V., ed. *Essays in Peace Studies*. Tempere, Finland: Tempere Peace Research Institute, 1987; Harris, Ian M. *Peace Education*. Jefferson, NC: McFarland and Co., 1988.; Kurtz, Lester. "Peace Studies: A Brief Sketch." Bethel, KS: Peace Studies Association Meeting, Bethel College, 1998.

5. Reardon, Betty A. *Comprehensive Peace Education*. New York and London: Teachers College, 1988, preface.

6. UNESCO. *UNESCO Yearbook on Peace and Conflict Studies*. Westport, CT: Greenwood Press, 1981.

7. Galtung, Johan. *Peace: Research-Education-Action: Essays in Peace Research*. Vol. 1. Copenhagen: Christian Ejlers, 1975; Harle, V., ed. *Essays in Peace Studies*. Tempere, Finland: Tempere Peace Research Institute, 1987; Kurtz, Lester. "Peace Studies: A Brief Sketch." Bethel, KS: Peace Studies Association Meeting, Bethel College, 1998; Stomfay-Stitz, Aline. *Peace Education in America, 1828–1990: Sourcebook for Education and Research*. Metuchen, NJ: Scarecrow Press, 1993.

8. Galtung, 1975; Kurtz, 1998.

9. Adams, Judith Porter. *Peacework: Oral Histories of Women Peace Activists*. Boston: Twayne Publishers, 1991.

10. Brock-Utne, Birgit. *Feminist Perspectives on Peace and Peace Education*. New York: Pergamon Press, 1989; Forcey, Linda Rennie. "Women as Peacemakers: Contested Terrain for Feminist Peace Studies." *Peace and Change* 16, no. 4, October 1991: 331–354; Reardon, Betty A. *Comprehensive Peace Education*. New York and London: Teachers College, 1988.; Stomfay-Stitz, Aline. *Peace Education in America, 1828–1990: Sourcebook for Education and Research*. Metuchen, NJ: Scarecrow Press, 1993.

11. Brock-Utne, Birgit. *Educating for Peace: A Feminist Perspective*. New York: Pergamon Press, 1985.

12. UNESCO. *UNESCO Yearbook on Peace*

and Conflict Studies. Westport, CT: Greenwood Press, 1981.

13. Alonso, Harriet Hyman. *Peace as a Woman's Issue: A History of the U.S. Movement for World Peace and Women's Rights*. Syracuse: Syracuse University Press, 1993.

14. Belenky, Mary F., Blythe M. Clinchy, Nancy R. Goldberger, and Jill M. Tarule. *Women's Ways of Knowing: The Development of Self, Voice and Mind*: Basic Books, 1986; Gilligan, Carol. *In a Different Voice: Psychological Theory and Women's Development*. Cambridge, MA: Harvard University Press, 1982; Miller, Jean Baker. *Toward a New Psychology of Women*. Boston: Beacon Press, 1986.

15. Forcey, 1991; Ruddick, Sara. *Maternal Thinking: Toward a Politics of Peace*. Boston: Beacon Press, 1995.

16. Elise and I had a conversation about this following the submission of my research proposal, which included some of this information.

PART I

Chapter 1

1. Norborg, Sverre. *An American Saga*. Minneapolis: Sons of Norway, 1970.

2. Christianson, J.R., ed. *Scandinavians in America: Literary Life*. Decorah, Iowa: Symra Literary Society, 1985.

3. Nelson, O.N., ed. *History of the Scandinavians and Successful Scandinavians in the United States*. Vol. 1. New York: Haskell House, 1969.

4. *Ibid.*

5. Boulding, Elise. Personal interview, June 21 1999.

6. Boulding, Elise. Personal interview, May 28, 1997

7. *Ibid.*

8. *Ibid.*

9. *Mor*, 1981.

10. *Ibid.*

11. *Ibid.*

12. Boulding, Elise. Personal interview, May 28, 1997.

13. Graham, Christine Boulding. Personal Interview, December 8 1999.

14. *Mor*, 1981.

15. EB Journals, November 14, 1974.

16. Boulding, Elise. Personal interview, June 21, 1999.

17. *Ibid.*

18. *Ibid.*

19. *Ibid.*

20. EB archives, Bentley Historical Library, University of Michigan at Ann Arbor, Box 19, "Music Criticism."

Chapter 2

1. "Born Remembering." *One Small Plot of Heaven: Reflections on Family Life by a Quaker Sociologist*. Wallingford, PA: Pendle Hill Press, 1989.

2. *Ibid.*

3. *One Small Plot of Heaven: Reflections on Family Life by a Quaker Sociologist*. Wallingford, PA: Pendle Hill Press, 1989, 50.

4. *Ibid.*, 53.

5. *Ibid.*, 47.

6. Brinton, Howard. *Friends for 300 Years*. Wallingford, PA: Pendle Hill Publications, 1994.

7. Lacey, Paul. *Education and the Inward Teacher*. Pendle Hill Pamphlet #278. Wallingford, PA, Pendle Hill Publications, 1988

8. *Ibid.*, 6.

9. Brinton, *Friends for 300 Years*, 29.

10. From *Fox Journals*, Nickalls, John, ed. in New England Yearly Meeting of the Religious Society of Friends, *Faith and Practice (Book of Discipline)*. Worcester, MA: New England Yearly Meeting, 1985, 183.

11. *Ibid.*

12. *Ibid.*

13. *Ibid.* This information was also given to me by a colleague of Elise's as well as in conversation with Elise.

14. Kerman, Cynthia Earl. *Creative Tension: the Life and Thought of Kenneth Boulding*. Ann Arbor: University of Michigan Press, 1974.

15. *Ibid.*, 144.

16. *Ibid.*

17. *Ibid.*, 290.

18. *Ibid.*, 251.

19. These sonnets were obtained through the services of the Bentley Historical Library at the University of Michigan, E Boulding archives, Box 20, folder marked E Boulding papers 1957.

20. Kerman, 290.

21. Interview at the home of Ann and George Levinger 6-7-99.

22. Johnson, Richard. "The Peacemakers." *Denver Post Magazine* 37, no. 9, March 2 (1986): 10–14.

23. E. Boulding Archives, University of Colorado at Boulder, Box 18, folder 1.

24. Graham, Christine Boulding. Personal Interview, December 8, 1999.

25. Scarecrow Press, scheduled for publication 2001.

26. Boulding, Elise and Boulding, Kenneth. *The Future: Images and Processes*. Thousand Oaks, CA: Sage, 1995.

27. *Ibid.*

28. Eynon, B. and Fishman, E., unpublished interview, Hanover, New Hampshire,

November 1978. EB archives, Bentley Library, University of Michigan, Box 21, folder marked "oral history."

29. Boulding, Elise. "Family Adjustments to the Crises of Wartime Separation and Reunion." *Annals of the American Academy of Political and Social Science*: Symposium on Family Stability, 1950; Hill, Reuben with chapters in collaboration with Elise Boulding. *Families Under Stress*. New York: Macmillan, 1949.

30. Boulding, Elise. Personal interview, May 28, 1997.

31. "Where Is Our Sense of Sin?" *Friends Intelligencer: A Quaker Weekly* 104, June 21 (1947): 320–321.

Chapter 3

1. This quote is from *One Small Plot of Heaven: Reflections on Family Life by a Quaker Sociologist*. Wallingford, PA: Pendle Hill Press, 1989, p. 159. These ideas are also found in an essay "The Family as Practice Ground in Making History: some autobiographical reflections." *The Friendly Woman* 4 no. 2, Fall (1979): 3–6.

2. Graham, Christine Boulding. Personal Interview, December 8, 1999.

3. Giffin, Holly. Personal interview, July 15 1999.

4. *Building a Global Civic Culture: Education for an Interdependent World*. New York: Teachers College Press, 1988.

5. See *Building a Global Civic Culture*, 1988; also *One Small Plot of Heaven*, 1989 and "Enlivening our Social Imagination." In *Citizen Summitry: Keeping the Peace When It Matters Too Much to Be Left to Politicians*, edited by Don and Comstock Carlson, Craig, 309–328: Ark Communications Institute Book, 1986.

6. *One Small Plot of Heaven*, 1989.

7. *The Personhood of Children: Nonviolence and Children in the Technological Society*. Religious Education Committee of Friends General Conference, *Rufus Jones Lecture*. Philadelphia, 1975.

8. *One Small Plot of Heaven*, 1989, 161.

9. *Ibid.*

10. See "Children's Rights." *Human Rights*, November/December (1977): 39–43; "Children's Rights." in *Human Rights and World Order*, edited by Abdul Azziz Said. New Brunswick, NJ: Transaction Books, 1978; *Cultures of Peace: The Other Side of History*. Syracuse: Syracuse University Press, 2000; *Our Children our Partners: A New Vision for Social Action in the 21st Century*. Kelvin Grove, Queensland, Australia: Margaret Fell Bookshop, 1996.

11. EB Archives, Bentley Library, University of Michigan, Box 20, folder marked "Calendars." (undated)

12. Boulding, Russell. Personal interview, June 1997.

13. *Mor: A Memoir of Birgit Marianne Johnsen Biörn-Hansen*. unpublished, 1981.

14. *Ibid.*

15. *One Small Plot of Heaven*, 1989, 118–119.

16. Boulding, Russell. Personal Interview, June 1997.

17. Elise has written extensively on women, nurturing and peacemaking. For further information see "Changing Gender Roles in Familial, Occupational and Civic Settings," in *Society as Educator in an Age of Transition* edited by Kenneth Benne and Steven Tozer. National Society for the Study of Education, 1986; *Cultures of Peace*, 2000; "The Culture of Peace in Everyday Life." *Friends Bulletin* 66, no. 6, April (1988): 86–87. "Feminist Inventions in the Art of Peacemaking." *Peace and Change* 20, no. 4, October (1995): 408–438; "Peace Behaviors in Various Societies," in *From a Culture of War to a Culture of Peace*, edited by UNESCO Peace and Conflict Studies. Paris: UNESCO, 1996; "Peace Culture," in *Encyclopedia of Violence, Peace and Conflict*. Academic Press, 1998; *The Underside of History: A View of Women Through Time*. Revised ed. Vols. 1 and 2. Newbury Park: Sage, 1992; *Women in the Twentieth Century World*. New York: Sage Publications, 1977; *Women the Fifth World*. Edited by H. Morganthau, *Headline Series of the Foreign Policy Association*. New York: The Foreign Policy Association, 1980.

18. *One Small Plot of Heaven*, 160.

19. "Mother, Father, Child: Reflections on the Social Status of Family Roles." *Transition* 27, no. 2, June (1997): 4–6.

20. See *Building a Global Civic Culture*, 1988.

21. *One Small Plot of Heaven*, 163.

22. *Building a Global Civic Culture*, 1988, 35.

23. "The Family as a Small Society." Annual Schumacher Lecture, published by the Schumacher Society, 1982.

Chapter 4

1. She alludes to this in a 1973 letter to Dorothy Steffens, Executive Director of the U.S. Section of the WILPF. EB Archives, University of Colorado at Boulder, Box 11, folders 7/8.

2. Gordon, Frank J. "Brief History of WILPF." Found in archives, University of library at Boulder, in its *Guide to Microfilm Edition*, undated. Gordon quotes from two other sources: Randall, Mercedes. *High Lights in WILPF History from the Hague to Luxembourg 1915–1946*, Philadelphia: WILPF National

Literature Department, 1946, and *Women's International League for Peace and Freedom, 1915–1938: A Venture in Internationalism*, Geneva: WILPF, 1938, 5–7.

3. Gordon, undated.

4. Foster, Catherine. *Women for All Seasons: The Story of the Women's International League for Peace and Freedom*. Athens: University of Georgia Press, 1989.

5. *Ibid.*

6. *Ibid.*

7. *Ibid.* Foster uses a WILPF circular edited by Elise for her information.

8. *Ibid.* Information taken from a 1970 copy of the WILPF newsletter "Peace and Freedom."

9. *Ibid.*, 115.

10. V. 17, no. 4, November (1955): 303–305.

11. 1958.

12. Eynon and Fishman interview, Hanover, NH, 1978.

13. *Ibid.*

14. Kerman, Cynthia Earl. *Creative Tension: The Life and Thought of Kenneth Boulding*. Ann Arbor: University of Michigan Press, 1974.

15. *Ibid.*

16. Kerman, Cynthia Earl. *The Image of Knowledge Life and Society*. Ann Arbor: University of Michigan Press. 1956; Ann Arbor Paperbacks, 1961.

17. Kenneth Boulding archives, University of Colorado at Boulder, Box 17, folder marked "Center for Research on Conflict Resolution"; additional information on the history of peace studies and the CRCR obtained from the following: Fink, Clinton. Personal interview, June, 1997; Kerman, Cynthia Earl. *Creative Tension: The Life and Thought of Kenneth Boulding*. Ann Arbor: University of Michigan Press, 1974; Harris, Ian. *Peace Education*. Jefferson, NC: McFarland, 1988.

18. K. Boulding archives, Bentley Library, University of Michigan, Box 33, folder marked "CRCC."

19. *Ibid.*

20. Boulding, Elise. Personal interview, March 20, 1997.

21. *Ibid.*

22. Foster, Catherine. *Women for All Seasons: The Story of the Women's International League for Peace and Freedom*. Athens: University of Georgia Press, 1989.

23. EB archives, University of Colorado at Boulder, Box 10, folder 25

24. *Ibid.*

25. EB archives, University of Colorado at Boulder, Box 10, folder 6.

26. EB archives, University of Colorado at Boulder, Box 10, folder 24.

27. *Ibid.*

28. EB archives, University of Colorado at Boulder, Box 11, folder 5.

29. EB archives, University of Colorado at Boulder, Box 10, folder 24.

30. "Friends Lake Community," descriptive pamphlet, in possession of Elise Boulding

31. EB archives, University of Colorado at Boulder, Box 27, folder marked "Friends-AFSC conflict dialogue."

32. Eynon and Fishman interview, 1978.

33. *Ibid.*

34. "The Place of the Child in the Society of Friends." *The American Friend*. July 1960. "A Quaker Journey, a Talk with College Students." Friends General Conference, 1961 (listed in archives as a 1954 talk: "my notes." *Children and Solitude*. Pendle Hill pamphlet no. 25. 1962. *Friends Testimonies in the Home*. Friends General Conference, Philadelphia, 1962.

35. See Chapter 5 for more in-depth discussion of Elise's Quaker involvements.

36. "Who Are These Women? Report on Research on New Women's Peace Movement." *Behavioral Science and Human Survival*. M. Schwebel, ed., Palo Alto: Science and Behavior Books, Inc. 1965.

37. This information was handed to me by Elise in a March 1963 report she wrote up about the research, presumably written for funding purposes and as a preliminary to her later publication.

38. EB archives, Bentley Library, University of Michigan, Box 27, folder marked "Japan."

39. "Japanese Women Look at Society." *The Japan Christian Quarterly*, 32, no. 1, January (1966).

Chapter 5

1. EB archives, University of Colorado at Boulder, Box 41, folder marked "Danforth."

2. Eynon and Fishman interview, 1978.

3. EB archives, University of Colorado at Boulder, Box 18, folder 1.

4. Eynon and Fishman interview, 1978.

5. EB archives, Bentley library, University of Michigan, Box 20, folder marked "Peace Candidacy."

6. *Ibid.*

7. *Ibid.*

8. EB archives, University of Colorado at Boulder, Box 11, folder 4.

9. Elise mentioned this anecdote several times in my contacts with her.

10. EB archives. Bentley Library, University of Michigan, Box 20, folder marked "Activities 1965–67."

11. Eynon and Fishman interview, Hanover, 1978.

12. *Ibid.*
13. *Ibid.*
14. *Ibid.*
15. Vol. 68: 4, Summer (1973). Found in EB archives, University of Colorado at Boulder, Box 18, folder 1.
16. Clements, Kevin. Personal Interview, June 1997.
17. "International Newsletter on Peace Research," E. Boulding, ed., 1:1, Winter (1963). Copies obtained from EB private collection; also found in EB archives at the University of Colorado in Boulder, Box 1, folder 21.
18. *Ibid.*
19. *Ibid.*
20. "Building a Global Civic Culture." *Twentieth Century Thought*, edited by R.P. Cuzzort and Edith King. New York: Harcourt, Brace College Publishers, 1989.
21. "International Newsletter on Peace Research," E. Boulding, ed., 1:1, Winter (1963).
22. "International Peace Research Newsletter," E. Boulding, ed., 2:2 June (1964). EB Private papers, also found in EB archives, University of Colorado at Boulder, Box 1, folder 21.
23. Kerman, Cynthia Earl. *Creative Tension: The Life and Thought of Kenneth Boulding*. Ann Arbor: University of Michigan Press, 1974.
24. "Peace Research: Dialectics and Development." *Journal of Conflict Resolution*. 16, no. 4, December 1972: 469–475.
25. EB archives, the University of Colorado at Boulder, Box 1, folder 21.
26. IPRA. *IPRA Studies in Peace Research: Proceedings of the International Peace Research Association Inaugural Conference*. Netherlands: Van Gorcum, Ltd., 1966.
27. *Ibid.*
28. "The Effects of Industrialization on the Participation of Women in Society." Doctoral Dissertation, University of Michigan, 1969.
29. *Ibid.*, 307–308.
30. EB archives, University of Colorado at Boulder, Box 28, folder marked "Activities."
31. Greenstein, Michael. Personal Interview, May 1999.
32. First published in 1969 in *Non-Governmental Organizations and National Development*, Report of the Workshop of Non-Governmental Organizations in Consultative Status with UNICEF, Santiago, Chile. New York: United Nations E/IECF Misc. 154. Reprinted in *International Associations*. 11 (November), 1969, 549–552.
33. EB archives, University of Colorado at Boulder, Box 11, miscellaneous loose material.
34. EB archives, University of Colorado at Boulder, Box 11, folder 18.
35. *Ibid.*
36. EB archives, University of Colorado at Boulder, Box 12, folder 41.
37. "Reflections on COPRED's Fourth Birthday," EB archives, University of Colorado at Boulder, Box 9, folder 48.
38. Words by Elise Boulding, in UNESCO. *UNESCO Yearbook on Peace and Conflict Studies*. Westport, CT: Greenwood Press, 1981.
39. Elise's report of the first year of activities of COPRED, in EB archives, University of Colorado at Boulder, Box 6, folder 12.
40. *Ibid.*
41. COPRED pamphlet, undated, in EB archives, University of Colorado at Boulder, Box 6, folder 10.
42. Letter from EB to AFSC Peace Education Secretaries, August 29, 1975, in EB archives, University of Colorado at Boulder, Box 8, folder 18.
43. "Reflections on COPRED's Fourth Birthday," 1974, EB archives, University of Colorado at Boulder, Box 9, folder 48.
44. *Ibid.*
45. *Ibid.*
46. *Ibid.*
47. EB archives, University of Colorado at Boulder, Box 6, folder 1.
48. *Ibid.*
49. *Ibid.*
50. *Ibid.*

PART II

Chapter 6

1. EB Journals, December 24, 1958.
2. KB. "Sonnet for a Quaker Wedding." This is one of many sonnets he wrote and is used in the introduction to *One Small Plot of Heaven: Reflections on Family Life by a Quaker Sociologist*. Wallingford, PA: Pendle Hill Press, 1989.
3. White, Gilbert. Personal interview, July 20, 1999.
4. EB personal interview, March 20, 1997.
5. *Ibid.*
6. "Criteria for a Transnational Curriculum in the Twenty-First Century." *The Peace Studies Bulletin*. 1, no. 1, Spring (1991): 1–5, 1.
7. Boulding, Elise and Kenneth. *The Future: Images and Processes*. Thousand Oaks, CA: Sage, 1995.
8. EB Journals, March 1974.
9. Spradlin, Anna L. "Elise Boulding and the Peace Movement: A Study of Leadership Rhetoric and Practice Within Social Movement Organizations." Dissertation, University of Denver, 1990.
10. EB archives, University of Colorado at

Boulder, Box 34, folder marked "UNESCO Peace Forum."

11. *Ibid.*

12. Stomfay-Stitz, Aline. *Peace Education in American, 1828–1900: Sourcebook for Education and Research.* Metuchen, NJ: Scarecrow Press, 1993.

13. Stomfay-Stitz, 1993, p. 216.

14. Stomfay-Stitz, 1993.

15. "The Child and Non-Violent Social Change." In *Handbook on Peace Education*, edited by Christoph Wulf, 101–133. Frankfurt-Main: International Peace Research Foundation Education Committee, 1974.

16. EB Archives, University of Colorado at Boulder, Box 32, Women's Strike for Peace Material.

17. "Who Are These Women: A Progress Report on a Study of the Women's Strike for Peace." Ann Arbor: University of Michigan Center for Conflict Resolution, 1963.

18. See the autobiographical introduction in *One Small Plot of Heaven*, 1989.

19. This quote, or one closely resembling it, is found in many of her writings on the family. For a more complete listing of these, see the endnotes in Chapter 8.

20. Giffin, Holly. Personal interview, July 15 1999.

21. *One Small Plot of Heaven*, 1989, 163.

22. Boulding, Elise. *Our Children, Our Partners: A New Vision for Social Action in the 21st Century*. Kelvin Grove, Queensland, Australia: Margaret Fell Bookshop, 1996.

23. *Ibid.*, Robert Coles. *The Spiritual Life of Children*. Boston: Houghton Mifflin, 1990.

24. EB Journals, August 18, 1935.

25. EB Workshop at Holy Cross College, Worcester, MA, November 19, 1999.

26. *My Part in the Quaker Adventure*. Philadelphia: Religious Education Committee of Friends General Conference, 1958.

27. EB archives, University of Colorado at Boulder, Box 36, WILPF material.

28. *Ibid.*

29. *Ibid.*

30. *Ibid.*

31. "The Child and Non-violent Social Change," 1974.

32. EB archives, University of Colorado at Boulder, Box 36, WILPF material.

33. *Building a Global Civic Culture: Education for an Interdependent World*. New York: Teachers College Press, 1988.

34. Stomfay-Stitz, *Peace Education in America*, 1993; Transnational Academic Program Institute for World Order. *Peace and World Order Studies*. 1981.

35. EB, informal conversations.

36. *Building a Global Civic Culture: Education for an Interdependent World*. New York: Teachers College Press, 1988. 28. As Elise has pointed out, the numbers in each of the categories are substantially higher now than when the book was written.

37. *Building a Global Civic Culture*, 35.

38. *Ibid.*

39. EB personal interview, September 14, 1999.

40. *Building a Global Civic Culture*, 49.

41. *Ibid.*, 54.

42. See *The Underside of History: A View of Women Through Time*. Revised ed. 2 vols. Newbury Park: Sage, 1992; *Women in the Twentieth Century World*. New *York: Sage Publications, 1977*; *Women: The Fifth World*. Edited by H. Morganthau, *Headline Series of the Foreign Policy Association*. New York: The Foreign Policy Association, 1980.

43. *Building a Global Civic Culture*. 1988, 138; Mary F. Belenky, Blythe M. Clinchy, Nancy R. Goldberger, Jill M. Tarule. *Women's Ways of knowing: The Development of Self, Voice and Mind*: Basic Books, 1986.

44. "Life Ways and Values." *Technology, Education and Society: Future Directions*. Melbourne, Australia: Royal Melbourne Institute of Technology, 1987.

45. Loomis, Rosemary. "Conversation with Professor Elise Boulding." *Newsletter of the Boston Research Center for the 21st Century*. No. 9, Fall (1997): 8–11.

46. "Life Ways and Values," 1987.

47. "Learning to Make New Futures." *Educational Reform for a Changing Society: Anticipating Tomorrow's Schools*. Edited by Louis Rubin. Boston: Allyn and Bacon, 1978.

48. *Cultures of Peace: The Other Side of History*. Syracuse University Press, 2000.

49. Her ideas on this are expanded upon in *Cultures of Peace*.

50. *Ibid.*

Chapter 7

1. Lacey, Paul. *Growing into Goodness: Essays on Quaker Education*. Wallingford, PA: Pendle Hill Publications, 1998, introduction. Lacey is using phrases he credits to Howard Brinton.

2. *Ibid.*, 28.

3. Lacey, *Education and the Inward Teacher*, 26.

4. *One Small Plot of Heaven*, 15.

5. *Ibid.*, 21.

6. *Ibid.*, 43.

7. Boulding, Elise. Personal interview March 20, 1997.

8. Palmer, Parker. *To Know As We Are Known: Education as a Spiritual Journey*. San Francisco: Harper San Francisco, 1993, preface.

9. *Ibid.*, 43.

10. EB archives. University of Colorado at Boulder, Box 27, folder marked "Contemplatives."

11. This comes from Homan, Walter J. *A Study of the Place of Children in the Theory and Practice of the Society of Friends, Commonly Called Quakers.* Berkeley, CA: Gillich Press: 1939. Originally a doctoral dissertation at Yale University.

12. *Ibid.*

13. Brinton, Howard. *Quaker Education in Theory and Practice.* Pendle Hill Pamphlet. Wallingford, PA: Pendle Hill Press, 1958.

14. For an excellent historical overview of the history of Pendle Hill, see Eleanore Price Mather's *Pendle Hill: A Quaker Experiment in Education and Community.* Wallingford, PA: Pendle Hill Press, 1980.

15. *Ibid.*

16. Lester, John. *The Ideals and Objectives of Quaker Education.* Philadelphia: Friends Council on Education, 1949.

17. Loukes, Harold. *Friends and Their Children, A Study in Quaker Education.* London: Friends Home Service Committee (first ed. by George Harrap and Co.), 1958.

18. Brinton, Howard. *The Function of a Quaker College.* Greensboro, NC: Guilford College, published as a Ward Lecture, 1951.

19. Giffin, Holly. Personal Interview July 15, 1999.

20. Proceedings of the First International Theological Conference of Quaker Women. London: Da Costa Print, 1991.

21. "Where Is Our Sense of Sin?" *Friends Intelligencer: A Quaker Weekly* 104, no. June 21 (1947): 320–321.

22. "The Joy That Is Set Before Us." Philadelphia: William Penn Lecture, 1956.

23. Listing by Elise Boulding at request of author for key people in her life, August 1997.

24. Quote from EB in "Newsletter of the Ad Hoc Committee on Friends Responsibilities in Higher Education and Research, 1:1, August (1965), 1.

25. EB archives, University of Colorado at Boulder, Box 27, "Friends."

26. *Ibid.*

27. *Ibid.*

28. "Newsletter of the Ad Hoc Committee on Friends Responsibilities in Education and Research." 2, September (1966).

29. Letter from Doris Darnell to EB. EB archives, University of Colorado at Boulder, box 1, folder 35.

30. "Whom Are We Trying to Reach?" Paper given at AFSC MAC Peace Education Workshop Retreat, September 11, 1965. EB archives. Bentley Historical Library, University of Michigan, Box 20, "EB Papers."

31. EB archives, University of Colorado at Boulder, Box 29, folder marked "AFSC Working Party."

32. White, Gilbert. Personal interview, July 20 1999.

33. Though the Friends Council on Education (FCE) and FAHE are distinct organizations, periodically they hold joint annual gatherings, a practice that began some years after the talk given by Elise.

34. "Mapping the Inner Journey of Quaker Women." Carol and John Stoneburner (eds). New York: Edwin Mellon Press, 1986.

35. "Coming Down to Earth in Peace Education," unpublished, 1994.

Chapter 8

1. EB, taped workshop at Wellesley College conference, September 1998.

2. *Ibid.*

3. *Ibid.*

4. UNESCO. *UNESCO and a Culture of Peace.* Paris: UNESCO Publishing, 1995. This monograph provides a complete description, including a historical overview, of the Culture of Peace Program.

5. *Ibid.*

6. *Building a Global Civic Culture: Education for an Interdependent World.* New York: Teachers College Press, 1988. This book, of all those written by her, most encapsulates her philosophy of education. Included at the end are "global exercises" for use in classrooms.

7. UNESCO, 1995.

8. Further information on UNESCO's program may be found at the following web site: http://www.unesco.org

9. EB Archives, University of Colorado at Boulder, Box 34, folder marked "UNESCO Peace Forum."

10. For an excellent source of information on the UNESCO and UN initiative, as well as other related material, see *Fellowship*, published by the Fellowship of Reconciliation, 65: 5–6, May–June (1999).

11. Syracuse, 2000.

12. *Cultures of Peace*, 3.

13. *The Underside of History: A View of Women Through Time.* Revised ed. 2 vols. Newbury Park: Sage, 1992.

14. *Cultures of Peace*, 6.

15. For further reading, the following titles are suggested. It should be noted, however, that, as in most of her work, women, families and children are not isolated to only a few writings but found thematically throughout much of her work. *Building a Global Civic Culture: Education for an Interdependent World.* 1988; *The Family as a Small Society.* Schumacher Society, based on annual Schumacher lecture, 1982;

"The Family as an Agent of Social Change." *The Futurist* 6, no. 5, October (1972): 363–378; "Female Alternatives to Hierarchical Systems, Past and Present: A Critique of Women's NGOs in the Light of History." *International Association*, no. 6–7, June–July (1975): 340–346; "Feminist Inventions in the Art of Peacemaking." *Peace and Change* 20, no. 4, October (1995): 408–438; *One Small Plot of Heaven: Reflections on Family Life by a Quaker Sociologist*. Wallingford, PA: Pendle Hill Press, 1989; *The Underside of History: A View of Women Through Time*. Revised ed. 2 volumes. Newbury Park: Sage, 1992; *Women in the Twentieth Century World*. New York: Sage Publications, 1977; *Women: The Fifth World*. Edited by H. Morganthau, *Headline Series of the Foreign Policy Association*. New York: The Foreign Policy Association, 1980.

14. 16. For further reading, see "The Child and Non-Violent Social Change." In *Handbook on Peace Education*, edited by Christoph Wulf. Frankfurt-Main: International Peace Research Foundation Education Committee, 1974, 101–133; *Children's Rights and the Wheel of Life*. New Brunswick, New Jersey: Transaction Books, 1987; *Our Children, Our Partners: A New Vision for Social Action in the 21st Century*. Kelvin Grove, Queensland, Australia: Margaret Fell Bookshop, 1996.

17. "Peace Culture." In *Encyclopedia ov Violence and Conflict*, edited by Lester Kurtz, 653–667: San Diego: Academic Press, 1999.

18. *Cultures of Peace*, 118.

19. "Toward a Culture of Peace in the 21st Century." *Peacework*, no. 259, January (1996): 12–14.

20. "Peace Culture: The Problem of Managing Human Difference." *Cross Currents: Journal of the Association for Religion and Intellectual Life* 48, no. 4, Winter (1999): 445–457.

21. Westview, 1976

22. Interview at the home of Ann and George Levinger June 7, 1999.

23. Russell Boulding interview June 1997.

24. Spradlin, Anna L. "Elise Boulding and the Peace Movement: A Study of Leadership Rhetoric and Practice Within Social Movement Organizations." Dissertation, University of Denver, 1990.

25. Irwin, Robert. Personal interview, Cambridge, MA May 26, 1999.

26. Anna Spradlin, in her dissertation on Elise's leadership rhetoric, outlines three interrelated characteristics to describe Elise's style: empowerment, connectedness and enactment. These, according to Spradlin, "create a stamp, an Elise Boulding imprint ... within the contemporary peace movement." For further information see Spradlin, 1990.

27. Herman, Theodore. Personal interview, Washington, D.C., June 1997.

28. "Women's Visions of the Future." *Visions of Desirable Societies*. E. Masini, ed. NY: Pergamon Press, 11–12. Interview with Robert Irwin, Cambridge, MA 5-26-99.

Chapter 9

1. *Image of the Future*. 2 volumes. English version published by Oceana Press, 1961. There is a one volume abridgement by Elise Boulding. San Francisco: Jossy-Bass/Elsevier, 1972. Translated from *De Toekomst is Verleden Tyd* by Fred Polak. Utrecht, W. DeHaan N.V., 1953.

2. Thousand Oaks, CA: Sage Publications

3. Most of her writings on women include one or more of these ideas regarding feminine contributions to peacemaking. See particularly *Cultures of Peace: The Hidden Side of History*. Syracuse: Syracuse University Press, 2000. "Feminist Inventions in the Art of Peacemaking." *Peace and Change* 20, no. 4, October (1995): 408–438. "The Role of Education in Building a Peaceful World Order." *The New Era* 46, no. 3, March (1965): 72–77. *The Underside of History: A View of Women Through Time*. Revised ed. 2 vols. Newbury Park: Sage, 1992; *Women in the Twentieth Century World*. New York: Sage Publications, 1977. "Women, Peace and the Future: Personal Reminiscences." *Fellowship* 64, no. 11–12, November–December (1998): 4–5. *Women: The Fifth World*. Edited by H. Morganthau, *Headline Series of the Foreign Policy Association*. New York: The Foreign Policy Association, 1980. "Women's Experiential Approaches to Peace Studies." In *The Knowledge Explosion: Generations of Feminist Scholarship*, edited by Kris and Spender Kramarae, Dale. New York: Teachers College Press, 1992.

4. *Cultures of Peace: The Hidden Side of History*. Syracuse: Syracuse University Press, 2000.

5. Irwin, Robert. Personal interview, May 26, 1999.

6. Graham, Christine Boulding. Personal interview, December 8, 1999.

7. Elise has often spoken on this in our work together.

8. See *Building a Global Civic Culture: Education for an Interdependent World*. New York: Teachers College Press, 1988. "Coming Down to Earth in Peace Education." Unpublished, 1994. "Criteria for a Transnational Curriculum in the Twenty-First Century." *The Peace Studies Bulletin* 1, no. 1, Spring (1991): 1–5. *Cultures of Peace: the Hidden Side of History*. Syracuse: Syracuse University Press, 2000. "Feminist Inventions in the Art of Peacemaking." *Peace and Change* 20, no. 4, October (1995): 408–438. "Women's Experiential Approaches to Peace

Studies." In *The Knowledge Explosion: Generations of Feminist Scholarship*, edited by Kris and Spender Kramarae, Dale. New York: Teachers College Press, 1992.

9. See Addams, J. "Twenty Years at Hull House" *Liberating Women's History: Theoretical and Critical Essays*. B. Carroll, ed. Urbana: University of Illinois Press, 1990.

10. Addams, J. *The Long Road of Women's Memory*. Urbana: University of Illinois Press, 2002 edition.

11. New York: Macmillan, 1922, p. 153.

12. Davis, A.F., ed. *Jane Addams on Peace, War and International Understanding 1899–1932*. New York: Garland Publications, 1976.

13. Belenky, Mary F., Blythe M. Clinchy, Nancy R. Goldberger, Jill M. Tarule. *Women's Ways of knowing: The Development of Self, Voice and Mind*. Basic Books, 1986. Gilligan, Carol. *In a Different Voice: Psychological Theory and Women's Development*. Cambridge, MA: Harvard University Press, 1982. Miller, Jean Baker. *Toward a New Psychology of Women*. Boston: Beacon Press, 1976, 1986. Ruddick, Sara. *Maternal Thinking: Toward A Politics of Peace*. Boston: Beacon Press, 1989.

14. See S. Ruddick, *Maternal Thinking*, 1989 and E. Boulding, *The Underside of History: A View of Women Through Time*. Revised ed. 2 vols. Newbury Park: Sage, 1992.

15. See Forcey, Linda Rennie. "Women as Peacemakers: Contested Terrain for Feminist Peace Studies." *Peace and Change* 16, no. No. 4, October (1991): 331–354.

16. The use of the word "underside" comes from the title *The Underside of History*, Sage, 1992.

17. Ruth, Sheila. *Issues in Feminism: A First Course in Women's Studies*. Boston: Houghton Mifflin: 1980.

18. *Ibid.*

19. *The Underside of History: A View of Women Through Time*. Revised ed. 2 vols. Newbery Park: Sage, 1992.

20. EB journals, Jan. 21, 1974

21. EB journals

22. *Ibid.*

23. "The Cooperative Nursery and the Young Mother's Role Conflict." *Marriage and Family Living* 17, no. 4 November (1955): 303–305.

24. The addition of the last part of the sentence is a direct addition inserted by Elise to the original manuscript as doctoral dissertation, authored by MLM. Elise carefully edited the original manuscript, adding to and commenting on various items. This provided many hours of fruitful discussion between MLM and EB, prior to the revisions done for final publication as a book.

25. Boulding, Elise. "The Effects of Industrialization on the Participation of Women in Society." Doctoral dissertation, University of Michigan, 1969.

26. Belenky, Mary F., Clinchy, Blythe M., Goldberger, Nancy R., Tarule, Jill M. *Women's Ways of Knowing: The Development of Self, Voice and Mind*: Basic Books, 1986, 112.

27. Miller, Jean Baker. *Toward a New Psychology of Women*. Boston: Beacon Press, 1976.

28. Boulding, Elise. "Feminist Inventions in the Art of Peacemaking." *Peace and Change* 20, no. 4, October (1995): 408–438.

29. "Feminist Inventions in the Art of Peacemaking," p. 422.

30. "Feminist Inventions in the Art of Peacemaking," p. 421.

31. Boston: Beacon Press, 1961.

32. See "Female Alternatives to Hierarchical Systems, Past and Present: A Critique of Women's NGOs in the Light of History." *International Association* no. 6–7, June–July (1975): 340–346.

33. As previously noted for other themes in her life and work, it is difficult to pinpoint specific citations for Elise's ideas on NGOs. She discusses this idea in many of her writings. Suggested citations are *Building a Global Civic Culture: Education for an Interdependent World*. New York: Teachers College Press, 1988, where her ideas are well articulated; "Criteria for a Transnational Curriculum in the Twenty-First Century." *The Peace Studies Bulletin* 1, no. 1, Spring (1991): 1–5; *Cultures of Peace: The Hidden Side of History*. Syracuse: Syracuse University Press, 2000, and "NGOs and the Search for Economic Justice." *International Associations* no. 6, June–July (1971): 360–367.

34. "The New Non-Governmental Order." *The Economist* December 11–17 (1999): received via electronic list-serve, no author listed.

35. See *Cultures of Peace: The Hidden Side of History*. Syracuse: Syracuse University Press, 2000.

36. *Ibid.*, 111, 117.

37. Moore, LeRoy. Personal Interview, July 9 1999.

38. When I interviewed Elise during one of our early times together, she felt it important to write down for me all of the newsletters she had begun.

39. EB personal interview, May 28, 1997.

40. Boulding, Russell. Personal interview, June 1997.

41. Garman, Mary. Personal interview, June 1997.

42. Schneider, Laurel. Personal interview, February 24, 2000.

43. "Women, Peace and the Future." www.peacecouncil.org/womenBoulding.html (First

published in *Fellowship*. FOR, November–December [1998]).

44. *Ibid.*

45. See "Image and Action in Peace Building." *Journal of Social Issues*, Vol. 44, No. 2, (1988): 17–37.

46. *Ibid.*

47. Boulding, Elise and Kenneth Boulding. *The Future: Images and Processes*. Thousand Oaks, CA: Sage, 1995, 100.

48. "The Joy That is Set Before Us." Philadelphia Yearly Meeting, Young Friends Movement, 1956.

49. See "The Family as Agent of Social Change." *The Futurist* 6, no. 5, October (1972).

PART III

Chapter 10

1. No. 6 (June–July) 1971, 360–367. E. Boulding archives, University of Colorado at Boulder, Box 18.

2. *Ibid.*

3. *The Underside of History: A View of Women Through Time*. Revised ed. 2 vols. Newbury Park: Sage, 1992 (reprinted, first published in 1976). *Women in the Twentieth Century World*. New York: Sage Publications, 1977.

4. "The Child and Non-Violent Social Change." In *Handbook on Peace Education*, edited by Christoph Wulf. Frankfurt-Main: International Peace Research Foundation Education Committee, 1974, 101–133.

5. EB archives, University of Colorado at Boulder, Box 1, folder 6.

6. *Ibid.*

7. *Ibid.*

8. Reply to A. Eide from EB, EB archives, University of Colorado at Boulder, Box 1, folder 6.

9. Reading, MA: Addison-Wesley Publishing, 1980.

10. EB archives. The University of Colorado at Boulder, 3rd Accession, Box 8, folder 10 marked "ASA Section on World Conflicts."

11. EB. Personal Interview, December 17, 2003.

12. Co-edited with Robert Chen and Stephen Schneider. D. Reidel Publishers, Netherlands, 1983.

13. EB personal interview, December 17, 2003.

14. Found in an organizational pamphlet in EB archives, University of Colorado at Boulder

15. EB Journals, June 29, 1975.

16. EB Journals. May–July 1975, quoted entry July 25.

17. Clements, Kevin. Personal interview, June 1997.

18. Boulding, Russell. Personal interview, June 1997.

19. Graham, Christine Boulding. Personal interview, December 8, 1999.

20. Giffin, Holly. Personal interview, July 15, 1999.

21. EB to KB, dated February 15, 1985.

22. Compilation of informal conversations between the author and EB.

23. Kerman, Cynthia E. *Creative Tension: The Life and Thought of Kenneth Boulding*. Ann Arbor: University of Michigan Press, 1974.

24. Letter to EB from KB, February 27, 1985.

25. EB. Personal Interview, August 2, 2000.

26. EB. Personal Interview April 15, 1999.

27. Information found in EB archives, University of Colorado at Boulder. 3rd Accession: Box 8, folder 9 marked "UNESCO."

28. *Ibid.*

29. *Ibid.* The quote reveals her strong identification with IPRA and its founding.

30. Letter from EB to D. Bazin, Acting Director, International Research and Training Institute for the Advancement of Women, United Nations. February 27, 1980. EB archives, University of Colorado at Boulder, Box 38, unprocessed material.

31. EB. Personal Interview, April 15, 1999.

32. *Ibid.*

33. 1999 Annual Report of the United Nations University.

34. *Ibid.*

35. Osborn, Wayne. "United Nations University in Costa Rica: History and Prospects." *Peace and Change* 25, no. 3, July (2000): 309–338.

36. *Ibid.*

37. EB. Personal Interview, August 2, 2000.

38. Osborn, 310.

39. Letter from EB to Helvi Sipila, Assistant Secretary-General for Social Development and Humanitarian Affairs, United Nations. February 26, 1980. EB archives, University of Colorado at Boulder, Box 38, unprocessed material.

40. New Brunswick, NJ: Transaction Books, 1987 (second printing).

41. Written report by EB. Undated. EB archives, University of Colorado at Boulder, Box 38, folder marked "IPAPAGA."

42. "Proposal for UNU Interprogramme Advisory Panel of Women Scholars." EB archives, University of Colorado at Boulder, Box 38, folder marked "IPAPAGA."

43. Johnson, Richard. "The Peacemakers." *Denver Post Magazine* 37, no. 9, March 2 (1986): 10–14.

44. Lyons, Gene M. *Putting ACUNS Together:*

ACUNS Reports and Papers 1999. No. 2 ed. New Haven: Yale University, 1999.

45. *Ibid.*

46. EB personal interview, August 2, 2000.

47. EB letter to Tom Weiss. July 24, 2000.

48. EB personal interview, August 2, 2000.

49. Boulding, Elise. "The U.S. Academy of Peace." *Teachers College Record* 84, no. 1–2, Fall (1982).

50. *Ibid.*

51. Resolution, Commission on Proposals for the National Academy of Peace and Conflict. *To Establish the United States Academy of Peace*. Washington, D.C.: U.S. Government Printing Office, 1981, 60.

52. *Ibid.*, 125.

53. EB personal interview, March 5, 1999.

54. EB letter to Richard Solomon, July 24, 2000.

55. EB letter to KB, February 20, 1985.

56. Boulding, Russell. Personal interview, June 1997.

57. KB letter to EB, February 27, 1985.

Chapter 11

1. Letter from Elisabeth Gerle to EB. August 10, 1993. EB archives, University of Colorado at Boulder. 4th Accession "WOMP."

2. Shuman, Michael, and Julia Sweig, eds. EXPRO Press, Washington D.C. Information on the content of the book was obtained from the web site of reviewer Brian Martin: www.uow.edu.au/arts/sts/ bmartin/pubs.

3. Information found in EB archives. University of Colorado at Boulder, Accession 4, Box 5, Folder 15 marked "EXPRO."

4. LR. Personal interview, July 1999.

5. Correll, Ruth. Personal interview, July 11, 1999.

6. EB archives. University of Colorado at Boulder. 3rd Accession, Box 6, folder 11 marked "IMYM-AFSC Joint Service Projects Committee."

7. EB personal interview, August 2, 2000.

8. Letter from AB to JS, January 5, 1990. EB archives, the University of Colorado at Boulder, 3rd–4th Accession, "Nobel Nomination."

9. EB archives. University of Colorado at Boulder, Accession 4, Box 5, file marked "Woodbrooke."

10. *Ibid.*

11. Spradlin, Anna L. "Elise Boulding and the Peace Movement: A Study of Leadership Rhetoric and Practice Within Social Movement Organizations." Dissertation, University of Denver, 1990.

12. Gonzales, Marty. Personal Interview, July 7, 1999.

13. EB. "Peacebuilding in the Middle East." Paper presented to the Peace Studies Association, University of Colorado February 27, 1992. EB archives. The University of Colorado at Boulder, Accession 3, Box 9, folder 5 marked "Kyoto Meeting."

14. Introduction to "Peace and Justice for the Peoples of the Middle East: Perspectives of the Peace Research Community, undated. EB archives. University of Colorado at Boulder, Box 46, folder marked "Middle East Commission."

15. Boulder, CO: Lynne Rienner Publishers, 1994.

16. See Harris, Ian. "Editor's Introduction." Special issue of the *Peabody Journal of Education. Peace Education in a Postmodern World* (1996).

17. *Ibid.*

18. *Ibid.*

19. EB. "Women's Experiential Approaches to Peace Studies." In *The Knowledge Explosion: Generations of Feminist Scholarship*, edited by Cheris Kramarae and Dale Spender. New York: Teachers College Press, 1992.

20. Abstract of the talk to be found in "Peace Education: Theory and Practice." *Peace Research Abstracts* (1987), pp. 104–105. Betty Reardon authored *Comprehensive Peace Education*, 1988. Another feminist peace educator with similar views is Birgit Brock-Utne.

21. 1993, unpublished. EB files, Needham, MA.

22. "Friends Peace Teams: Skills and Action in the Face of Violence and Oppression." *Peacework* no. 276 (1997): 25–27.

23. *Ibid.*

24. *Ibid.*

25. EB archives. University of Colorado at Boulder, 4th Accession, Box 2, folder 2 marked "Peace Council."

26. EB journal, December 20, 1995.

27. EB journal, November 22, 1996.

28. *Cultures of Peace: The Hidden Side of History*. Syracuse University Press, 2000.

29. *Ibid.*

30. EB journal, May 17, 2000.

Bibliography of Selected Writings by Elise Boulding

"Adolescent Culture: Reflections of Divergence." In *Social Force and Schooling*, edited by Nobuo Kenneth Shimahara and Adam Scrpski. New York: David Kay, 1975. Pp. 187–220.

"Age and Gender Differentiation and Social Inequality." In *Global Inequality: Politics and Socioeconomics*, edited by John Grove. Boulder, CO: Westview Press, 1979.

"Building a Global Civic Culture." In *Twentieth Century Thought*, edited by R.P. Cuzzort and Edith King. New York: Harcourt, Brace College Publishers, 1989.

Building a Global Civic Culture: Education for an Interdependent World. New York: Teachers College Press, 1988.

Can Peace Be Imagined? Edited by Linda Forcey. New York: Praeger, 1989.

"Changing Gender Roles in Familial, Occupational, and Civic Settings." In *Society as Educator in An Age of Transition*, edited by Kenneth Benne and Steven Tozer: National Society for the Study of Education, 1986.

"The Child and Nonviolent Social Change." In *Strategies Against Violence: Design for Nonviolent Change*, edited by Israel Charny. Boulder, CO: Westview Press, 1978.

"The Child and Non-Violent Social Change." In *Handbook on Peace Education*, edited by Christoph Wulf, 101–133. Frankfurt-Main: International Peace Research Foundation Education Committee, 1974.

"The Child as Shaper of the Future." *Peace and Change: A Journal of Peace Research* 1, no. 1, Fall (1972): 11–17.

"Children's Rights." In *Human Rights and World Order*, edited by Abdul Aziz Said. New Brunswick, NJ: Transaction Books, 1978.

"Children's Rights." *Human Rights*, November/December (1977): 39–43.

Children's Rights and the Wheel of Life. New Brunswick, New Jersey: Transaction Books, 1987.

"The Cold War in the Classroom." *War/Peace Report*, June (1963).

"The Concept of Peace Culture." In *Peace and Conflict Issues after the Cold War*, edited by UNESCO, 107–133. Paris: UNESCO, 1992.

"The Cooperative Nursery and the Young Mother's Role Conflict." *Marriage and Family Living* 17, no. 4 November (1955): 303–305.

"Criteria for a Transnational Curriculum in the Twenty-First Century." *The Peace Studies Bulletin* 1, no. 1, Spring (1991): 1–5.

"The Culture of Peace in Everyday Life." *Friends Bulletin* 66, no. 6, April (1998): 86–87.

Cultures of Peace: The Hidden Side of History. Syracuse: Syracuse University Press, 2000.

"The Earth Charter and the Culture of Peace." In *Women's Views on the Earth Charter*, edited by Helen Marie and Morgante Casey, Amy. Cambridge, MA: Boston Research Center for the 21st Century, 1997.

"Educating Children and Youth for Peace." Childhood Education Section of the Women's International League for Peace and Freedom, 1962.

"Education for Inventing the Future." In *Alternative to Growth 1: A Search for Sustainable Futures*, edited by Dennis Meadows, 297–300. Cambridge, MA: Ballinger Publishing Company, 1977.

"Education for Peace." *Bulletin of the Atomic Scientists* 38, no. June/July (1982): 59–62.

"The Effects of Industrialization on the Participation of Women in Society." Doctoral Dissertation, University of Michigan, 1969.

"Enlivening our Social Imagination." In *Citizen Summitry: Keeping the Peace When It Matters Too Much to Be Left to Politicians*, edited by Don and Comstock Carlson, Craig, 309–328: Ark Communications Institute Book, 1986.

"Familial Constraints on Women's Work Roles." *Signs: Journal of Women in Culture and Society* 1, no. 3, part 2, Spring (1976): 95–117.

"Families" (with Elizabeth Moen). In *Women and the Social Costs of Development: Two Colorado Case Studies*, edited by Charles P. Wolf. Boulder, CO: Westview Press, 1981.

"Families as Centers of Peace and Love: Paradoxes and Contradictions." In *Current Quaker Concerns*, edited by Leonard Kenworthy. Richmond, IN: Friends United Press, 1987.

"Family Adjustments to the Crises of Wartime Separation and Reunion." In *Annals of the American Academy of Political and Social Science*: Symposium on Family Stability, 1950.

The Family as a Small Society: Schumacher Society, based on annual Schumacher lecture, 1982.

"The Family as an Agent of Social Change." *The Futurist* 6, no. 5, October (1972): 363–378.

"The Family as Practice Ground in Making History: some autobiographical reflections." *The Friendly Woman* 4, no. 2, Fall (1979): 3–6.

"Family Wholeness: New Conceptions of Family Roles." In *Working Women and Families: Sage Yearbooks in Women's Policy Studies*, edited by Karen Feinstein. Beverly Hills: Sage Publications, 1979.

"Female Alternatives to Hierarchical Systems, Past and Present: A Critique of Women's NGO's in the Light of History." *International Association*, no. 6–7, June–July (1975): 340–346.

"Feminist Inventions in the Art of Peacemaking." *Peace and Change* 20, no. 4, October (1995): 408–438.

"Friends Peace Teams: Skills and Action in the Face of Violence and Oppression." *Peacework*, no. 276 (1997): 25–27.

Friends Testimonies in the Home. Philadelphia: Religious Education Committee of the Friends General Conference, 1953.

The Future: Images and Processes (with Kenneth Boulding). Thousand Oaks, CA: Sage, 1995.

"Futurism as the Galvinizer of Education." In *Educational Reconstruction: Promise and Challenge*, edited by Nobuo Shimura. Columbus, OH: Charles E. Merrill, 1973.

"Global Altruism and Everyday Behavior." In *Humatriotism: Human Interest in Peace and Survival*, edited by Theodore Lentz, 39–65. St. Louis: The Futures Press, 1974.

"Learning Peace." In *The Quest for Peace: Transcending Collective Violence and War Among Societies, Cultures and States*, edited by Vayrinen. London: Sage Publications, International Social Science Council, 1987.

"Learning to Make New Futures." In *Educational Reform for a Changing Society: Anticipating Tomorrow's Schools*, edited by Louis Rubin. Boston: Allyn and Bacon, 1978.

"Life Ways and Values." In *Technology, Education and Society: Future Directions*. Melbourne, Australia: Royal Melbourne Institute of Technology, 1987.

"Mapping the Inner Journey of Quaker Women." In *The Influence of Quaker Women on American History*, edited by Carol Stoneburner and John Stoneburner. Louiston, New York: Edwin Mellen Press, 1986.

"Mother, Father, Child: Reflections on the Social Status of Family Roles." *Transition* 27, no. 2, June (1997): 4–6.

My Part in the Quaker Adventure. Philadelphia: Religious Education Committee of Friends General Conference, 1958.

"Myopic View from Olympus." In *Ecology and the Quality of Life*, edited by Sylvan Kaplan and Evelyn Kivy-Rosenberg. Springfield, IL: Charles C. Thomas, 1973.

New Agendas for Peace Research: Conflict and Security Reexamined. Boulder, CO: Lynn Rienner Publisher, 1992.

"NGO's and the Search for Economic Justice." *International Associations*, no. 6, June–July (1971): 360–367.

"The Nurture of Adults by Children in Family Settings." In *Research in the Interweave of Social Roles: Women and Men*, edited by Helena Lopata, 167–187. Greenwich, CT: JAI Press, 1980.

One Small Plot of Heaven: Reflections on Family Life by a Quaker Sociologist. Wallingford, PA: Pendle Hill Press, 1989.

Our Children, Our Partners: A New Vision for Social Action in the 21st Century. Kelvin Grove, Queensland, Australia: Margaret Fell Bookshop, 1996.

"Peace and Justice for the Peoples of the Middle East—Perspectives of the Peace Research Community." International Peace Research Association, 1993.

"Peace at Home, Peace Abroad." *Friends Bulletin* 64, no. 4, December (1995): 56.

"Peace Behaviors in Various Societies." In *From a Culture of Violence to a Culture of Peace*, edited by UNESCO Peace and Conflict Studies. Paris: UNESCO, 1996.

"Peace Culture." In *Encyclopedia of Violence and Conflict*, edited by Lester Kurtz, 653–667. San Diego: Academic Press, 1999.

Peace Culture and Society: Transnational Research and Dialogue. With Clovis Brigagao and Kevin Clements in cooperation with IPRA, eds. Boulder, CO: Westview Press, 1991.

"Peace Culture: The Problem of Managing Human Difference." *Cross Currents: Journal of the Association for Religion and Intellectual Life* 48: 4, Winter (1999): 445–457.

"Peace Education: Theory and Practice." *Peace Research Abstracts*, no. 178315 (1987): 104–105.

"Peace Research: Dialectics and Development." *Journal of Conflict Resolution* 16: 4, December (1972): 469–475.

The Personhood of Children: Nonviolence and Children in the Technological Society, Rufus Jones Lecture. Philadelphia: Religious Education Committee of the Friends General Conference, 1975.

"Perspectives of Women Researchers on Disarmament, National Security and World Order." In *Approaching Disarmament Education*, edited by Magnus Haavelsrud. Guilford, England: Westbury House, IPC Science and Technology Press, 1981.

"The Process of Peacebuilding." *Waging Peace Worldwide: Journal of the Nuclear Age Foundation* 9, no. 1, Spring (1999): 6–7.

"Reflections on Guenter Lewis's "Peace and Revolution." In *Quaker Service at the Crossroads*, edited by Chuck Fager, 101–108. Falls Church, VA: Kimo Press, 1988.

"Religion, Futurism, and Models of Change." *The Humanist* 33, no. 6, November–December (1973): 35–39.

"The Role of Education in Building a Peaceful World Order." *The New Era* 46, no. 3, March (1965): 72–77.

The Social System of the Planet Earth (with Kenneth Boulding and Guy Burgess). Reading, MA: Addison-Wesley, 1980.

"Toward a Culture of Peace in the 21st Century." *Peacework*, no. 259, January (1996): 12–14.

The Underside of History: A View of Women Through Time. Revised ed. 2 vols. Newbury Park: Sage, 1992.

"The U.S. Academy of Peace." *Teachers College Record* 84, no. 1–2, Fall (1982).

"Warriors and Saints: Dilemmas in the History of Men, Women, and War." In *Women and the Military System*, edited by Eva Isaksson. London: Harvester Wheatsheaf, 1988.

"What Can We Do for Our Children?" *Liberation* 6, no. 10, December, 1961 (1961): 14–16.

"What Is a Peace Culture?" *Breakthrough News*, no. January–February (1999): 3–4.

"Where Is Our Sense of Sin?" *Friends Intelligencer: A Quaker Weekly* 104, June 21 (1947): 320–321.

"Women and Peace Work; for International Workshop on Changing Sex Roles in Family and Society, Dubrovnik, Yugoslavia." In *International Women's Year Studies on Women*: Institute of Behavioral Sciences, University of Colorado, 1975.

"Women as Role Models in Industrializing Societies: A Macro-System Model of Socialization for Civic Competence." In *Cross-National Family Research*, edited by Marvin Sussman and Betty Cogswell. Leiden: E.J. Brill, 1972.

Women in the Twentieth Century World. New York: Sage Publications, 1977.

"Women, Frugality and the Planetary Household." *Christian Ministry* 4, no. 5, September (1973): 12–16.

"Women, Peace and the Future: Personal Reminiscences." *Fellowship* 64: 11–12, November–December (1998): 4–5.

Women: The Fifth World. Edited by H. Morganthau, *Headline Series of the Foreign Policy Association.* New York: The Foreign Policy Association, 1980.

"Women's Experiential Approaches to Peace Studies." In *The Knowledge Explosion: Generations of Feminist Scholarship*, edited by Kris Kramarae and Dale Spender. New York: Teachers College Press, 1992.

Index